YOU'RE HIRED!

CVs, INTERVIEW ANSWERS
& PSYCHOMETRIC TESTS

YOU'RE HIRED!

CVs, INTERVIEW ANSWERS & PSYCHOMETRIC TESTS

CORINNE MILLS, CERI RODERICK,
JAMES MEACHIN AND STEPHAN LUCKS

You're Hired! CVs, Interview Answers & Psychometric Tests

This book first published in 2011 by Trotman Publishing, a division of Crimson Publishing Ltd., Westminster House, Kew Road, Richmond, Surrey TW9 2ND

© Trotman 2011

Authors Corinne Mills, Ceri Roderick, James Meachin and Stephan Lucks

British Library Cataloguing in Publication Data
A catalogue record for this book is available from the British Library

ISBN 978 1 84455 421 8

Typeset by RefineCatch Ltd, Bungay, Suffolk
Printed and bound in the UK by Ashford Colour Press, Gosport, Hants

CONTENTS

Part III: Psychometric Tests

LIST OF ACTIVITIES

ABOUT THE AUTHORS

CORINNE MILLS

Corinne Mills is MD of Personal Career Management, one of the UK's leading and most innovative career-coaching companies, specialising in helping individuals make informed career decisions and obtain the role they want. She also works with organisations on their talent-management programmes and outplacement.

As a qualified career coach, she has worked with thousands of individuals during her 12 years in the career management field, ranging from people on million pound salaries, to those at the start of their career. Previously working in senior HR roles, she is uniquely positioned to understand both from the candidate's and the organisation's point of view, what makes a good fit.

Corinne appears regularly in the media as a spokesperson and author on career management issues. Appearances include being the career-coaching expert on the Tonight with Trevor MacDonald series, BBC News, for the *Guardian*, Monster and frequent radio appearances. She has also written many articles and columns for newspapers and professional journals and been a guest speaker at many industry events on a range of career-management topics. She is a member of the Chartered Institute for Personnel and Development with an MA in Human Resources and is a CIPD committee member and external adviser for their courses.

Corinne's book, *You're Hired! CV,* is available from Trotman.

CERI RODERICK

Ceri Roderick is a Partner and Head of Assessment at business psychologists Pearn Kandola, and has been designing and delivering tough interviews for over 20 years. After a period with Deloittes, he joined Pearn Kandola in 2000, working with blue chip companies and government departments, nationally and internationally, on all aspects of assessment.

Ceri's books, *You're Hired! Interview Answers* and *You're Hired! Psychometric Tests,* are available from Trotman.

JAMES MEACHIN

James Meachin is Principal Psychologist at the business psychology consulting firm Pearn Kandola, where he specialises in the design and delivery of assessment processes. He is a chartered occupational psychologist and holds a master's degree from Cardiff University.

James's book, co-authored with Ceri Roderick, *You're Hired! Psychometric Tests,* is available from Trotman.

STEPHAN LUCKS

Stephan Lucks is a Managing Psychologist at Pearn Kandola where he specialises in the design and implementation of assessment and development processes for organisations, management and senior management development, and one-to-one coaching. He is a Chartered Occupational Psychologist with over 17 years' experience.

Stephan's book, co-authored with Ceri Roderick, *You're Hired! Interview Answers,* is available from Trotman Publishing.

ACKNOWLEDGEMENTS

Corinne Mills

To Jonathan, Elliot and Louis

Thank you for your love and patience

Ceri Roderick, Stephan Lucks and James Meachin

With thanks to our clients and colleagues with whom we gained the valuable experience to write this book

INTRODUCTION

The job-hunting process can be a job in its own right: this book brings together the best from the You're Hired series and helps you to tackle the three most fundamental parts of today's job application process; the CV, the interview and the psychometric test.

The book is divided into three separate parts, each covering one of these key areas. You can dip into a section if you're concentrating on a particular aspect of your job application or read it right through to give yourself a step-by-step guide to the whole process.

Don't let these stages of the job application faze you. Follow the expert guidance from this book and you can improve your employability and win the job you want.

Good luck!
The Trotman Team

CVs

INTRODUCTION

CV writing looks like it should be easy to do. However, anyone who has tried it knows that it is not as straightforward as it seems. This is because the seemingly innocuous CV works on many different levels. On the one hand, it is a straightforward historical record of your skills, qualifications and employment history. While on the other, it is a carefully crafted business proposal that sets out the business case for why you should be invited to interview.

It is deceptively tricky.

The chances are that you are reading this because you have realised this, either because you are writing your CV for the first time, up-dating your old one or because your existing one isn't getting you shortlisted. Whether you are a first-time job-seeker or a seasoned employee, you are also likely to be aware that the quality of your working life and the career opportunities that you can access are likely to be influenced by the effectiveness of your CV. Your CV can mean the difference between falling at the very first recruitment fence or going on to win the race.

The aim of Part I is to help you create a CV that is going to get you to the interview for the job you want and position you as a front-runner for the interview finishing line.

Part I helps you gather the information you need and then build a CV which offers a meaningful and highly persuasive portrait of you as an ideal candidate. All the chapters are clearly signposted in terms of content so that you can either read through Part I from start to finish or dip into the sections of most relevance to you. Also included are activities to help you research the information you need in a more fun and accessible way. It is highly recommended that you complete these activities as you will find them invaluable as the main building blocks for your CV and as preparation for interview. You can complete them within this part or copy them onto paper or your computer. Keep them handy because you will need them often.

A CV that works is time efficient, can increase your earning potential and job satisfaction, and improves your employability and choices for the future. Well worth it!

Happy job-hunting!

Corinne Mills
www.personalcareermanagement.com

1 GATHERING THE FACTS

At its most simple level, your CV is a historical record of who you are, what you have done and your contact details. The first step therefore in writing a new CV, or even revising an old one, is to ensure that the facts are complete, accurate and appropriate. This chapter is going to help you gather together and check that you have all of the factual information about yourself that is needed.

This chapter will help you:

■ identify the essential information you need to include on your CV

■ decide which optional information you want to include

■ identify information that should definitely be left out

■ collect the information you need for easy reference.

Fact not fiction

Every CV should include the following factual information:

- name and full contact details
- details of your career history
- educational record
- any professional qualifications and/or professional memberships
- relevant skills and knowledge
- relevant training and development.

Although this seems very straightforward, getting it wrong, as candidates frequently do, can have serious implications. Factual information that has been supplied by a candidate and which is found to be false, may exclude you from any other applications to that organisation. Even if it is discovered *after* you have been employed for some time, the employer could still legitimately dismiss you for gross misconduct.

So let's go through each of the above items in the list in turn to make sure there are no omissions or gaffes.

Contact details

Name
Decide the name you want to be referred to and stick to this throughout. In your private life people may call you something slightly different, e.g. Robert or Bob, but try to ensure that you refer to yourself in a consistent way to avoid any confusion. If you have a fairly common name, e.g. John Brown, then you may wish to add an initial to differentiate yourself.

Telephone contact number(s)
It is now acceptable just to quote your mobile number as your preferred point of contact. However, if you do this, ensure that you keep your mobile charged, topped up with credits if you are on a 'pay as you go' plan, and check for voicemails regularly.

The voicemail may be the first time that a potential employer hears your voice, so make sure the message is suitably clear and professional. Jokey voicemails may be fun but are not going to set the right tone for you as a serious candidate. Employers who are unable to contact you immediately or leave a message will be unlikely to ring back. Their view will be that if you could not organise a working voicemail, you are unlikely to have the professional approach that they are looking for.

If you provide your home number, then ensure that anyone who could pick up the phone is ready and equipped to take messages. They need to note down the person's name, company, contact number and pass it on to you quickly. Opportunities do get missed because messages are not passed on promptly or properly, so make sure that you leave clear instructions.

If you are currently working, do not give your current work telephone number as a contact number unless your manager is aware that you are looking for a job and is supportive. It's too risky.

Email address

Try using a personal email address for your job-searching activities rather than a current work email address (if you have one). Many companies now have an internet and email policy that warns employees that their facilities are for company business only and they will take action over inappropriate use.

It's not a great idea to risk disciplinary proceedings when you are looking for your next job, so just play it safe and set up your own personal email facility. You can set one up quickly and easily using services such as Gmail, Hotmail or Yahoo. The advantages of these email addresses are that they are free, confidential and you can access them from anywhere that has internet access. You can also set up this email address specifically for job-searching and close it down at a later date if you have no need for it, or if it becomes a magnet for spam.

Make sure that your email address is suitably professional. Your surname with initials or numbers usually works best. However, avoid using 'O' or 'I' unless they are part of a recognisable word. This is because it can be difficult for email senders to distinguish between the letters 'O' or 'I' and the numbers 'zero' or 'one', respectively. For example, Olivia222@hotmail.com is clear whereas OliviaIII@hotmail.com makes it difficult to see whether the 'I' is a capital 'i' or a lower case 'L' or the number '1'.

Be aware also that email addresses you currently use, perhaps with your friends, may be inappropriate for prospective employers, e.g. jonathan@

sexanddrugs.com. This will certainly create a strong impression, but just not necessarily the right one.

I'm just under average height and so called myself 'little Alex' in my email address. However, it wasn't until it was pointed out to me, that I realised that this could be creating a false impression and was potentially very sensitive. I changed my email address.

Alex Care
Project Manager
Real-life Projects

Many couples share an email, e.g. simonandliz@email.com especially when it is a shared home computer account. However, this is now considered old fashioned and rather twee. Employers want to write to you, not your family. Obtain your own email address.

Career background

Employers will want to know details of your work experience, educational background, professional memberships, etc. Each aspect is discussed below and you can use the forms in Activity 1 on page 23 at the end of this chapter to record all of your relevant information.

Career history
- **Previous employers:** list all of your previous employers with some additional information about their size, turnover, key products or services. You can use this information later to draw attention to any similarities between your previous organisation and the one you are applying to, e.g. similar turnover, products, multi-site locations.
- **Dates of employment:** these are essential to get right. You can enter the dates as month to month or even year to year if you want to cover gaps of a few months. However, these must be 100% accurate. Employers will check with previous employers the dates that you worked for them and your P45 will clearly state your date of leaving. Some companies even hire external specialists to double-check information on previous employment supplied by candidates. Any doubt about the date you have given them may lead them to question whether the other information you have supplied is

accurate. Don't be caught out by some casual error that could cost you the job offer.

- **Key duties and responsibilities:** for each role, include some brief bullet points about the key duties you performed. Employers want to know the scope and size of your role so try to quantify this, for example:
  - What staff responsibilities did you have? How many staff did you recruit, train, appraise, manage, etc.?
  - Did you manage a budget and if so for how much?
  - Who were your customers? How big were their accounts?
  - How often did you need to write reports, correspondence, give presentations, etc.
  - Did you have any national, international or cross-organisational responsibilities?
  - Did you help bring business into the company, and if so, what did you do and how much was it worth?

Vocational qualifications and/or professional memberships

List any qualifications you have achieved which are industry related or recognised by professional associations. These could include certificates, diplomas, BTECs, NVQs, degrees or post-graduate training, e.g. certificate in counselling, diploma in social care, post-graduate degree in education.

If you are already working in a specific field, you should also list any memberships of compulsory and voluntary organisations, e.g. the General Medical Council, the Chartered Institute of Public Relations. Such organisations often require members to work to certain standards and ethics and take professional exams. Listing your memberships and membership grade if appropriate (e.g. Fellow) will demonstrate your professional credibility and commitment to standards.

Training and development

Note any training or development that you have undertaken. This could include any of the following:

- in-house courses, such as customer service
- external courses, such as PRINCE2
- e-Learning packages, such as MCSE Microsoft engineer packages
- ongoing courses, such as Open University study
- extensive reading on particular subjects such as diversity issues
- being on the fast-track 'talent pool' at work

- workplace or career coaching
- voluntary work training, such as learning listening skills as a Samaritan
- distance-learning courses
- attendance at conferences and seminars
- participation in action-learning groups
- mentoring or being mentored
- secondment opportunities
- health and safety, first aid, risk assessment.

Make a note of any courses you are currently undertaking and their estimated completion date. Employers like to see that you are continually learning and updating your skills.

University or college education

Write down details of any degree or college courses for which you have studied. Note the grade achieved, the dates of study and the name of the institution. Where you have more than one degree, list them all, with the most recent or the most relevant first.

Secondary school education

Write down all of the qualifications you attained at school and your dates of study and exam achievements. Normally, your CV should include information on your secondary school achievements only if you have less than five years' job experience and/or do not have a higher academic qualification such as a degree.

However, you could include your secondary school education if you had excellent A level results but disappointing university grades. If you do this, then be prepared to talk at interview about why your degree results were poor by comparison. The fact that you were too busy partying is not going to impress the employer. However, they may well have sympathy for other mitigating circumstances.

If you are a first-time job-seeker, you should also make a note of other school activities in which you were involved to show off your capabilities. Examples include:

- any awards or prizes gained
- any relevant projects undertaken, e.g. participation in school business challenge
- any sports achievements
- any voluntary work undertaken

11

- being head girl or boy
- being a school council member or holding another position of responsibility
- organising events, e.g. summer fairs.

MAKING THE GRADE!

If you've ever been tempted to 'improve' your grades on your CV…

■ Employers will often check your academic record and may ask you to bring in your certificates.

■ If you lie and are found out, then any job offer is likely to be withdrawn.

■ You can be dismissed at any time if you are found to have lied at the recruitment stage. High-profile examples include Patrick Imbardelli, who in 2007 was about to be promoted to the main board of Inter-Continental Hotels when it was discovered that he had lied about his academic qualifications. He was fired in disgrace from his £300,000 job by his long-standing employer. Imagine trying to get a reference after that!

■ Academic qualifications are most important at the start of your career, but become less important the more experienced you become.

■ Many successful people have risen to the top despite poor academic qualifications, for example Richard Branson and Bill Gates.

■ There are lots of opportunities to continue your education and training while you work, including Open University and distance-learning programmes. There are even schemes to accredit your work experience and translate this into academic points.

■ If you have relevant experience, showing that you are working towards a qualification even if you have not achieved it yet, it can sometimes be sufficient to get you on the shortlist for a job where this is a requirement.

Knowledge

Write down the specific areas of knowledge you have of a subject, including specific industry or sector knowledge, for example:

- advising managers on employment law
- change management within the mobile telecommunications sector
- direct marketing for charities
- financial databases used for budget management and forecasting
- maintenance of home burglar alarm systems
- merchandising for fashion stores
- software programing languages for data warehousing
- understanding the workings of the National Health Service (NHS) including recent government initiatives.

Information technology (IT) packages

These are such an essential skill that it is worth noting all IT capabilities and your level of ability.

Publications/research/conferences/working groups

This is usually more relevant for academic staff, consultants or anyone who is seeking to position themselves as an acknowledged authority in a particular area. How do you show you are a leading industry expert? One way to demonstrate your prowess is by listing research papers and publications, consultancy projects, media activities or conferences you have attended as a speaker. Write down any industry- or subject-related working groups in which you participate. Include any instances where your advice has been sought outside your current organisation.

> If you want to claim 'industry expert' status then you need to demonstrate that your knowledge is highly regarded by others apart from your immediate employer. Articles, original research, participating in relevant committees can help to raise your industry profile and look impressive on your CV.
>
> *Delia Goldring*
> *Visiting Professor, Middlesex University Business School*

Hobbies/interests

Write down all your hobbies and interests. It is not strictly necessary to include this on your CV, but it sometimes has advantages. If you are going for a job as a sales assistant in a bookshop, it makes sense to put down reading as one of your hobbies. Interesting hobbies can also enliven an otherwise conventional CV. A secretary who is a champion water-skier – fantastic! Sports and physical recreation activities are useful to include because they indicate you are fit and healthy. This is particularly relevant if you are more mature in years and want to demonstrate that you have bundles of energy. Listing only solitary activities such as bird-watching, stamp-collecting and playing video games may lead the recruiter to wonder how sociable you are.

Gaming and online networking are popular and fast-growing social activities. However, be aware that if you mention social networking websites, employers may well be prompted to investigate your online profile on sites such as Facebook. Be careful what you publish on the web as it may be seen by a prospective, or even your current, employer.

Most importantly, if you decide to include a hobby on your CV, then make sure it is genuine and that you can talk about it at the interview. Many a promising candidate has scuppered their chances by writing about their theatre-going or mountain-climbing activities, only for it to emerge at interview that they can't remember the last play they saw and the mountain-climbing was a one-off as a result of taking a wrong turning.

> Be wary as to what you put as your interests. When I see 'reading and socialising' as someone's only interests, I start to worry. Socialising is a basic human requirement so you might as well put 'eating, breathing, going to bathroom in spare time'.
>
> *Peter Lockhart*
> *Executive Recruiter, Ward Simpson*

Voluntary work

Think of all the voluntary activities you have been involved in over the past few years. This could include fundraising, helping out at your local school, running a local football team or sitting on a local committee.

Employers are often interested in socially responsible activities. They indicate energy and community spirit, the kind of behaviours they want you to employ for their organisation.

They can also demonstrate that you have capabilities over and above your paid work experience. Taking a strategic role on an advisory committee, using advanced interpersonal skills in working with vulnerable people, or using

VOLUNTARY WORK IS A GREAT WAY TO ENHANCE YOUR CV

- In the UK, there are currently 11.6 million people volunteering at least once a month and 17.9 million people at least once a year.

- Employers often want you to have experience – and volunteering can be a way of getting this experience. Most employers will see voluntary work as valuable as any paid job – the important thing is to sell your knowledge, skills and experience gained. Voluntary roles can cover anything from fundraising to befriending an isolated, vulnerable person or press work in a major national charity.

- As well as developing your work experience and building your confidence, you will learn new skills and you might be offered the chance to study or train for a qualification.

- For career changers, volunteering can provide the chance to sample a new role, and a way into working in a completely new field – including paid opportunities within the charity sector itself.

Katie Hall
UK Workforce Hub, National Council for Voluntary Organisations

financial skills as treasurer are good examples of ways in which you can help bridge perceived gaps in your paid work experience when applying for a new role. It helps to demonstrate to an employer that you are serious about your next career move because you have invested unpaid time and energy to progress your career in this direction.

If you aren't working currently and have a gap since your last job, enrolling yourself to do some voluntary work at least a few hours a week will be enormously beneficial. It will give you an answer to the interview question 'So what have you been doing since your last job?', and you will also develop skills and network contacts.

Additional information

Think about whether there is any other information about you which may be of use to an employer. These could include having:

- a driving licence
- dual citizenship
- language skills
- rights to work in the UK if you are a non-European Union (EU) citizen
- other roles undertaken, e.g. magistrate, non-executive director.

Referees

Identify two individuals who will be happy to act as a referee for you. Ideally they should be your current and past managers. If this is problematic, then you could use someone equivalent in seniority within the same organisation or someone with whom you had a key business relationship, for example a customer whose account you managed. If you are a first-time job-seeker, you can ask your course tutor to provide a reference.

Always check with your referees that they are happy for their details to be forwarded to prospective employers. Do not assume that they will be happy to do so. The last thing you want is a referee who is unhappy with you because you haven't extended them the courtesy of asking them.

Although you need to have your referee's details handy, do not include them on your CV. The only exception to this is if they are extremely well known in their field and likely to be well regarded by the recruiter. Then definitely show off your connections.

Why is it important to retain control of your referees? If your current manager is a referee and they are not yet aware that you are looking for a new role, you need to make sure that they are going to offer you the job before you hand over your manager's contact details. It also gives you an opportunity to brief your referees on the job you are applying for and what you think the prospective employer would like to know about you. You can then remind them of all the wonderful things you did for them that demonstrate how you meet the employer's requirements. This is especially helpful if you are going for a different type of job and need your referee to be 'on message' regarding your transferable skills.

If the employer says they want referees at the start of the recruitment process, say that you are happy to supply references after your interview. Most job offers are made subject to references so it's not usually a problem, and handling it this way means that you can use your referees to best advantage.

I had a candidate's referee on the phone who was very reluctant to give a reference for the applicant (who had specifically given me his name and number). When I asked whether the candidate had performed his duties to the company's satisfaction his reply was:

'I'm sure there was nothing wrong with his work, but since I found out he's been sleeping with my wife I'm finding it difficult to say anything nice about him.'

Michelle Foreman
Human Resources Manager

Optional information to include on your CV

Date of birth

Since the introduction of age discrimination legislation in the UK in 2006, it has been unlawful to discriminate against candidates because of their age. Employers must consider your suitability in terms of your skills and experience, not how young or how old you are. Some companies will actually ask you to remove your age from your CV to support their equal opportunities policies.

However, it is usually possible to determine roughly a person's age because of the dates of their qualifications and experience. So omitting your date of birth is not a foolproof method of avoiding direct or indirect age discrimination.

If you are concerned that your age may work against you, leave out your date of birth. You may also choose to omit any work experience or background over 20 years old unless directly relevant to the role in question. If you are relatively early in your career, putting your date of birth can help to quickly put into context why you haven't got much work experience yet.

Nationality/work status

The UK has strict guidelines regarding the employment of workers from outside the EU, and employers face legal prosecution if they employ someone without the right to work in the UK.

EU citizens have full rights to work in the UK, so if your background and experience are predominantly from outside the EU, it is helpful to state your citizenship/work status. This will help the employer know whether you are immediately available to work. The eligibility arrangements are subject to change, which means that international candidates need to proactively check their permissions to work.

Information you should definitely leave out of your CV

Marital/family status

There is no requirement to include your marital status, number of children or other dependants and little value in doing so. What were accepted stereotypes 15–20 years ago, no longer apply. Nowadays, married status is seen as no more an indicator of stability than single status guarantees that the individual is free of personal responsibilities.

Religion, sexuality, political affiliations

Do not include religion, sexuality or political affiliations in your CV. The only exception to this would be where these were specifically relevant to the role in question, for example working with a particular group or community. In this event, it would be more appropriate to include it in a covering letter as part of your supporting evidence about why you are a suitable candidate.

Religion is a sensitive issue within the workplace. Employers are legally required to abide by anti-discrimination legislation, but as a candidate it is sometimes difficult to know if or when during the recruitment process it is appropriate to raise religious requirements.

If the religious arrangements you require are likely to be fairly straightforward, for example taking annual leave during religious festivals, you may wish to raise it either at the interview or when the job has been offered. However, if the terms on which you are available to work are less easy to arrange and/or could impact on the company's business operations, it may be easier to raise it earlier in the recruitment process either in a covering letter or in a telephone conversation.

Disabilities

It can sometimes be a difficult decision whether to disclose a disability. However, if a disability is likely to be apparent to the employer, or you will need some additional arrangement at the interview or once you start work, it may be advisable to disclose it. This will of course depend on each individual circumstance.

As with any sensitive information, it is recommended that if you wish to raise this, do so by covering letter, telephone or in person, where you can explain in more detail. Do not include disability details on your CV where space is more limited as it should retain a clear focus on your skills and capabilities.

Ill-health

Do not refer in your CV to periods of ill-health, especially if it is unlikely to have any effect on your capacity to work in the future. However, if the illness does in some way impact on your work, then like a disability issue you may want to raise it, but it is best to do this in a covering letter. You may be required to undertake an occupational health assessment at which you will need to declare your health record. However, you may also have rights under the Disability Discrimination Act for certain conditions.

The Equality and Human Rights Commission (www.equalityhumanrights.com) has more information and guidance for people affected by disability or health issues.

Reasons for leaving

Some application forms ask for reasons for leaving an organisation. This is not required on a CV – so don't volunteer it. The recruiter is considering hiring you so they don't want to be reminded by your CV of all the times you left an organisation.

Criticisms and conflicts

Undoubtedly there will have been jobs you enjoyed more than others and some which were not enjoyable at all. You may have been made redundant, had a difficult relationship with a manager or colleague, or simply been bored by the job.

Regardless of any negative associations with previous employers, it is essential that you make no direct or implicit criticisms on your CV. Employers want to hire candidates who have had good and positive relationships with previous employers. So make sure that your CV does not contain any references or even hints of disciplinary proceedings, grievances, tribunals, complaints, bullying, harassment, personality clashes, etc. Any references to these, no matter how justified you are, will be likely to arouse suspicion by a recruiter that perhaps you could be the cause of the conflict. Speak only well of past employers.

Criminal convictions

Some, but not all organisations will ask their potential employees if they have any criminal convictions. The Rehabilitation of Offenders Act means that individuals do not usually need to disclose any convictions to an employer if their conviction is 'spent'. A conviction becomes spent when a stipulated amount of time has elapsed since the offence was committed. Prison sentences of over 2.5 years and certain offences never become spent.

If your conviction is spent and an employer asks you to disclose whether you have a criminal record then you are legally entitled to say no. It may be easier to explain any career gaps by saying that you were undertaking a training course or voluntary work or some other reason that you can part justify.

However, certain organisations are exempt from the Rehabilitation of Offenders Act, including those whose work involves contact with children or other vulnerable people, for example the NHS. These organisations will normally insist on a CRB (Criminal Record Bureau) check. For these organisations, all convictions must be declared including those deemed to be spent. So, criminal convictions need to be disclosed when:

■ the employer specifically asks you whether you have a criminal record and your conviction is not spent
■ you have a spent conviction but the organisation is exempt from the Rehabilitation of Offenders Act.

You may also decide to disclose any conviction voluntarily if you feel this is appropriate. Clearly, disclosure needs to be handled sensitively and the best place to do this is definitely not on your CV. If you are making an initial application to an organisation you know is exempt from the Rehabilitation of Offenders Act, you can include this in a covering letter. However, if the question is asked after the interview, then this is best handled in person, either by telephone call or a meeting if appropriate.

NACRO (www.nacro.org.uk) has lots of excellent information on job-searching for ex-offenders, including full details on when convictions become spent, etc.

Their freephone service on 0800 0181 259 offers advice and information on all aspects of employment, benefits, etc.

Caring responsibilities

If you have caring responsibilities then presumably you will only be applying for jobs that complement these. There is therefore no need to separately state that you have these responsibilities on your CV. If you do, then it cannot help but subconsciously raise a query in the employer's mind about your non-work commitments and availability. There is legislation in place to help employees who need time off for dependants and most organisations have some flexibility or policy about this, so there is no value in raising this as a potential issue when it is unlikely to be one.

However, if your caring responsibilities are likely to affect your ability to work the hours required, you will need to raise this. Again, this is best done in a covering letter or by telephone conversation in the first instance rather than via your CV.

A CV should be a positive reflection of your skills and experience, so if you have to disclose your criminal record, it is best to do this separately. You should remember that if you are not asked about your criminal record, you do not need to volunteer the information on your CV. We suggest writing a brief letter of disclosure to go with your CV or application form, so that you can give a full explanation of your criminal record and reassurance that you are still a great candidate for the job.

If you have an employment gap on your CV because of a criminal record, you could say 'not in employment' or 'unavailable to work due to personal circumstances'. You can then explain this further in a covering letter if it is necessary to disclose your criminal record, or at interview if you are questioned about it.

Ruth Parker
Helpline Manager, NACRO

TABLE 1: PERSONAL INFORMATION CHECKLIST FOR YOUR CV

	Include	Do not include	Optional
Name	✓		
Address	✓		
Telephone contact	✓ Mobile and/or home	Work telephone number	
Personal email address	✓	Work email address	
Nationality/rights to work in UK	✓ If non-EU background		
Career history	✓		
University/college education	✓		
Secondary school	✓ Only if less than 5 years' work experience		
Professional memberships	✓		
Knowledge	✓		
Training and development	✓ If relevant		
Publications, research, working groups	✓		
Voluntary work	✓		
Additional information			✓ If directly relevant
Hobbies and interests			✓
Date of birth		✓ Unless have less than 5 years' work experience	
Religion		✓	
Referees		✓	
Marital status		✓	
Sexuality		✓	
No. of children		✓	
Political affiliations		✓	
Reasons for leaving		✓	
Any conflicts with employer, colleagues, etc.		✓	
Disabilities		✓ Include in covering letter if affects ability to work	
Ill-health		✓ Include in covering letter if affects ability to work	
Criminal convictions		✓ If required to disclose these then do so in covering letter or in person, but not on CV	

INFORMATION GATHERING

Use Forms 1 and 2 to capture all the essential information given in this chapter. Alternatively you can re-create them on your computer and use them later when it comes to writing your CV or completing online applications.

FORM 1: CAREER HISTORY

Name of company and location	Company information, e.g. size, turnover, products, customers	Dates worked (m/m or y/y)	Key duties and responsibilities (no. of staff managed, budget size, projects)

FORM 2: PROFESSIONAL/VOCATIONAL QUALIFICATIONS, E.G. CIMA, NVQS

Qualification	Grade	Year achieved	Institution

Training and development, e.g. any formal or informal learning activities

Membership of professional associations (membership status)

University, college education
- University/college:
- Years attended:
- Qualification:
- Grade:
- Other achievements:
- Positions of responsibility held:

- University/college:
- Years attended:
- Qualification:
- Grade:
- Other achievements:
- Positions of responsibility held:

Secondary school(s)
- Name of school:
- Years attended:
- Qualifications achieved with grades:
- Additional information:
- Other achievements:
- Positions of responsibility held:

- Name of school:
- Years attended:

- Qualifications achieved with grades:
- Additional information:
- Other achievements:
- Positions of responsibility held:

Key knowledge (technical and sector)

IT packages

Publications/research/articles/media activities/conference speaking

Hobbies/interests

Voluntary work

Additional information, e.g. clean driving licence,
achievements outside work

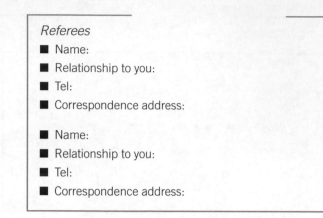

Referees
- Name:
- Relationship to you:
- Tel:
- Correspondence address:

- Name:
- Relationship to you:
- Tel:
- Correspondence address:

IN A NUTSHELL

This chapter has focused on ensuring that the factual information that you should include in your CV is complete, correct and appropriate. Remember to:

- make sure all the information on your CV is accurate
- ensure all of your contact details are fully functioning and business-like
- make sure that sensitive issues such as disability, criminal convictions, etc. are dealt with separately from the CV
- keep all your factual information easily accessible because you will be referring to it frequently.

2 PROVE YOURSELF

You may know that you are the best person for the job. You may feel 100% confident that your prospective employer will never find anyone as skilled as you to do the job. However, the employer doesn't know that. You have to prove it to them! This chapter looks at how you can give the employer the evidence they need that you have the skills they are looking for.

This chapter will help you:

- understand competencies and how they are used by employers

- collect the evidence to help prove your key skills and competencies

- discover the other ways that employers can test your aptitude and ability.

Are you competent?

The words 'competences' or 'competencies' are used frequently and often interchangeably throughout the recruitment process. They are also used in training and development and for promotion purposes, so it's helpful to know what these refer to and how they are used.

NB. In Part I I will refer to competencies, but please be aware that these are the same as (or similar to) competences.

Most popular organisational competency terms

- Communication skills
- People management
- Team skills
- Customer service skills
- Results orientation
- Problem-solving.

Survey by Chartered Institute of Personnel and Development (2007)

Competencies refer to behaviours that an organisation feels are required for effective performance in a particular role. They encompass not only the individual's technical skills, knowledge and abilities, but also the way in which these are applied in practice.

The ways in which employers will assess whether you have the competencies they are looking for are by:

- seeing if you can provide good examples of when you have demonstrated these competencies
- observing you perform tasks or activities designed to test those competencies, e.g. at interview, assessment centre or online
- giving you case studies or theoretical examples and asking you to outline your approach to the challenge set.

Unless you provide good examples in your CV giving evidence of your abilities, you are not going to get the chance to prove it to them at interview.

Which of the following two statements do you think is the more credible and why?

- I am good at handling conflict.
- My work in customer services helping clients who on occasion could be aggressive, means that I am highly experienced and able to handle conflict should it arise.

The second sentence seems much more credible because it supplies background and context. This is the key to providing the proof that an employer is looking for in your CV. If you can supply detail regarding when you have demonstrated a particular skill, the recruiter is much more likely to believe you.

At the end of this chapter, you will conduct a full self-assessment of your skills. It is likely to surface some obvious skills that you know you have, as well as ones that you might have forgotten or simply taken for granted.

Aptitude testing

Some roles require a high level of innate ability as a pre-condition for consideration as a candidate. An example is spatial awareness for a pilot. For these roles, the employer may use aptitude or ability tests to ascertain whether you have the abilities they require. These commonly are questions with a right or wrong answer.

Employers may also set practical tasks or simulations, for example a typing test or a mock sales presentation, to assess your abilities. These tests may be positioned at the start of the recruitment process so you complete these at the same time as sending in your CV. They may also accompany the interview process. Make sure you are confident that you can achieve in a test any claims you make about your abilities in your CV.

You can proactively test yourself in some key areas such as verbal reasoning by visiting some of the psychometric testing websites listed below. They feature lots of good advice and many have free practice tests for candidates to try, so you can conduct your own self-assessment. If you are considering paying for a test, it is highly recommended that before paying any money for a psychometric test you should read the guidance at the British Psychological Society website (www.psychtesting.org.uk).

Ability tests are a measure of maximum performance. They are designed to measure the extent to which candidates are able to perform specific aspects of a particular role, for example verbal or numerical reasoning.

Howard Grosvenor

Managing Consultant, SHL

- www.shl.com: includes lots of excellent advice and free practice aptitude tests from one of the UK's largest test publishers.
- www.morrisby.com: examples of ability tests found in the Morrisby Profile tests.
- www.gmac.com: the Graduate Management Admission Council provides advice and tests for graduates applying for MBA courses.
- www.ets.org: the Educational Testing Service gives advice and access to practice questions for Graduate Management Admissions Test (GMAT), Graduate Records Examinations (GRE) and the Test of English as a Foreign Language (TOEFL).
- www.savilleconsulting.com: Saville Consulting provides aptitude preparation guides and advice.
- www.learndirect.co.uk: Learn Direct offers some aptitude tests free and will signpost you to other providers where you may access low-cost aptitude assessments.

ACTIVITY 2

IDENTIFYING YOUR SKILLS

Once you have completed this activity, remember to keep this information ready to hand because you are going to need to refer to it when it comes to writing your CV and preparing for interview.

1. The skills list given here isn't an exhaustive list but is designed as a useful prompt. Use a coloured pen to highlight which, in your opinion, are your BEST skills.
2. Write down any other skills which you have, which are not on the list.

Skills list

adapting	diplomacy	interviewing
administering	directing	inventing
advising	displaying	investigating
analysing	disproving	judging
anticipating	dissecting	launching
appraising	disseminating	leading
articulating	documenting	learning quickly
assembling	drafting	lecturing
assessing	drawing	liaising
auditing	driving	lifting
briefing	editing	listening
budgeting	educating	making presentations
building	empathising	managing
calculating	empowering	managing people
certifying	enforcing	marketing
chairing	estimating	measuring
classifying	evaluating	mediating
coaching	examining	memorising
collaborating	experimenting	mentoring
collating	explaining	modelling
communicating	facilitating	moderating
(telephone)	filing	motivating
communicating (face-	finalising	negotiating
to-face)	financing	networking
computing	fixing	operating
conceptualising	forecasting	ordering
constructing	generating ideas	organising
consulting	growing plants	painting
controlling	guiding	persuading
coordinating	handling conflict	piloting
coping	helping	pioneering
counselling	illustrating	planning
creating	implementing	precision
cultivating	improving	presenting
customer service	improvising	prioritising
decision-making	influencing	problem-solving
delegating	informing	procuring
demonstrating	initiating	promoting
designing	innovating	proof-reading
detailing	inspecting	public speaking
detecting	inspiring	publicising
developing	installing	purchasing
diagnosing	interpreting	quantifying

raising animals	scheduling	time-management
reconciling	selling	training
recording	setting objectives	trouble-shooting
recruiting	simplifying	using tools
rehabilitating	sorting	versatility
relationship building	structuring	visualising
repairing	summarising	winning
report writing	supervising	working to deadlines
representing	systematising	working under
researching	teaching	pressure
restoring	team building	writing
risk assessment	testing	

ACTIVITY 3

PROVING YOUR SKILLS

1. Ask the opinion of someone whose opinion you trust to run through this with you. Often they will be able to remind you of examples that you have forgotten.
2. Write down at least 3 examples of how and when you used each one of the skills you have highlighted in Form 3. These may be skills you use every day or more occasionally.

FORM 3

Your key skills	Examples of when you have used these skills

IN A NUTSHELL

In order to write your CV you need to have a clear, objective view of the skills and competencies you are offering an employer. This chapter has helped you:

- identify your key skills
- provide evidence to prove these abilities, which you can use in your CV and in your interview
- understand that employers may also set ability tests so any claims you make on your CV regarding your abilities must be realistic.

3 HIGHLIGHTING YOUR ACHIEVEMENTS

Chapter 2 was about proving your skills and abilities to the employer. Using achievement statements in your CV is a way to show that you can use those skills, not just for their own sake, but to deliver meaningful results for the organisation. It shows employers they are likely to get a return on their investment if they hire you.

This chapter will help you:

■ understand why employers like achievements on CVs

■ identify the achievements you have made

■ write achievement statements for your CV

■ record your achievements in an easily usable form.

Value added: why employers like achievers

Many candidates write their CVs like a job description. They faithfully list the duties they performed and their responsibilities. However, they fail to show the positive impact of their work on the team or organisation as a whole.

The whole point of employing someone is that they can make a contribution to the organisation. Employers are interested in employing staff who can:

- solve a problem for them
- increase profits
- reduce costs
- sell more
- improve efficiency
- raise quality
- generate ideas
- enhance customer satisfaction.

If the employer can see that the salary they will be paying you will be more than offset by your contribution to organisational efficiency and profits, then it makes the hiring decision easier for them.

Including your achievements in your CV helps to present you as a person who:

- does over and above what is required in the role
- can see the relationship between their individual effort and the bigger organisational picture
- focuses on results
- likes a challenge
- gets things done.

Candidates who include achievements in their CV are much more likely to be seen as dynamic, business-aware, high performers and to be viewed as a potential asset rather than a cost.

Julia Gardner

Career Coach

TABLE 2: DUTY VERSUS ACHIEVEMENT

Statements indicating 'duty'	Statements indicating 'achievement'
Responsible for inducting new staff	Inducted over 20 new staff in departmental procedures to ensure consistency of approach and high-quality customer service
Introduced mentoring scheme	Introduced mentoring scheme to over 30 new staff per year, which improved staff retention and enabled new employees to quickly become effective in their new role
Trained staff in Excel	Trained 50 staff in Excel, which increased the capabilities of staff and their time efficiency in producing reports
Purchased new factory equipment	Researched and purchased new factory equipment, which led to a 30% increase in packaging efficiency
Responsibilities include credit control	Since taking over the credit control function over 95% of long-standing debts have been recovered, some of which had been owing for more than 2 years
Responsible for pool maintenance	Reduced leakages by changing sealant, which meant existing liner could be repaired rather than replaced, saving over £5,000 in materials and staff costs

Dutiful or high achiever?

If you are not convinced whether achievement statements make much difference on a CV, then compare the duty and achievement statements in Table 2 to see which you think are most attractive to any employer.

The achievement statements above reinforce the impression of the candidate as someone who understands and does their best to support the wider business needs of an organisation rather than an employee who is a 'jobsworth' doing the bare minimum.

So what have you achieved?

No matter what roles you have been working in or how long your career has been, there will be things that you have achieved and which you can use on your CV to create that positive impression. However, this is one of those activities where it is not always easy to be objective about yourself and realise the impact that you have made. So to help you, the following prompts have been designed to get you thinking about your achievements.

IDENTIFYING YOUR ACHIEVEMENTS

Think about the following questions and record your answers in Form 4 at the end of this activity.

For each role in which you have worked, aim to think of at least three to five achievements that you can include as a bullet point in your CV. You may find it helpful to reflect on the following questions.

- What positive feedback have you received at work and why?

- Have you received any awards, commendations or special mentions?

- What personal targets have you achieved?

- How have you contributed to team or organisational targets?

- What did you do that saved money, time, and resources for the organisation?

- What did you do that directly or indirectly increased profits, customers or sales?

- How did you improve the quality or efficiency in your own work or that of others?

- What did you do to improve customer service for both internal and external customers?

- What challenges or problems have you faced that you were able to overcome?

- What have you helped to change and what has been the impact?

- What ideas have you generated and what was the result?

Achievements should be predominantly work related but you can also include non-work activities that are either relevant to the type of role sought or reflect well on you in other ways.

If your role is an outcome-related one, for example sales and marketing, then your CV needs to focus heavily on results in terms of increased sales, market share, value of contracts won, etc. Try wherever possible to use numbers, percentages, size, pounds and pence, or hours to describe the results, making an estimate if the final amount is not clear-cut.

Complete the following form to help you capture the information you need.

FORM 4: YOUR ACHIEVEMENTS		
Problem, challenge, opportunity?	How you tackled it?	Impact/benefits

Writing your achievement statements

Now you need to think about how you are going to write this information in a way that you can use on your CV. Here are some guidelines to help you.

■ Try to use these formulas to help you write those statements:

Beneficial result   +   what you did that made this happen

Example: Saved management time and improved customer experience [beneficial result] by introducing an effective complaints escalation procedure [what you did].

or

What you did   +   beneficial result

Example: Introduced complaints escalation procedure [what you did] which saved management time and improved customer experience [beneficial result].

- Aim for at least six achievement statements for your CV.
- The statements should be between one and three sentences long.
- Start with a positive action verb (e.g. increased, promoted).
- Include some detail (but be succinct) about what you did and how you did it.
- State the difference that was made to the work/team/organisation as a result of this achievement. Quantify this with numbers, percentages if possible or using estimates if you don't have exact numbers.
- Ensure these are things that you can justify happened as a result of your contribution rather than being a more general achievement of the team or organisation.
- Be prepared to talk about these achievements in detail at an interview.

Table 3 lists some prompts to help get you started.

TABLE 3: PROMPTS FOR ACHIEVEMENT STATEMENTS

Won contract for...	Eliminated errors by...
Increased average weekly sales by...	Won award for...
Developed market share by...	Nominated for...
Reduced costs by...	Devised system which...
Graduated within the top 1%...	Tackled issue of... by... as a result...
Customer satisfaction rating of...	Implemented new... which...
Reduced overheads by...	Promoted because of my work...
Accelerated processes by...	Increased output by...
Improved productivity by...	Reorganised... which resulted in...

Here are some examples of Achievement Statements for two different roles to give you some ideas.

SECRETARY – SOME ACHIEVEMENTS

- Improved the ease and accuracy of recording customer enquiries by devising new client record sheets.

- Reorganised the office filing system, which greatly reduced the amount of time spent to retrieving and filing everyday paperwork.

- Achieved cost savings on bulk buying and delivery costs by systemising the ordering of stationery.

- Introduced mail-merge and window envelopes into our mass mailing campaigns, which substantially reduced time and costs.

MARKETING MANAGER – SOME ACHIEVEMENTS

■ Delivered an additional £150,000 profit per annum as a result of launching an up-sell programme for managers.

■ Achieved a brand re-launch within 4 months from inception, including a complete redesign of packaging and promotional materials, new television and press advertisements and consumer promotional activity. Product is on-track to deliver £750,000 over 2 years.

■ Increased sales by 32% in first year by developing a guest programme that extended distribution to 30 new outlets.

■ Led development of 5 new products in 2008, all of which have been green-lighted for roll-out throughout Europe.

ACTIVITY 5

WRITING YOUR ACHIEVEMENT STATEMENTS

It's now your turn. Try to write a minimum of six achievement statements for your own CV.

My achievement statements
1
2
3
4
5
6

IN A NUTSHELL

This chapter has focused on highlighting your achievements on your CV. You should now:

■ understand how achievements can create a positive impression on a CV
■ have written at least six achievement statements that you can include in your CV
■ be able to talk about your achievements in depth at an interview.

4 SO WHAT ARE YOU REALLY LIKE?

Skills and experience are not the only things being judged on your CV. Whether you like it or not, the employer is making a judgement about the kind of person they think you are. This chapter looks at how your CV needs to take personality factors into consideration, by helping you:

■ understand why employers are interested in your personality

■ identify your own personality and work-style preferences

■ provide examples for your CV that show the employer that you have the 'desirable' personality traits they are looking for.

Employers invest much time and money in recruiting new staff, so they are understandably keen to get a return on that investment. They want staff who can not only do the job, but are also motivated and get on with the other people they are working with. Most of us have had experience of working with someone who is disruptive, lazy or even dishonest, and know the negative impact they can have. Employers are right to be cautious about whom they let into their organisation. If you can reassure them on your CV that you are an asset, not a liability, then you can create a competitive advantage over other candidates.

THE THREE SHORTLIST QUESTIONS

- Can you do the job?

- Will you do the job?

- Are you going to fit in?

What every employer wants?

There are certain personal traits and behaviours that every employer will expect their employees to have. They may not explicitly state that they are looking for these, but they will be looking for clues in your CV and in your whole approach to your job search, that you understand what those desirable behaviours are, and that you can deliver them.

WANTED...

- Ability to handle pressure and conflict

- Ability to learn

- Adaptable to change

- Care about quality of work

- Communication skills

- Confidentiality

- Customer service approach

- Energy, enthusiasm, initiative

- Hard-working

- Honesty

- Professional approach

- Reliability

- Represents the company well

- Team player

PROVING YOU ARE A MODEL EMPLOYEE

So how can you prove on your CV that you have the personal qualities every employer looks for? Use Form 5 to identify some examples of when you have demonstrated these desirable personality traits. They can be everyday activities or more occasional occurrences.

FORM 5: YOUR TRAITS

Every employer wants	Your examples	Tips
Reliability		
Consistently meets deadlines or targets		Ensure CV arrives on time
Willing and ready to work		
Takes on additional tasks if required		
Excellent attendance record and punctuality		Do not claim excellent attendance or punctuality record unless you know that your previous employer will confirm this in their reference
Professionalism		
Takes care in the standard of work		Ensure your CV is well presented and clean, and supplies the information the employer needs
Displays business-appropriate behaviour even under pressure		Your CV will be seen as an illustration of your business approach
Understands business requirements		
Builds constructive working relationships		
Honesty, integrity and confidentiality		
Takes responsibilities of high trust, e.g. money, sensitive matters		Make sure all information supplied in your CV is accurate, including dates and grades

Every employer wants	Your examples	Tips
Deals with confidential information		
Follows an ethical code of practice		
Energy and adaptability		
Takes the initiative		Use positive action words throughout CV, which will give it more of an energetic feel, e.g. led, organised, created
Able to cope with change		
Willing to learn		
Ability to work well within a team		
Role within different team structures, e.g. departmental, external		If you are in a stand-alone role, you need to show you can work independently as well as within a team
Team projects worked on		
Customer service approach		
Represents the company positively		Show on your CV your understanding that customers are both internal and external and both require a customer service focus
Takes care of customers		
Problem-solving approach		
Diplomacy/handling conflict		

Use some of the examples you have identified above in your CV to show your personality 'in action'. The right column in the form shows that the employer will also be making judgements about your personality from the way that your CV is presented. As individuals, we all have our own unique style, preferences and behaviours. Some of these you will be aware of, others may be more unconscious. Your CV is likely to exhibit some of both kinds of characteristics, either overtly, for example in the kinds of achievements you include, or subconsciously, for example in your use of particular words or in how you

ly present your CV – an employer is unlikely to believe your examples
your high levels of professionalism if your CV is sloppily presented.

It is therefore worth taking a proactive approach and doing some self-research.
You can then identify and make a feature in your CV of some of the particular
personality characteristics you have that will be of positive advantage in the
role. You can also check (and get someone else to double-check) that any less
appropriate traits, for example lack of assertiveness, don't start inadvertently
creeping in and affecting the tone of your CV.

Activity 7 will help you start thinking about some of your key personality traits
and preferences. Because it is so difficult to be objective about yourself, it is
worth asking other people how they view you and seeing if their answers match
your own self-perception. Ask them to highlight what they think your personality
strengths and behaviours are – and the things you need to watch out for.

> A key point to remember in tailoring your CV is to make sure you
> communicate a sense of who you are and how you work best. To do
> this, seek to understand your work style, values and what motivates
> you at work. This means you can target organisations where you are
> likely to work well.
>
> *Janet Sheath*
> *Career Consultant*

ACTIVITY 7

YOUR PERSONALITY AND PREFERENCES

Think about the following questions and also ask others for their feedback.
Record your thoughts and findings either in this table or separately on
paper or on your computer.

- Think of the different teams in which you operate and how you
  and others would describe your contribution and approach. For
  example, leader, facilitator, creative, factual, technical, practical,
  theoretical, etc.

- Do you like working in detail or are you more of a 'big picture'
  person?

- What is your approach to planning and organising a future activity? Is it structured or more informal?

- Do you like an amount of routine or do you get easily bored?

- How comfortable are you when dealing with issues that are ambiguous, unclear or unstructured?

- How quickly do you tend to make decisions at work?

- How have you handled conflict at work?

- How good are you at persuading and influencing other people?

- How have you coped under pressure?

- How would other people at work describe you?

- How have you dealt with a mistake or a failure you have been responsible for?

- How have you dealt with mistakes made by others that affected you?

- How structured do you like your work to be?

- Do you prefer a logical approach with facts and data to support an argument?

- How much do you use 'gut feel' to make decisions?

- How important to you is it to be physically active in your work?

- How have you coped with change in the past – particularly when it has taken you out of your comfort zone?

- How easy do you find it to talk to new people?

From the information noted above:

1. Select the personal characteristics you think are particularly appropriate for your target role and employer.
2. Think of practical examples of when you have demonstrated these qualities.
3. Write down up to five examples in the space below that you can use on your CV to show how your personality is an asset. For example: I have the ability to remain calm under pressure as shown by times when I have had to deal with aggressive behaviour from members of the public.

Examples that show my personality/work style in a positive light:

1.
2.
3.
4.
5.

Personality testing or 'testing' personality?

There is a whole industry devoted to helping employers assess whether your psychological profile is the right one for their organisation. Personality testing, usually completed via online questionnaires, is often used in graduate recruitment, where the individual's capabilities and approach are relatively unproven. Organisations may also test candidates for certain jobs where they are looking for specific types of behaviour, for example stress resilience for high-pressure roles.

Personality tests have no right or wrong answers but reflect how a person taking the test would typically act or think.

It is beyond the scope of Part I to provide detailed information on personality testing, but as we have seen, all employers will be categorising you to some extent on how well they think your personality fits the role/organisation.

If you are due to take a personality test as part of a forthcoming process or you simply want to do some more self-research, check out the following websites for more information. Most have sample practice tests, many of which you can try for free.

■ www.shldirect.com: free practice personality assessments from one of the UK's largest test publishers, including sample questions for OPQ (Occupational Personality Questionnaire)
■ www.keirsey.com: complete the free online personality questionnaires: Keirsey Character Sorter and Keirsey Temperament Sorter
■ www.teamtechnology.co.uk: free practice personality test drawing on MBTI (Myers-Briggs Type Indicator).

As with aptitude tests, if you are considering paying for any kind of personality test, it is highly recommended that you check out the British Psychological Society website (www.psychtesting.org.uk) for information and guidance.

Personality at work is all about 'how' you go about doing your job – are you practical or theoretical? Will you follow your own approach regardless, or go along with the majority? Do you prefer to be around others all the time, or do you value your own space more? In this way, personality is an essential part of fitting people to jobs. Personality questionnaires are designed to assess a candidate's perception of their typical or preferred behavioural style. They can focus specifically on a person's behaviour in the workplace and therefore give an indication of likely performance at work and an objective perspective on a person's suitability for a particular role.

Howard Grosvenor
Managing Consultant, SHL

IN A NUTSHELL

This chapter has focused on how your personality is part of the selection criteria for shortlisting and helped you to:

- understand that employers will often make a judgement about your personality on the basis of your CV alone
- recognise how you can influence that perception by using examples within your CV that show your personality in a positive light
- ensure that the image you present is a consistent and genuine one, so that the content and presentation of your CV match the person they will be meeting at the interview.

5 HOW TO SHOW YOU ARE THE PERFECT FIT

A role in one organisation can be very different from another with the same job title in another company. Assumptions about what a role may entail can be very misleading. This chapter is going to look at how you can find out what the job involves and what the employer is looking for in a candidate. You can then use this information to present yourself as their ideal new member of staff.

This chapter will help you:

■ decode job advertisements

■ use job descriptions and person specifications effectively

■ research target organisations and their markets

■ research the larger job market for your ideal role

■ use all this information to tailor your CV specifically to the employer's requirements.

R ecruitment is a matching exercise. The easier it is for the employer to match your CV with their requirements, the greater the likelihood you will be shortlisted. So let's look first of all at how we can find out what they are looking for.

Reading job advertisements

When you are looking to understand what an employer wants, then the most obvious place to look first is at the job advertisements. Let's review a couple of job advertisements for a corporate legal secretary. Look at the following job advertisement for a corporate legal secretary and highlight what you think are their main requirements.

Corporate legal secretary
£30,000–£31,000 per annum

Looking for involvement? This exciting role would suit a legal secretary/ personal assistant who is looking for just that! The position is working for two dynamic partners who specialise in corporate finance. They are often abroad on business hence they are looking for a very experienced legal secretary with extensive experience of corporate finance within a renowned City or West End law firm.

The ideal candidate will be an excellent communicator as you will be liaising with high-profile clientele. A born organiser is required for this exciting role, as lots of travel arrangements and diary management skills are needed.

Very generous staff benefits on offer: 30-day holiday; subsidised staff restaurant; pension scheme; Bupa health insurance; life insurance; gym membership.

Rise to the challenge and email your CV immediately.

The advertisement seems fairly straightforward and up-front about its requirements. However, if we start to analyse it further what other information can we glean and what implications might there be for writing a CV to apply for this role?

TABLE 4: ANALYSING THE ADVERTISEMENT FOR A CORPORATE LEGAL SECRETARY (1)

Advertisement	Analysis
Corporate legal secretary: £30,000–£31,000 per annum	Salary level indicates the seniority level for the job. If seniority level unclear, check on internet and benchmark salary with other jobs to see how it compares
Looking for involvement? Then this exciting role would really suit a legal secretary/personal assistant who is looking for just that!	This suggests they want someone with initiative and energy who is willing to take responsibility rather than waiting to be told what to do
The position is working for two dynamic partners who specialise in corporate finance	This relationship is key to the role. They will want someone capable of building a strong trusted relationship with the partners. Use examples on CV of previous close working relationships with other managers. Given that relationships take some time to build, they will probably want someone prepared to be around for the longer term. The use of the word 'dynamic' in this context also suggests high energy, demanding pace, and changeable situations. Emphasise in CV about how you are used to working in such environments
They are often abroad on business...	Think of examples where you had to hold the fort while your manager was absent, e.g. sickness, in meetings or where your boss was frequently out of the office. Their absence means that you need to present a confident, highly professional image as well as being self-reliant and able to work on your own initiative
... hence they are looking for a very experienced legal secretary	State legal secretary qualifications early in CV with the number of years of experience.
... with extensive experience of corporate finance	Need to highlight prominently any experience you have of working in these areas, even if this was a relatively small part of what you were doing previously. If you have no experience in this area, then they may not consider you unless you can show them that you have transferable knowledge in this area
... within a renowned City or West End law firm...	If you have not worked within a well-known City/West End firm before, they may not consider you. However, any examples you can give of working in a similar quality, first-class, legal organisation may be helpful
The ideal candidate will be an excellent communicator...	State examples of where you have had to communicate with different audiences, e.g. clients, suppliers, other departments, external bodies. Be specific about communication skills used, e.g. answering queries from clients, writing legal correspondences, taking minutes, etc.

Advertisement	Analysis
… as you will be liaising with high-profile clientele	State any experience working with 'very important persons' (VIPs), not necessarily their names if you need to keep those confidential, but their status, e.g. senior business leader, key figure in entertainment industry
Also, a born organiser is required for this exciting role as lots of travel arrangements and diary management skills are needed.	Even if this was a relatively small part of previous jobs, use separate bullet points to give examples of travel and diary arrangements experience
Very generous staff benefits on offer: 30-day holiday; subsidised staff restaurant; pension scheme; Bupa health insurance; life insurance; gym membership	They want to attract and retain good-quality staff so they are offering good benefits. Make sure that in your CV, it comes over that you are someone looking for a long-term role
Rise to the challenge and email your CV immediately	The whole style of the advertisement is upbeat, dynamic and fast paced. Match this style by using positive action words on your CV to reinforce that you have the energy for the job, e.g. led, organised, created

As you can see, there is lots of information packed in a relatively short advertisement. So for this role, the advice would be that your CV and covering letter should focus on:

- relevant legal qualifications
- previous role with City law firm or similar prestigious legal organisation
- specific experience/knowledge of corporate finance
- experience of liaising with VIP clients
- specific verbal and written communication skills, e.g. accurate message-taking, liaison between partners and clients
- experience of acting as representative for manager or others
- strong secretarial skills including diary management
- experience of organising travel
- IT skills
- use of active, high-energy words throughout the CV to show that you are the right personality for the job.

Now let's compare this with another job for a corporate legal secretary. Same job title, so how different can it be?

Corporate legal secretary, WC1

An experienced, versatile and efficient legal secretary with strong corporate finance experience is urgently required to join this mid-sized commercial law firm based in Central London, where your fast typing and experience in churning out lengthy documents will be highly regarded.

Strong Word and typing skills and command of English grammar is essential. Knowledge of DeltaView and billing is desirable.

If you are looking for work–life balance within a professional environment, then please email us for immediate consideration.

TABLE 5: ANALYSING THE ADVERTISEMENT FOR A CORPORATE LEGAL SECRETARY (2)

Advertisement	Analysis
Corporate legal secretary WC1	As there is no salary advertised it is more difficult to gauge the level at which the job is pitched
An experienced... versatile... and efficient... legal secretary	State how many years' experience you have as a legal secretary. Versatile could mean varied organisational duties or it could just mean that you get asked to make the tea. In your CV show your flexibility, your duties involving welcoming visitors, liaising with IT, etc. Efficient – important to convey your speed and accuracy. Use words such as 'quickly, fast turnaround'. State your legal qualifications in full
... with strong corporate finance experience	State in your career profile your corporate finance experience. If you do not have this or any directly related experience, they may not shortlist you
... is urgently required to join this mid-sized commercial law firm based in Central London	They may be prepared to be flexible on some of their selection criteria if you can start soon. State your availability – especially if it is immediate
... where your fast typing, and experience in churning out lengthy documents will be highly regarded	State your typing speeds. Emphasise your fast working and give examples of meeting deadlines. Give examples of the type of long documents you have produced. This is clearly the central part of the job

Advertisement	Analysis
Strong Word and typing skills… and command of English grammar essential	State that you have excellent Word and typing skills – however, only apply for this role if this is true as it is such a key component of the job that they are likely to test this at the interview. Include on CV any English academic qualifications and specify your grades if they were especially good. Ensure the spelling and grammar in your CV and covering letter are perfect.
Knowledge of DeltaView and billing is desirable	State your experience of DeltaView in your career profile. If you do not have this experience, find out specifically about DeltaView and then draw on any transferable knowledge you may have, e.g. 'I have extensive experience of ABC, which is a comparable system to DeltaView and am confident that as a fast learner, I can pick up and apply DeltaView very quickly.' Equally state billing experience and knowledge
If you are looking for work–life balance within a professional environment, then…	The work–life balance is an important statement as it implies that you should be able to go home on time – not always the case in law firms
… please email us for immediate consideration	The 'immediate' reinforces their need for someone quickly. Send them your CV as soon as possible, as they are likely to recruit the first suitable candidate

When responding to this advertisement, the key requirements that should be focused on are:

- relevant legal qualifications
- corporate finance experience
- typing speeds, e.g. of producing long documents against tight deadlines, able to work quickly and efficiently
- immediate availability
- good written English skill
- knowledge of DeltaView or equivalent
- knowledge and experience of billing
- applying as quickly as possible.

You can see from the two legal secretary examples that although these are both advertisements for jobs with the same title, there are very different expectations of the post-holder. This shows how important it is to avoid making assumptions about what you think the job is. Try to gain as much information as you can to help you tailor your CV to what the employer really wants.

Job descriptions and person specification forms

More detailed information on a particular job is often given in a job description and person specification form. These are usually, but not always, made available to candidates before they apply for the post – either the organisation will send it to you or you can access it via its website. It is always worth asking if there is one available for you to look at because although job descriptions will vary in the amount of detail provided, their aim is to tell you exactly what the employer wants. This makes your task of matching their requirements on your CV much more straightforward.

Recruitment agencies may not always supply this information either because they don't have it or because they are trying to protect the employer's anonymity or their commission. However, it is always worth asking them if there is a copy they could send.

Job description

This will usually list the job duties, responsibilities and reporting structure for the role. You can see the kind of activities you will be involved in as well as any people management and financial responsibilities. Organisations will have their own format for their job descriptions and all their recruitment forms but they will usually look something like the examples given here.

SAMPLE JOB DESCRIPTION

Client side developer
Reporting to: Client side manager
Location: Pulham
Staff reports: None

Gladstone Computer Technologies is looking for an experienced, professional and enthusiastic front-end developer to join a world-class team.
Key responsibilities
- To write complex code using semantic X/HTML, CSS, object-oriented JavaScript and other equivalent client side technologies.
- To liaise with the product manager to ensure that all technical possibilities are explored and that products achieve the best possible look, feel and functionality.

- To work with designers and software engineers to ensure that interactive elements of designs work.
- To work with all relevant parties on the deployment of code to the live site.
- To monitor work against the production schedule closely and provide progress updates and report any issues or technical difficulties to the Senior Client Side Developer on a regular basis.

The person specification (Table 6) is usually attached to the job description and it summarises the criteria that the employer will use to determine whether you meet the shortlisting requirements.

TABLE 6: SAMPLE PERSON SPECIFICATION CRITERIA FOR CLIENT SIDE DEVELOPER

	Essential – E Desirable – D
Knowledge	
Knowledge of semantic X/HTML, JavaScript and CSS	E
Experience of commercial web development processes	E
Working knowledge of JavaScript libraries, XSLT/XML, Flash/ActionScript, Template Toolkit, PHP	E
Knowledge of information architecture principles and techniques	D
Qualifications and training	
Relevant degree	D
Appropriate web development qualifications/training	E
Key competencies	
Ability to simplify complex problems or projects into component parts, exploring and evaluating them systematically, and identifying and resolving problems	E
Ability to present well-reasoned arguments to effectively convince others	E
Able to take initiative, taking a proactive approach to work without close supervision	E
Ability to communicate with technical and non-technical audiences	E
High-performance working under the pressure of demanding deadlines	E

The person(s) responsible for shortlisting candidates will either use the person specification form as shown in Table 6 or they will have a slightly amended form like the following one, which they will use to assess each candidate's CV.

TABLE 7: SAMPLE PERSON SPECIFICATION CRITERIA FOR CLIENT SIDE DEVELOPER

	Essential – E Desirable – D	Assessment method	
		CV	Interview
Knowledge			
Knowledge of semantic X/HTML, JavaScript and CSS	E	☐	☐
Experience of commercial web development processes	E	☐	☐
Working knowledge of JavaScript libraries, XSLT/XML, Flash/ActionScript, Template Toolkit, PHP	E	☐	☐
Knowledge of information architecture principles and techniques	D	☐	☐
Qualifications and training			
Relevant degree	D	☐	☐
Appropriate web development qualifications	E	☐	☐
Key competencies			
Ability to simplify complex problems or projects into component parts, exploring and evaluating them systematically, and identifying and resolving problems	E	☐	☐
Ability to present well-reasoned arguments to effectively convince others	E	☐	☐
Able to take initiative, taking a proactive approach to work without close supervision	E	☐	☐
Ability to communicate with technical and non-technical audiences	E	☐	☐
High performance working under the pressure of demanding deadlines	E	☐	☐

As you can see from the forms, shortlisting is a systematic process whereby a 'tick' is obtained only if you have proved on your CV that you meet the specific requirement the employer is looking for. The more ticks you get, the more likely you are to be shortlisted.

Many good candidates fail to get on the shortlist pile because they make assumptions about what employers will 'read into' a CV. For instance, consider an experienced secretary who is applying for a role where diary management skills are a key requirement. They feel that the employer will know that diary management was a key part of their last job and so they do not itemise it separately. However, the employer's perception is likely to be that secretarial roles vary greatly and if the candidate has not made explicit reference to diary management skills, it is an unknown quantity and therefore unproven. The candidate will then fail to get their 'tick', which means that they may not get shortlisted.

So, never assume that employers will just 'know' that you have what they are looking for. Spell it out loud and clear with examples, focus on getting the 'tick' and placed on the shortlist pile.

If you find that you meet the majority of the criteria, but not all, then you may not get shortlisted. However, you could always try a covering letter using one of the following strategies.

- Admit that you don't have a particular criterion, but list ways in which you could easily bridge the gap: 'although I do not currently have Sage experience, I have investigated suitable courses and have enrolled on a course for next month'.
- Use transferable experience: 'although I have not worked in account management, I have always worked in customer-facing environments where relationship management was essential'.
- Show your motivation and research: 'although I do not have direct experience of working in advertising, I have read extensively on the subject and spoken with many individuals working within the industry, including your own organisation. This has given me an understanding of the particular challenges, expectations and operations of an organisation like yourself. I believe that this research combined with my keen interest and enthusiasm will enable me to quickly become an asset to your organisation'.

Sometimes, these strategies may just work.

Researching the organisation

Just like people, organisations tend to have particular characteristics or behaviours that differentiate them. As we saw earlier, employers will select candidates who they believe will fit in within their organisation. It is therefore useful to see if you can find clues about how the organisation as a whole likes to operate.

If you know anyone who works in your target organisation, or is one of their suppliers, competitors etc., try to talk with them to find out more about what it is like to work there. Sometimes, organisations give a contact name for you to ring so that you can find out more about the job. Always take up this opportunity as it enables you to gain a more realistic picture of what the job entails and also to hear, usually from one of the recruitment panel, exactly what they are looking for in their ideal candidate. Just remember that this is also a chance to sell yourself in person so as well as asking questions, prepare a sales pitch to tell them why you think you are a good candidate.

Edgar Schein, an eminent organisational psychologist, wrote in his book *Organisational Culture and Leadership* that you could get a sense of an organisation's culture by:

■ the way the organisation looked and its visual symbols, e.g. its logo
■ how the company talked about itself
■ the assumptions and beliefs taken for granted by the people who work there.

Many of these aspects you will unconsciously register when applying to a particular organisation. The way it handles the recruitment process, the information it sends to candidates, its website, all reveal essential information about the company's culture.

ACTIVITY 8

DISCOVERING AN ORGANISATION'S PERSONALITY

If you are thinking of sending your CV to a particular organisation, then it's worth thinking about the answers to the following questions to help you discover a little more about the organisation's culture and the kind of employee it wants.

■ What impression does the organisation's website give about it?

■ How does the organisation represent itself in its literature?

■ What are the organisation's values?

- What are its ambitions?
- How are employees dressed?
- What does the location, building, office décor or use of space tell you?
- How are people hired and what does that tell you about the organisation?
- How does it compare with its competitors?
- What is the organisation's approach to its customers?
- What is the reception area like for the organisation?
- What does its staff say about what it's like to work there?
- What is the organisation's approach to training and development?

How do you translate this insight into helping you write your CV?

Table 8 gives some examples of different types of organisational culture with some advice on how you can tailor your CV to match both the individual job requirements and the larger cultural fit.

TABLE 8: ADAPTING YOUR CV TO DIFFERENT TYPES OF ORGANISATIONAL CULTURE

Organisational culture	Emphasise in your CV
Bureaucratic	
Importance of following processes, rules, procedures, paperwork, e.g. civil service	Activities involving rules, policies and procedures that needed to be followed
	Applications that have needed to be completed for achievements of quality standards, accreditations, awards, grants, etc.
	Membership of committees, institutes
	Any liaison with trade unions, professional bodies
	Compliance activities, e.g. helping the organisation meet legal, health and safety, and financial obligations
Altruistic	
Focus is on a higher value, i.e. an outcome that is other than monetary gain, e.g. charity organisation	Your strong identification with the organisation's service, product or cause
	Emphasise voluntary work or community activities undertaken, e.g. fundraising, charity committees
	Achievements should focus on quality outcomes as well as financial ones

Organisational culture	Emphasise in your CV
Entrepreneurial	
Innovative, risk taking, quick to act upon opportunities, e.g. business start-ups	Use words such as initiated, created, identified
	Include examples of where you came up with an idea which worked
	Emphasise speed, tight timescales, the need to act quickly
	Talk about how you have helped identify opportunities, helped the business to grow, return on investment
	Show how you have helped your employers make money, retain or win new customers
	Highlight strong commercial and business acumen
	Mention any dealings with external investors
Expert culture	
Organisations where knowledge is prized, e.g. universities	Highlight particular expertise, qualifications, technical knowledge, specialisms, sector insight, professional memberships
	Emphasise your continuous updating of knowledge, learning and development activities
	Include examples of when your advice was sought both internally and externally
	Reports, recommendations, books, publications, guidance materials, manuals produced
Task culture	
Project based/ action orientated, team approach, e.g. management consultancy	Emphasise involvement with tasks/projects and their outcomes
	Include lots of examples of working in a team, including cross-department or cross-organisational
	Focus on objective and goal-setting activities and their achievement
	Influencing skills, time-management skills, matrix working-structures
	Examples of building a team, supervising, organisational abilities, handling conflict

Organisational culture	Emphasise in your CV
Power culture	
Organisations where decisions made quickly either by one person or a few key players with little or no consultation, e.g. some family businesses	Include examples of being asked by your manager/chief executive officer (CEO) to lead an activity, work on a project
	Highlight close working relationships
	Give examples of briefing senior management team/CEO
Creative	
Where ideas, originality, aesthetics are important, e.g. advertising, publishing	CV design should be visually pleasing and look different from a standard CV. Perhaps use PDF or web CV (see Chapter 8)
	Include ideas you have proposed and outcomes
	Include more creative hobbies and interests
	Show how up to date you are in your field, refer to industry trends
	Let your personality come through on CV, your approach to your work
	Use the jargon appropriate for the organisation/industry
Reward culture	
Where staff are rewarded for performance rather than length of service, e.g. sales-driven organisations	Focus on performance targets which have been met
	Include examples of any awards, recognition or positive feedback from management, customers
	Examples of how you have added value to the organisation, e.g. new customers, repeat business
	Use energy, action-orientated words such as led, initiated
Strategic	
Focused on longer-term objectives, e.g. economic think tank	Emphasise research and planning approach to activities
	Include examples of longer-term gains achieved
	Include change management activities, e.g. reviewing work processes, restructuring responsibilities

Organisational culture	Emphasise in your CV
Short-term focus	
Organisations focused on the here and now, e.g. telesales organisations	Use 'energy' words and phrases such as fast-paced, quick turnaround
	Focus on results achieved within short timescales
	Emphasise short-term projects

There are many other types of organisational culture, but once you become attuned to what to look for, then you can weave hints into your CV that show you understand and can fit in with how the organisation operates.

Researching the employer's market

You only need to read the business news to see how organisations are continually adjusting to external pressures whether it is a market downturn, new opportunities, competitive pressures, etc.

An organisation's staff requirements will depend, for instance, on whether it's looking to grow the business, trying to keep its head above the water or needing to innovate to stay ahead. You can use this information to good effect on your CV by focusing on those areas likely to be important for the future, e.g. your international experience because you can see they are looking to grow their business abroad.

ACTIVITY 9

ANALYSING AN EMPLOYER'S MARKETPLACE

- Is the employer's product or service in a market that is buoyant or in recession?
- Who is the market leader in its sector and how does this company compare with competitors?
- What does the organisation see as its competitive edge?
- Who are the target customers?
- What are the greatest challenges, opportunities and threats in the sector?
- What are the projected trends in the market for the future?
- What will it need from its employees in the future?

Understanding where the organisation is in relation to those external pressures will help you anticipate what the employer may be looking for right now, as well as for the future. If you are going to post your CV on an internet recruitment site or send it speculatively to employers on the off-chance that they may have a suitable job, then you need to do your research slightly differently, as shown in Activity 10.

ACTIVITY 10

RESEARCHING THE JOB MARKET

First, aim to find five to six advertisements for jobs similar to the one that you are looking for and try to determine the following employer requirements from the information provided:

- Skills, knowledge and experience
- Qualifications/training
- Personal characteristics
- Salary range
- Key duties and responsibilities
- Any other particular requirements.

Second:

- Talk to people you know, ideally managers, who are working in your chosen field. Ask their opinion on the recruitment market and what they would look for in a potential employee for this role.

- Ask recruitment agencies – they are on the front line and can tell you what skills are in demand and what differentiates the successful candidates.

- Check whether your professional association or trade journal monitors recruitment trends for its members – many do.

- Search the internet for online salary surveys, of which there are many. Simply type in 'salary survey' and your job title or sector into a search engine and this is likely to bring up some good examples.

- NB: internet job sites can give a false impression of the supply of actual jobs because some recruitment agencies advertise in more than one place or don't remove filled jobs from their lists of available jobs. Advertisements that have been placed by or on behalf of named employers are more likely to be reliable.

Third, use this information to help you:

- Check whether you are being realistic in what you are looking for

- Identify the common recruitment requirements for your target role and show how you meet these in your CV

- Focus your energy on sending your speculative CV to the sectors most likely to be recruiting for your type of skills

- Ascertain if there is anything else that you could do to give yourself a competitive edge. If so, go out and do it and then highlight it on your CV

- Benchmark the salary levels so that you know what you are worth and can negotiate.

ACTIVITY 11

WHO IS THE IDEAL CANDIDATE?

Gather all of your research from this chapter and record it in Form 6 to identify the employer's ideal candidate. You can use the form given here or create it separately on paper or on your computer.

Record your research findings on your target job(s) from:

- Job advertisements, job descriptions and person specification forms

- Talking to people who know the target job(s) or organisations

- Getting feedback from agencies on the current market for this type of job

- Benchmarking to compare with similar jobs in different organisations

- Viewing the employer's website, their marketing material, core values, etc.

- Finding out what is happening in the employer's market or the sector generally

- Comparing target organisations with their competitors.

FORM 6: THE IDEAL CANDIDATE

	The ideal candidate will have:
Skills/competencies	
Experience	
Knowledge	
Education/qualifications	
Training	
Personal characteristics, e.g. personal qualities, working style	
Organisational characteristics, e.g. bureaucratic	
Any other requirements, e.g. professional memberships	

MATCHING YOU TO THE ROLE

Use your research from Chapters 1–4 and the findings from Activity 10 to show how you can prove to the employer that you are the ideal candidate. If there are any areas that don't match, identify what you can do right now or in the future to bridge any gaps in suitability.

FORM 7: SHOW YOU'RE THE IDEAL CANDIDATE

Key requirements (see notes from Activity 11)	Examples of how you meet the requirements	Are there any gaps? If so how are you going to bridge them? For example, training, voluntary work, reading, secondment, work-shadowing, enrolling on a course

IN A NUTSHELL

This chapter has focused on the different ways you can research what an employer is looking for in a candidate. It has helped you to:

- check rather than assume that you know who the employer's ideal candidate is
- provide examples of how you meet their stated selection criteria
- identify other aspects that might influence candidate selection
- identify gaps and work out how you might bridge them.

6 THE FIRST HALF PAGE OF YOUR CV

This is the most important part of your CV because it will determine whether the rest of it is read by the employer or not. You need to create an opening for your CV that is functional and smart, and gains the employer's interest.

This chapter will help you:

- select an appropriate title for your CV

- ensure your contact details are complete, appropriate and functional

- write a career profile and career objective statement that will grab the employer's attention.

Your CV is essentially a sales document. The aim is to generate the employer's interest so that they will invite you to an interview. You are competing not only with other applicants but also with other demands on an employer's time. Typically an employer will scan your CV in less than 15 seconds, paying most attention to the top half of the first page. If you grab their attention early on with lots of relevant information, then they are likely to read through the rest of the CV. If you bury all of the relevant experience on page 2, then there is no guarantee that they will read that far before placing you on the reject pile.

Let's look at how you can make the first half page work in your favour.

CV headings

Curriculum vitae/résumé?

There is one heading that you are not going to need. Do not head your CV with either Curriculum Vitae or Résumé. It's not wrong, just old-fashioned. There is also a danger that if this is the first heading on your CV a computer could scan your name as 'Mr Curriculum Vitae'.

Personal information

Your name

This should always be at the very top of your CV, usually in a bigger font than the rest of the CV, for example, size 14 if you are using 12 elsewhere. You could also use capital letters.

Always include your name as a footer at the bottom of the CV with the page number and the total number of pages. This way, if any pages become detached as they often do during photocopying, they can easily be reassembled.

Address

Always include a contact address if you are sending your CV directly to an employer. If you leave this out, then an employer will wonder where you are located, whether you have a permanent address at all and therefore how ready you are to start working for them.

> If I can make one simple plea to anyone writing a CV, it is to remember that it is a marketing tool not an autobiography. When applying for a role, ensure that everything on your CV sells you for that job. I do not want to spend time looking for some hint of why an individual is applying for a particular job.
>
> *Cathy Earle*
> *Head of Human Resources*

However, recruitment agencies will usually leave your contact details out to ensure that all offers from an employer come through them rather than directly to the individual.

If you are posting your CV online in a public forum then you may want to include just your email address rather than all of your personal contact information, in order to maintain privacy and safety.

Telephone number

It is now acceptable just to provide your mobile number if this is the best number to contact you on. Remember not to give your current work telephone number as a contact number unless your manager is aware that you are looking for a new job. It is too risky.

Email address

Use an individual personal email address for your job-searching activities rather than your current work email address or a shared address. Set up a free Gmail, Hotmail or Yahoo address if needed (see p. 8).

UK rights to work

You need only state this if your background and experience is clearly non-EU.

What you shouldn't include

Don't include any of the following:

- date of birth
- religion
- sex
- marital status
- number of children
- disabilities
- political affiliations.

Examples of layout for personal information

> Hanif Kotecha
> 58 Elms Avenue, Sawbridge
> SW9 ABC
> Mobile: 0777 777 555
> Email: hk@hotmail.com
>
> Footer:
> CV   H. Kotecha   page 1 of 2

> John Brown
>
> Address: 7983 South Boulevard, Gladstown,
>   South Africa
> Mobile: +44 0777 666 555
> Email: johnb@yahoo.com
> Work status: Approved to work in UK under the
>   Highly Skilled Migrant Programme
>
> Footer:
> CV   John Brown   1/2

Writing a career profile

A career profile is a mini-advertisement that is placed directly after your personal details to try to capture the attention of the employer and summarise why you are a great candidate. It consists of approximately three to five sentences describing the skills, knowledge and experience you have that are relevant to the job sought. It usually sits in its own section on the first page, situated directly under the personal contact details. A career profile is optional, but used thoughtfully, it can be very effective to quickly create a positive first impression.

So what should go in a career profile?

Job title

Employees can get very hot under the collar about job titles and what they feel their role should be called. However, job titles are notoriously misleading. There is no standardisation across organisations about job titles. Even departments within the same organisation will often use job titles differently. Recruiters will look to confirm the seniority of your role by looking at your salary, scope of responsibilities, staff responsibilities, etc. rather than your job title alone.

However, given this, wherever possible, use the title of the job you are applying for, to describe yourself within the career profile. If they are looking for a 'customer services assistant', then call yourself this even if your previous job title was actually 'customer liaison officer'. This is justifiable if your previous roles have been similar in function. Psychologically, if the recruiter sees a candidate with the right job label in the career profile, even if your job title is listed differently in your career history, then they are more likely to believe in your suitability. Of course this has to be substantiated by the rest of your CV. It's no use calling yourself 'customer services manager' when your CV shows no evidence of management skills.

Key experience

The career profile should include how many years' experience you have in the area they are looking for. For example:

- *sales adviser with over 20 years' sales experience within the computer retail sector.*
- *5 years' post-qualification experience internationally as a chartered surveyor.*
- *10 years' experience working as a technical engineer within the UK telecommunications sector.*

Relevant qualifications, education, professional affiliations

Where professional qualifications are required, put these in the profile. For example:

- CIMA qualified accountant
- RICS qualified surveyor
- part-qualified paralegal secretary
- Full Member of the Chartered Institute of Purchasing and Supply (MCIPS)
- Associate Fellow of the British Psychological Society
- MSc in Engineering

You can also include relevant degrees, e.g. MBA, and/or chartered status if you belong to a professional institute.

Key knowledge
Itemise any relevant specialist knowledge you have:

- industry expert on network architecture
- specialist in crime prevention for businesses
- excellent knowledge of arboriculture.

Relevant training
Include any training that supports your work:

- trained mediator
- trained in health and safety risk assessments
- trained in CAD design.

Personal attributes
As we have seen in Chapter 4, employers do like to get a sense of what you are like as a person/employee.

Many candidates will include in their career profile some personality traits which they think will impress the employer. Some attributes that frequently appear on CVs are: dynamic, charismatic, team player, excellent communicator, hard-working, visionary, capable, dependable, people person, innovative.

However, without evidence to back these up, they are pretty meaningless. There is also a real danger that if you go over the top, it can have a counter-productive effect. The most over-used phrases in career profiles are 'good communication skills' and 'team player'. This isn't going to give you much of a competitive edge as 99.9% of candidates assume, rightly or wrongly, that they have these attributes. However, specifying what type of communication skills you have can be an important differentiator (Table 9).

TABLE 9: INSTEAD OF 'STRONG COMMUNICATION SKILLS' SPECIFY THE TYPE OF COMMUNICATION SKILLS YOU HAVE

Verbal	Written
Persuading individuals	Writing correspondence
Influencing stake-holders	Writing reports
Selling to customers	Accurate message taking
Presenting to an audience	Shorthand
Mediating conflict	Summarising information
Negotiating in person	Presenting research findings
Dealing with complaints	Writing copy for promotional materials
Making visitors feel welcome	Producing technical manuals
Relationship building	Filling in forms
Articulating needs	Producing newsletters
Translating	Transcribing
Advocacy	Writing policies and procedures
Training	Proof-reading

What kind of person is the employer looking for? Focus on identifying the particular interpersonal skills and abilities that you think they want and provide evidence to demonstrate that you have them. For example:

- strong relationship-building skills that have resulted in three of our biggest customers increasing their orders by 25%
- used to dealing with confidential and sensitive information while secretary for the executive board meetings
- highly creative thinker whose innovative presentation ideas have attracted new customers such as Jonas Lighting, Gladhouse Electricals, The Bulb Company.

You can use words such as 'results orientated' or 'commercially focused' only if your CV includes examples of where you achieved concrete goals and/or made money for the company. Equally, if you are using words such as dynamic then your CV should back this up, for example fast-track promotions, new customers won, changes implemented, awards, etc. Unless your CV shows evidence of this, then 'dynamic' is going to look more of a wish than a reality. So remember, any trait used in the career profile must be borne out by the rest of your CV.

TABLE 10: IDENTIFY PARTICULAR INTERPERSONAL SKILLS AND ABILITIES

Good negotiator ✘	Highly experienced in negotiating favourable contract terms with software suppliers ✓
Strong communication skills ✘	Highly developed interpersonal skills acquired as a result of working with individuals under stress ✓
Excellent written skills ✘	Adept at liaising between technical and non-technical staff to produce user-friendly guidance materials ✓

EXAMPLES OF CAREER PROFILES

■ Industry award-winning Marketing Director with over 15 years' experience of working in the consumer food industry. Proven track record in turning under-performing brands into market leaders within very short timescales. Responsible for many innovative and successful new product launches, e.g. Double Chocolate Cookies, which took 15% market share within 12 weeks against a dominant market leader.

■ Chartered Institute of Personnel and Development (CIPD)-qualified human resources (HR) officer with over 3 years' experience of working in the public sector. Used to working closely with line managers on a wide range of HR issues, including staff recruitment and disciplinary and grievance handling. Excellent interpersonal skills, particularly in dealing with sensitive issues such as redundancy situations.

■ Technical operations manager with over 10 years' experience of working with fast-paced organisations in the telecommunications market with X-mobile. Highly knowledgeable about new and emerging technologies and used to managing the roll-out of new products from inception to delivery in-store. Used to managing both technical and people resources to deliver complex projects within demanding timescales, e.g. the up-scaling of all mobile web-based technologies within a 6-month period.

■ 4 years' experience as a graphic designer working for prestigious, image-aware organisations such as the Creative Solutions Group. Specialist areas include the redesign and branding of annual reports, sales and marketing information and ensuring brand consistency throughout the organisation. Enjoy working as part of a creative team to innovate and refresh an organisation's visual messages.

Additional information

Think of anything else that you can put in the career profile that will make you stand out from the crowd.

- Have you won any awards?
- Do you speak relevant languages?
- Have you created something well known?
- Did you work for prestigious companies, individuals or projects?
- Have you appeared in the media in your professional capacity?
- Have you published any research or books?

If there is something that is particularly impressive or even quirky that shows you in a good light, include this in the career profile.

Writing a career objective statement

A career objective statement can be used either as part of or instead of a career profile statement. Simply put, it says what kind of job you are looking for and why. Opinions vary as to their usefulness and they do seem to be more common outside the UK and for certain candidate groups such as first-time employees.

A career objective statement is particularly helpful when:

- you have just left school or university and have little or no work experience
- you are applying to a company with lots of potential routes
- you don't want to be pigeon-holed in the area that your CV suggests
- you are applying for promotion and want to justify why you are suitable even if you do not have all of the experience required for working at the new level
- you are posting your CV on a public website and want to be clear about the kinds of roles you are interested in
- you are sending your CV speculatively to organisations.

Some typical examples of career objective statements are given below.

- Experienced programme developer seeking a role that requires extensive liaison between technical teams and non-technical end-users.
- Technical Project Manager looking for a management position that utilises my analytical and organisational skills alongside my people management abilities.

- Following completion of my Certificate in CIPD, I am looking for a role in an HR department where my substantial administrative skills can help me further my career in the HR field.

The disadvantage of career objective statements is that if you state too narrow a job focus, it could mean that you exclude yourself from other potentially interesting opportunities which the employer could have in mind. Also, if you choose to include a career objective statement, then make sure that the job you say you are looking for, is compatible with the one for which you have just applied.

CAREER PROFILE VERSUS CAREER OBJECTIVE STATEMENTS

Career profile: Useful attention-grabber highlighting your suitability

- Use if role is relevant to previous career history

- Can help you keep your options open

- Use on a speculative CV if you want to avoid narrowing your options.

Career objective: Use if you want to be considered only for specific roles or employers

- Provides opportunity to justify why ready for promotion

- Can use to highlight transferability of skills if changing career direction

- Use to explain that looking for first job/graduate entry role

- Can highlight your wish to work for a particular employer rather than a defined role

- Use if expressly asked for by employer

- More commonly used in some countries than others, e.g. USA.

NB: You can always combine the two. This enables you to retain the attractive sales pitch of the career profile while being clear about the roles you are interested in.

WRITING A CAREER PROFILE/CAREER OBJECTIVE STATEMENT

Choose whether you are going to write a career profile or career objective statement or a combination of the two. Write your statement in the space provided or separately on your computer.

1 Look through your research from Chapters 1–4 to help you cherry-pick your relevant career experience, significant achievements and personal qualities.
2 Review your research from Chapter 5 to focus on your target employer's key requirements. Aim to show in your statement how you meet these.
3 Use three to five carefully chosen sentences with a confident tone.
4 Use job title to describe yourself in a way that is relevant to the job sought and which you can justify.
5 Remember to keep all claims factual and specific and consistent with the rest of your CV.
6 Do not refer to yourself in third person.
7 Be realistic if stating the role you are looking for next.

IN A NUTSHELL

This chapter has helped you write the first half page of your CV so that you:

- can follow a format to write your CV headings including contact details and footers
- know what personal information to include
- have a career profile/objectives statement to quickly focus the employer's attention on your suitability.

7 CHOICE LANGUAGE

You will have noticed from writing the career profile statement that finding the right words to use is not always easy. So before we go on to write the main body of your CV let's look at some tips and techniques to make this easier.

This chapter will help you:

■ know how to refer to yourself within your CV

■ choose words to reinforce the image you want to portray

■ decide whether to use bullet points or full sentences

■ understand how and when to use technical words

■ find the right pitch – be confident but not over the top.

Speaking volumes

The language you use in your CV works on many different levels. It:

- conveys factual content
- directly and indirectly expresses what the individual thinks about that content
- creates associations for the reader, some of which are fairly predictable whereas others will be more personal to the individual.

Most importantly, careful and deliberate use of language in your CV can influence all three points in your favour.

This chapter looks at how you can use language cleverly within your CV to not only convey the factual information but to reinforce an image in the employer's eye of you as an ideal candidate.

Me, myself and I: using the personal pronoun

How you refer to yourself within the CV is going to influence what the reader thinks about you and how they think you view yourself. So choose wisely.

The 'I' option
This is used for a more formal approach, when you are writing in full sentences. However, it usually means that you have to repeatedly use the personal pronoun as in 'I did this' and 'I was responsible for that', which tends to look clumsy, egocentric and quickly becomes tiresome to read.

The 'We' option
Within an organisation, people frequently use the word 'we' in conversations as there is often an emphasis on team and organisational teamwork. However, in recruitment, the employer is interested in what *you* did. If you use the pronoun 'we' within your CV or the interview, then it becomes unclear what contribution you made.

The third person option
Some CVs refer to the individual in the third person as though someone else has written the CV on their behalf, e.g. 'Jones spent 10 years working with...'.

If you are thinking of writing it in this style then be careful. It frequently trips people up and they get themselves in all kinds of grammatical confusions and then start using the 'I' pronoun later on. There can also be a tendency to pile on the superlatives, e.g. 'Jones is a master of his craft…'. However, most of the time we know Jones has written it and it makes him look like a complete egomaniac.

It is appropriate to use this option if someone else really is writing it for you, e.g. a head-hunter creating a profile for you or something produced by your organisation as part of their sales and marketing, e.g. management consultancy.

No pronoun

Perhaps the easiest solution is to try to avoid personal pronouns altogether. Rather than writing full sentences, the use of bullet points led by strong action words reduces the need for any pronoun at all. The advantages of bullet points over full formal sentences are given below.

BULLET POINTS VERSUS FULL SENTENCES

■ Won a £2 million contract for new service arrangements by leading the bid team. Responsibility for writing and presenting the contract bid and project-managed its successful implementation within an ambitious 6-month time-frame.

or

I was responsible for the project team which won the £2 million pound contract for new service arrangements. Appointed to lead the team, I was involved in writing the contract proposal and I also presented the bid. I was then asked to manage the implementation of the new arrangements which I successfully achieved within an ambitious 6-month time-frame required by the customer.

Which do you think works best?

The bullet point is clean and succinct with no personal pronoun. The paragraph is longer, clumsier, repeatedly uses 'I' and full sentences which makes it seem long-winded. In the words of the Elvis song '*A little less conversation and a little more action*' will stand you in good stead.

Choose bullet points without personal pronouns, to make your message in an action-orientated and economical way.

The magic of words

A study by the psychology department of University of Hertfordshire in 2005 showed that specific words and phrases used in CVs and application forms were a key influence in determining which candidates were shortlisted.

TABLE 11: UNIVERSITY OF HERTFORDSHIRE 2005 STUDY, WORDS TO INCLUDE IN A CV	
Top 10 words to include	Top 10 words to exclude
Achievement	Always
Active	Awful
Developed	Bad
Evidence	Fault
Experience	Hate
Impact	Mistake
Individual	Never
Involved	Nothing
Planning	Panic
Transferable skills	Problems

> Every recruiter and admissions office will have to assess hundreds, if not thousands, of personal statements from hopeful applicants and will make their decision based on what they can see on paper. Choosing the right words is, therefore, vitally important if your application is to stand out from the rest.
>
> *Karen Pine*
> *Professor of Developmental Psychology, University of Hertfordshire*

Here is a list of words that you can sprinkle throughout your CV to help reinforce the message that you are a positive, upbeat, 'can-do' type of candidate – the kind that every employer wants.

Useful action words for your CV

accelerated	adapted	aligned
accomplished	advised	allocated
achieved	advocated	analysed

applied	developed	forecast
arbitrated	devised	formulated
arranged	diagnosed	fortified
assessed	differentiated	founded
attained	directed	generated
attracted	discovered	guided
audited	disseminated	handled
authored	distinguished	harmonised
awarded	diversified	headed
balanced	documented	helped
boosted	doubled	highlighted
briefed	drafted	identified
broadened	educated	illustrated
built	eliminated	implemented
calculated	enabled	improved
canvassed	encouraged	incorporated
centralised	enforced	increased
chaired	engineered	influenced
clarified	enhanced	initiated
coached	enjoyed	innovated
collaborated	enlarged	inspired
communicated	enriched	instigated
compiled	ensured	integrated
completed	equipped	introduced
constructed	established	invested
contributed	evaluated	investigated
controlled	examined	launched
convinced	exhibited	led
coordinated	expanded	liaised
created	experimented	located
cultivated	explained	managed
customised	explored	marketed
decreased	extended	maximised
defeated	facilitated	mediated
defined	filtered	mentored
delivered	finalised	minimised
demonstrated	fine-tuned	mobilised
designed	fixed	modernised
determined	focused	modified

monitored
motivated
navigated
negotiated
nurtured
operated
orchestrated
organised
originated
outlined
overcame
overhauled
oversaw
persuaded
piloted
pinpointed
pioneered
planned
prepared
presented
prioritised
promoted
proved
publicised
published
qualified
raised
ran
recommended

reconciled
recruited
rectified
reduced
refined
regulated
rehabilitated
reinforced
renewed
reorganised
repaired
replaced
researched
reshaped
resolved
restored
retained
revamped
reviewed
revitalised
saved
scheduled
secured
selected
set goals
set up
shaped
shared
simplified

sold
solved
sorted
spear-headed
specialised
standardised
straightened
stream-lined
strengthened
structured
summarised
supervised
supported
surpassed
taught
tested
trained
transformed
uncovered
unified
updated
upgraded
utilised
validated
verified
visualised
volunteered
won
wrote

Useful adverbs

accurately
assertively
astutely
capably
carefully
clearly

cleverly
collaboratively
competently
consistently
consultative
cooperatively

creatively
decisively
effectively
efficiently
energetically
enthusiastically

ethically	promptly	selectively
inclusively	quickly	sensitively
positively	rapidly	successfully
powerfully	resourcefully	well-judged
proactively	responsibly	

Use these and similar words to describe how you approached your tasks and achievements. The more positive words you can include, the more positive an impression you will create.

Toxic words

In the University of Hertfordshire study, the researchers also identified certain words it was best to avoid in a CV (see Table 11). Interestingly, the words 'always' and 'never' were often viewed by employers as negative because it suggested that the applicant was exaggerating their abilities.

Here are some other words that it is probably best to avoid in your CV, unless you are showing how you achieved a positive from a negative, e.g. 'successfully launched design previously thought unworkable'.

Words to avoid

abandoned	difficult	hopeless
absurd	disagreement	idiotic
argued	disciplined	impossible
attempted	dismissed	impractical
avoided	disorganised	incapable
bullying	down-sized	inconceivable
bureaucratic	empty	indecisive
closed down	exasperating	ineffectual
confined	failed	inept
conflicted	fired	infuriating
criticised	fought	intolerable
decline	futile	irreparable
decrease	gave up	irreversible
defeated	grievance	isolated
denied	harassed	lost

maddening	slump	unreasonable
miserable	stress	unruly
non-viable	stupid	unsuccessfully
objectionable	succumbed	unworkable
opposed	tried	weak
preposterous	ugly	withdrew
recession	unbearable	wrestled
ridiculous	unendurable	
shoddy	unmanageable	

Technical words

Most industries or professional/technical jobs have their own jargon or buzz words. These should be used to show your relevant knowledge. However, often the person shortlisting is not a technical expert, so care needs to be taken that they can understand what you are talking about.

It is safe and desirable to use jargon that has already been used in the job description or advertisement. Where you describe in detail other technical skills or knowledge, make sure that you clearly link it to a particular skill or competence described in the job description or advertisement so a non-technical recruiter can see its relevance.

Pitch perfect

The language used in your CV needs to be positive and confident. However, it also needs to avoid being 'over the top'. How can you judge the difference? Compare these sentences:

■ Managed a charity event attended by 100 people that raised £15,000 for charity and generated excellent PR in the local paper for the company
■ Superb organiser, fundraiser and event manager. Excellent PR skills.

The first statement is anchored with evidence – you know what the event was, its size and scale and the outcomes. The second sentence may equally be true but there is no evidence provided to back up the claims. Therefore the use of words such as 'superb' and 'excellent' are seen to reflect only the candidate's view which is unsubstantiated.

As a result the first sentence is credible – the second sentence is 'over-the-top'. Other 'over-the-top' language could include describing yourself as:

- talented
- brilliant
- born leader
- visionary
- wonderful
- the best salesperson in Europe
- the most capable graduate of their generation.

As stand-alone statements, these are highly subjective and unconvincing. On the other hand if these superlatives are true, then you should provide examples of these skills in action, e.g.: 'Achieved the highest sales figures in the entire European department'; 'Led organisation from verge of bankruptcy to profit within three years as a result of re-shaping the business process and developing profitable product lines'; 'Talented designer who won 2008 industry award for best website and received nominations in two other categories'.

Now let's start writing the main body of your CV. The following chapters present a number of different CV formats you can use. Read through the chapters to decide which of these suit you best.

IN A NUTSHELL

This chapter has focused on helping you choose language that will support and complement the content of your CV. Remember to:

- use positive language throughout your CV, including action-orientated and positive descriptive words, e.g. 'created' or 'sensitively'
- use negative words only if showing how you improved the situation, e.g. 'Achieved 30% sales increase for a product line that had previously performed badly'
- always provide evidence of any claims about your excellent performance
- results-orientated bullet points reinforce the sense of energy in the CV and help avoid the over-use of the 'I' or 'we' pronoun
- technical CVs should be understandable by a non-technical person who has only the person specification in front of them
- pare down the detail to the bare minimum. Avoid flowery and over-wordy sentences.

8 CV TEMPLATES

CVs come in many formats; which one you use will depend on your work history and target role. This chapter covers the main CV formats.

You can choose to present your CV in one or more of these formats depending on which ones sell your skills most effectively and suits you best.

This chapter will help you:

- understand when to use each different format of CV

- write your CV in each of these formats.

Chronological CVs

A chronological CV organises its content according to a historical timeline. Employers like them because they can see very easily what your work history and career progression has been. They can also see any career breaks, the length of each employment and any changes in career path.

If you are looking for a role which is a natural progression given your career to date, then the chronological CV format will be appropriate and will highlight your suitability for the role, for example a conference assistant who is looking for a similar role in the same industry or for the next step. Under the most recent employment it should be possible to demonstrate relevant skills and experience that the employer will be interested in. It is also helpful in highlighting the names of your previous employers. This can be advantageous if they are prestigious brands or competitors of your target employer and therefore likely in themselves to attract interest.

However, if your last employment(s) have not been directly relevant to the role you are applying for, then a chronological CV will do you no favours. It will instead raise questions about why you are applying. Equally, if you have had several jobs, gaps between jobs or career breaks, then this CV format could make what is a very legitimate work history look irregular and troublesome. In this case, you would be advised to look at one of the other CV formats, such as a functional CV, which is covered in this chapter on pages 111–115.

Let's look at how you would write a chronological CV using all of the information you have gathered when doing the activities in this part.

PROS AND CONS OF CHRONOLOGICAL CVs

Advantages of a chronological CV

- A chronological format is liked by most employers.

- It is a clear and simple format.

- It is easy to chart your career progression, e.g. promotions or growing specialisation.

- It is more in line with application forms with experience, dates, employment history laid out in a straightforward manner.

Disadvantages of a chronological CV

- A chronological CV will show up any inconsistencies or variations in your career path.

- It can reveal unimportant or inconsequential jobs.

- It can reveal periods of unemployment or brief job tenure.

- It may emphasise your lack of wider experience if you have stayed in one job for a long time.

Template for a chronological CV

Name

Address
Tel:
Email:
Date of birth (optional):

Career profile

(use or adapt the career profile you wrote in Activity 13)
Describe yourself using the same or a similar title to the job you are applying
for and give details of your experience in the sector. Follow with a few lines
(approximately three to five) which summarise what you have to offer in relation
to the job, e.g. key skills and experience. Include a mix of technical, professional
and softer skills. Include prestigious brand names, awards, etc. Your profile is the
most important part of your CV and it should encourage a prospective employer
to read further.

Career history

(use material from Activity 1 on information gathering and Activity 12 for your
research on matching you to the role)
- Most recent job title   • Organisation   • Date (year to year)
- Write a brief description: one to two sentences on the company, its size,
  products, location, structure (Activity 1).
- Describe your key achievements in your last post, bearing in mind the
  requirements for the job you are applying for. Quantify those achievements –
  what difference did it make to the organisation? (Activity 5).
- Do not write your job description here – cherry-pick skills and duties and
  personal qualities relevant to the role being sought.

Previous job title	Organisation	Date
Previous job title	Organisation	Date
Previous job title	Organisation	Date
Previous job title	Organisation	Date

Go back 10–15 years or more if your job previous to this still has relevance to the
job for which you are applying. You can give fewer details the further back you
go. Try not to repeat yourself. If you are in danger of doing this, a functional CV
may be more appropriate.

If you need to talk about a period where you had several jobs but do not wish to go into specifics you could group them together as 'a variety of roles, including Project Manager, Team Leader, Team Coordinator, which enabled the development of my ...'.

Qualifications and training

- List relevant professional qualifications/memberships first, e.g. Trained NVQ Assessor.
- Higher academic qualifications should be listed before others unless lower qualifications are of more immediate relevance.
- School qualifications do not need to be included on the CV where you have higher qualifications.
- Training can be a separate heading. Do not list all training courses but do include those that may have a direct benefit on new employers, e.g. first aid, project management. Remember training does not have to take place in a classroom to have value, e.g. distance learning, e-learning.

Additional information

- This section can be used to include any information that will show you in a good light as a candidate.
- You might like to include any voluntary work that you do, e.g. school governor.
- You can also include language skills, clean driving licence, inventions, achievements outside work.

Interests

This is optional, but can be useful if you have limited work experience and want to give the employer more of a sense about what you are like as a person. Also if you are more 'mature' in years, you can use this section to show that you are fit, energetic and up to date.

The CV should be no more than two pages long unless you need to include lists of publications or research.

Functional CVs

A functional CV format will enable you to highlight in the first page of your CV the skills and experience you have that are of most relevance to the employer. This can include paid and unpaid work, transferable skills, qualifications or any other additional information which will demonstrate your suitability.

This is a particular advantage if you know you have the skills and experience to do the job, but your current or past employment has been in an unrelated role. Where an employer has detailed specific competencies that are required, you can also use these competencies as headings and provide examples with accompanying evidence.

You can select your headings and order them according to how they will sell you best. Some examples of those you can use are:

- career profile
- career history
- work experience
- key achievements
- responsibilities
- key skills
- key competencies
- education
- qualifications
- training
- innovations
- publication
- additional information
- hobbies/interests
- project experience
- IT skills
- specialist knowledge
- positions of responsibility.

Depending on your experience and the job in question, it may make sense to prioritise some areas rather than others. For example, for jobs in the higher education or research sector, it makes sense to put your educational details first and then include headings for any publications, research, conference speaking events and continuous professional development activities, etc. If you are selling yourself as an IT technical expert, you should specify your technical skills and knowledge up-front.

Chronological detail regarding your employment history is generally relegated to the second page. This means that any gaps in employment, unconnected jobs, etc. are downplayed as you will hopefully have persuaded the employer on the first page that you are suitable for shortlisting.

If you feel that the functional format is a good format for your CV then you can follow the template provided here as a guide.

PROS AND CONS OF FUNCTIONAL CVs

Advantages of the functional CV

- It prioritises the areas of most relevance to the employer.

- You can combine skills and experience used in different jobs to strengthen what could otherwise come across as rather thin experience.

- You can use paid and unpaid work experience to support your application.

- You can omit or downplay any work history that could be seen as a distraction.

- Employment gaps or lots of short-term jobs are not as noticeable as in a chronological CV.

- It allows you to show your transferable skills, which is essential if you are seeking to change career direction or are a less than obvious candidate.

Disadvantages of the functional CV

■ Employers are slightly more suspicious of this format given its usefulness in hiding things that the candidate would rather the employer didn't know.

■ You will still need to supply the detail of employment dates, qualifications, etc. because the employer will want verification of whom you worked for and when.

■ It can sometimes be unclear about the skills you gained from a particular job or experience.

■ If you have had good career progression in an appropriate field, a functional CV will not show this to as good an advantage as the chronological CV.

■ It can be tricky to get the balance of information right and not make the CV too long.

Template for a functional CV

Name

Address
Tel:
Email:
Date of birth (optional):

Profile
(use or adapt profile written in Activity 13)
Describe yourself using the same or a similar title to the job you are applying for and give details of your experience in the sector. Follow with a few sentences (approximately three to five) that summarise what you have to offer to the job, e.g. key skills and experience. Your profile is the most important part of your CV and should encourage a prospective employer to read further.

Key skills and experience/key achievements or other relevant heading
(use research from Activity 12 on matching you to the role)
* From reading the advertisement or person specification for the job, show directly how you meet the selection criteria, choosing examples of how you demonstrate the competencies required.
* Put the information in bullet points, putting those most relevant to the job you are applying for at the top.
* Think of the skills you have developed from different jobs and even from activities outside work that show the competencies the employer is looking for.
* You can also include sub-headings that match the selection criteria, e.g. financial management, training, etc.
* Include a mix of technical, professional and interpersonal skills.
* Include memberships or affiliations as appropriate.
* For key achievements, use the information you gained from Activities 4 and 5 in Chapter 3 to pick out two or three particular achievements that show your capabilities for the role, e.g. if the employer wants organisational skills, choose an example that shows this off to good effect.
* Quantify those achievements, e.g. increased sales by 30% over 2 months.
* This section will probably take up most of the first page.

Career summary
Most recent job title	Organisation	year to year
Previous job title	Organisation	year to year
Previous job title	Organisation	year to year

You can summarise your jobs or put a couple of lines about key responsibilities under each one. If you need to include a period where you had several jobs but do not wish to go into specifics you could group them together, e.g. '1995–1999, worked in a variety of office-based roles including Personal Secretary, Corporate Secretary, Team Coordinator, which helped me develop my administrative skills and my IT capabilities.'

Qualifications and training

- If qualification is highly relevant include it in the career profile or on the first page. Otherwise list relevant professional qualifications/memberships first, e.g. Trained NVQ Assessor.
- Higher academic qualifications should be listed before others unless lower qualifications are of more immediate relevance.
- School qualifications do not need to be included on the CV where you have higher qualifications.
- Do not list all training courses but do include those that may have a direct benefit on new employers, e.g. first aid, project management.
- Remember training does not have to take place in a classroom to have value, e.g. distance learning, e-learning.

Other information

This may include any other relevant information, e.g. clean driving licence, languages, and any other piece of information which is significant.

Interests

This is optional. Three or four are usually sufficient but do think about whether you would be happy to talk about them and what they say about you. Make sure that they genuinely are your interests.

The CV should be no more than two pages long unless you need to include lists of publications or research.

One-page CVs

First a warning: do not send a one-page CV as part of an application for an advertised job unless you have been specifically requested to do so. The two-page format is the default standard.

However, there are particular instances when a one-page CV can be very effective. Most commonly they are used as a 'teaser' advertisement to gain interest or a meeting without giving too much away in the first instance.

Following your research on potential employers, you might use it to send speculatively to an employer you are interested in working for. By carefully cherry-picking certain key skills, knowledge or achievements, which you know will benefit an organisation, you can gain interest and obtain meetings with your target employer.

The other advantage of this CV format is that you don't necessarily need to include your past employment details. You can refer to these indirectly such as '5 years' working as key account manager for well-known household brand'. This can be useful if the details of your employment history are either not helpful or if confidentiality is important. If you are approaching a competitor, you may want to be discreet.

You might also devise a one-page CV if you are self-employed or if your company supplies potential customers with career background on their staff as part of the company's sales pitch. This is particularly relevant for professional service providers, consultancies or any other enterprise where the individual's expertise is a key factor in winning new customers to the company, e.g. training specialist.

PROS AND CONS OF ONE-PAGE CVs

Advantages of a one-page CV

- It is quick and easy for employer to read.

- It has the ability to be highly selective in information included.

- It can hide details of current employer if still working for them.

- It is effective if making speculative approaches to potential employers, as it can be used to gain interest without giving too much information away.

- It can be used by your current employer to market their services to potential customers.

- If you are self-employed, you can use this format to show your credentials.

- It is appropriate for online forums such as social-networking websites.

Disadvantages of a one-page CV

- It is unsuitable for applying for advertised vacancies.

- It is unsuitable for applying to agencies.

- The balance of information can be tricky to get right.

- Any claims made still need to be substantiated.

Here is a template CV which you can use as a guide to write your own CV in this format.

Template for a one-page CV

Name

Address (optional)
Tel/Mobile:
Email:

Profile (optional)

Describe yourself in terms of your experience and specialisms. You could include key brand names, organisations worked with or impressive projects.

Key skills and experience or key achievements

- Focus on activities that you have undertaken and that have added value to the organisation, e.g. increased profitability, efficiency, quality.
- Quantify all achievements: use numbers, percentage points, budget size, etc.
- Relate all skills and experience directly to customer's/employer's anticipated needs

Career history

Present this in summary form, for example:

- 2002–2008: Training Consultant, Albin Training Consultancy
- 2000–2002: Training Director, The Shires Training Consultants
- 1995–2000: Training Manager, Train to Train

Alternatively your career history can be written in full sentences without naming organisations, e.g. 5 years' experience of working with organisations as diverse as high-street banks, large-scale accountancy practices and insurance companies, as a management development specialist.

Education/training

Give your highest qualifications and only relevant training.

Affiliations, professional memberships

Include any details that enhance your professional status and/or are prestigious in themselves.

Developing your own CV website

If you have a portfolio of work that prospective employers would find helpful to view, then consider creating your own website. You can use it to display all of your relevant information and background with examples of your work and testimonials from satisfied clients or employers. This approach is highly suitable for individuals in the following and similar fields:

- website developers
- designers
- journalists
- artists
- performers
- film-makers
- freelance employees, e.g. coaches

The links to the website can be included within a traditional CV that you send as normal to an employer or to a recruitment website. You can also include it on business cards. If you email companies directly with a covering email and the link to your website within the body of the email, then you may need to check that they received the email as spam filters can be sensitive to links.

PROS AND CONS OF HAVING YOUR OWN CV WEBSITE

Advantages

- It can replace physically carrying around a portfolio of your work (most of the time).

- There is now an expectation that if you are a creative professional, e.g. a designer, you will have a website with examples of your work.

- There are no limits on space or the type of material you can include.

- You can use photos, video, graphics, sound, links, etc.

- You have the chance to use your creativity in the design of the website, which in itself can impress your target audience as much as the content.

(continued)

(continued)

Disadvantages

■ It requires financial investment.

■ Developing the website can take from weeks to months.

■ It needs maintenance – a website where links don't work or the content is not displayed correctly can lose you business.

■ It needs regular updating.

■ Many roles will still need a conventional CV format.

How to build your own website

If you are interested in setting up your own website, there is a wealth of information available on the internet on how to do this. Simply search on 'how to set up your own website' in your preferred search engine.

The basic steps you will need to take are:

1. Choose a domain name, which will be your website name. It's like choosing a company name in that, first, you need to make sure it's available, and, second, you have to pay to register it. You can find domain name companies by searching on the web.
2. You will need a web host to host your website on the internet, for which another fee is payable, usually annually.
3. Design your website. This will depend on your ambitions, your capabilities and your budget. You can use website templates that you can customise. You can build it from scratch using specialist software if you are capable, or you can get someone else to design it for you. If you are thinking of using a professional, be aware that the costs could range from a few hundred pounds to several thousand for more complex projects.

What to include on your website

If you are using this website to obtain your next role or engagement, then it needs to pay as much attention as a regular CV to your key selling points, and what you think the target audience is looking for. The visual presentation may be more sophisticated, but there is still no margin for error. Poor layout, spelling mistakes, etc. will not be forgiven.

The website should include:

- your name
- how to contact you
- your credentials, e.g. technical skills, relevant qualifications, education
- what you can offer (do the sales pitch!)
- information to impress, e.g. exhibitions, prestige projects, well-known customers
- relevant work history (dates optional)
- photo of you, if you are a performer or you work in an area where a personal relationship is important, e.g. image consultant. Make sure the photo shows you in your professional capacity
- photos of your work (if artist, designer)
- video or sound clips if appropriate
- articles written by you or about you
- quotes, testimonials, glowing reviews or case studies.

A website also gives you the chance to express more personal information, perhaps about your approach to your work, e.g. 'My aim is to surprise and delight my clients with highly innovative design solutions that combine practicality and a sense of fun'.

However, resist the temptation to include irrelevant personal information, e.g. old family photos, early history unless it is directly of relevance. Keep it strictly professional. The audience want to know what you can do for them, not what your favourite bands are.

On the next page is an example of a website for a web designer. You can find many more examples by typing in 'online portfolio CV' into your preferred internet search engine. It is extremely useful to see what others have developed and what you think works and what doesn't. You can then start to devise your own.

A web designer's website

_MILLSYinc.

_Elliot Mills
_020 555 555
_em@yahoo.co.uk

_Download CV

_Client List

Gnomes Garden Industries
All-Year-Round Organic Vegetables
St Augustus Horticultural Society
Japanese Koi Fish
'Health Is Wealth' Lifestyle Magazines
Barrington Spa
The Interior Design Company
Just Gorgeous Ornaments
Wood Garden Centres
Garden Wall Art
C&A Landscaping
Greg Dymon Personal Training

Click on a client to show
more work

_Contact me

Name

Email

Query

Submit

MY BACKGROUND

My name is Elliot Mills and this is my portfolio of website and design work. I am a freelancer so I'm always interested in new projects. I have 5 years experience of website design work helping clients within the aspirational lifestyle sector to develop a customer-friendly, visually pleasing, professional and trouble-free website.

TECHNICAL SKILLS

Code includes xHtml, JavaScript, CSS, Action script versions 4, 5, ASP and VB and PHP, Perl. Good understanding of SQL database. Programmes include Photoshop, Image Ready, Illustrator, Dreamweaver, Flash, After Effects, Premiere, InDesign and Quark. Mac OSX and Windows 2000/XP platforms.

CURRENT WEBSITES

www.gnomesgi.com
www.candalandscapes.co.uk
www.ayrorganic.com
www.staugustus.horticulture.co.uk
www.jkfish.com

www.interiordesign.com
www.barringtonspa.co.uk
www.justgorgeous.org.uk
www.woodgardens.com
www.gregdymonpt.com

I take the time to really understand what you are looking for and will always provide you with a range of ideas from which you can choose. I have a real creative flair and the ingenuity to provide highly impressive websites which are inspiring, functional yet also low maintenance.

TESTIMONIALS

"We were delighted with our site. Elliot completed it in record time and he really got the essence of how we wanted the site to work. We were very pleased!" S. Moon ABC Ltd

"As complete beginners to the internet, Elliot helped us to understand our options and make great choices regarding the design and functionality of our site. He also kept costs within the budget we had set. We would highly recommend him!" M. Malone RST UK

IN A NUTSHELL

Now you have a good idea of which type of CV to use for certain job applications.

Use a chronological CV when:
- your last few roles/employers are directly relevant to the job being sought
- you have been promoted and/or been given additional responsibilities throughout your career

Use a functional CV when:
- your career path has been more haphazard than steady progression
- changing career direction to display your transferable skills.

Use a one-page CV when:
- you are self-employed, to use alongside other company marketing material
- you wish to upload your CV to a social networking website

The way your CV looks on a website is as important as the content. Make sure you:
- avoid a feature-heavy layout, unless sending as PDF
- check, double-check and triple-check spelling.

9 HOW TO MAKE YOUR CV LOOK GOOD

Employers will judge your professionalism not only by the content of your CV but also by the standard of its presentation.

This chapter will help you to:

- produce a CV that is visually attractive as well as functional

- know the etiquette for sending your CV by post

- decide whether to send a photo

- quality check your CV so that it is error free.

A nicely presented CV says to the recruiter that you have taken care in your application, and therefore you are likely to:

- want the job because you have clearly made an effort
- have good quality standards because of your attention to detail
- act as a good representative for the company because you understand how to make a good impression.

Your CV must be produced using a computer – even if the role for which you are applying does not require IT skills. A CV or covering letter that is hand-written, or which shows poor IT skills, will make you look very old-fashioned and is almost certainly going to end up on the reject pile.

The relative ease with which documents can be produced and amended electronically also means that there are high expectations regarding the aesthetics of the CV and a low tolerance of mistakes.

If you don't have strong IT skills, there are several ways to improve and this is a very worthwhile investment. Check out www.learndirect.co.uk for more information on online programmes and also courses at your local college. IT facilities can also be found at libraries and internet cafés.

However, if you are really struggling with the IT demands of writing a CV, then ask someone else if they can type it for you as a favour, or pay to have it done professionally through a local secretarial service or CV service. Then, go and get yourself on a course.

Making your CV look attractive

The following guidelines are designed to help you lay out your CV in a way that reinforces the highly professional image you are trying to convey.

BEAUTIFY YOUR CV

■ **Compatibility:** formatting options such as columns, shading, boxes, etc. may look nice, but they could interfere with the recruiter's software package. Avoid these formatting options, unless you have checked that the format will be compatible.

■ **Font size:** choose one font to use throughout. Arial or Times New Roman 10–12 pt always work well.

■ **Margins:** use margins of at least 2.5cm on either side and on the top and bottom of the page.

■ **Headings:** use a consistent style for headings, either bold, all capitals and/or slightly bigger font. Underlining looks messy and can confuse some recruitment and scanning software.

■ **Bullet points:** use standard bullet point formats as unusual symbols can confuse software.

■ **Punctuation:** be consistent in the use of full stops at the end of bullet points and/or paragraphs.

■ **Alignment:** make sure all headings, paragraphs, etc. are in line with each other.

■ **Justification:** text looks better if it is not justified as this can leave odd spacing in the copy.

■ **White space:** make sure that around headings and paragraphs of text there is plenty of white space to make it look aesthetically pleasing. If you are struggling to get your information into two pages, it is better to edit and remove text rather than pack it in too tightly so it looks cramped.

■ **Colour:** your CV will be printed out and photocopied in black and white so make sure it works well in monochrome format.

■ **Length:** aim for a CV that is no longer than two A4 pages. The only exception are academics who need to list their publications, presentations, etc.

- **Footers:** include your name and the page number in the footer of each page in case they get muddled once printed out.

- **Creatives:** if you are in a creative profession, you may want to demonstrate your design abilities within your CV. Do this in a PDF format but make sure that the recipient can read it, as photos or Jpegs may be blocked by spam filters.

Say 'cheese!'

In certain countries it is standard procedure to send a photo with your CV. However in the UK, strong anti-discrimination legislation means that photos are not encouraged as they can potentially leave the employer open to accusations of bias. The only time a photo is normally requested is in those fields of entertainment where appearance is a justifiable selection criteria.

Sending in an unrequested photo will lead the employer to question whether you understand basic UK business principles and legislation. It will show naivety, and that in itself could be a reason to reject you. So don't include a photo unless it is expressly asked for. If it is required, perhaps because the employer's recruitment function is handled abroad, then use a photo that shows you in the clothes and environment similar to that in which you would be working, i.e. business appropriate.

Quality control

Spelling
The odd spelling error in everyday email communication may be forgivable – but when you are job-hunting, it becomes a reason to place you on the reject pile. In a 2007 survey by the UK Department for Education and Skills, it was revealed that as many as one in four CVs contained spelling mistakes. One of the most regular mis-spellings were the misuse of their, they're and there.

Does this matter? Well, 58% of employers in south-east UK who were asked, said that they would reject applicants who made such mistakes. So why is it so common to see spelling mistakes? There may be a number of reasons.

- It's not always easy to pick up spelling mistakes on a computer screen.
- Spell-checkers don't pick up every mis-spelling, particularly if the mis-spelt word is a valid word in its own right or is okay in American English.
- Spelling and grammar is a weak point for many people and therefore more challenging to get right.

While there are several good reasons why there could be mistakes in your CV, there are even better reasons why you should ensure it is 100% accurate. The spelling mistake that is so easily missed by you will stick out like a sore thumb to anyone else who reads it. To the recruiter it will smack of sloppiness and lack of attention to detail – and your CV will be heading for the reject pile.

So if you want your CV to be read and considered, make sure that you:

- use the spell-check facility on your computer
- check the spelling yourself
- print the page off and then check each page carefully
- get someone else to check it for you.

IN A NUTSHELL

The way your CV looks is as important as the content. Make sure you:

- avoid a feature-heavy layout, unless sending as PDF
- take time to make the layout look professional
- do not include a photo unless specifically requested
- check, double-check and triple-check spellings.

10 CVs FOR SPECIFIC CAREER CHALLENGES

Everyone has a different career situation, but there are certain categories of job-hunter who face particular CV challenges. This chapter features advice and CVs for some of those including:

■ graduates and school-leavers

■ career changers

■ people with career gaps

■ technical staff

■ creative and media

■ managers

■ internal promotions.

The basic principles of CV writing apply no matter what your personal situation. Research the job, demonstrate you have what they are looking for and then organise the information on the page in an attractive and professional manner.

This chapter offers additional tips for where organising and presenting the content presents its own challenges.

CVs for graduates and school-leavers

Looking for your first 'proper' job is exciting and daunting. How do you convince an employer you are a great person to hire, when you have limited work experience to draw on?

Well, everyone has to start somewhere. What employers are looking for in their young staff is potential: the capacity to learn, the motivation to work hard and the ability to get on with people. They also want to see that you have thought about why you are suitable for the role and that you genuinely want to do it.

So, let's look at how your CV can help convince them that you have got what it takes.

Career objective/career profile

If you are using your CV for a specific role, include a career objective that states you are looking exactly for that role. For example, a graduate with experience of working Saturdays with an electrical retail store might apply for a sales-type role with this career profile:

'Business graduate experienced in retail sales and customer service environments. Used to advising customers on a range of complex technical products, processing sales and helping with merchandising. Regularly earned bonuses as a result of meeting personal and team targets. Looking for a position where I can further my interest in sales and business development.'

However, if they wanted to apply for an accountancy role then they could try:

'Business graduate seeking trainee accountancy role to further my interest in the financial aspects of running a business. Used to dealing with cost calculations, payment processes and following strict financial procedures as a result of my experience working for large electrical retailer.'

Academic studies

You may want to put this as one of your first headings so that they can see you are a new job-hunter.

Include details about the components of your course only if it is directly relevant to the job sought, e.g. you have a marketing degree and are applying for a marketing-related role or your course has given you an awareness of the organisation's industry or product.

You may want to highlight under your studies any involvement in the following highly transferable skills:

- data analysis, interpreting statistical information
- IT skills
- team-working, group project work
- communication and presentation skills
- report writing
- creativity, initiative and design ability.

Employers particularly want good communication skills, so this is an area to emphasise throughout your CV.

If your courses were completed abroad indicate the level to which they are equivalent, e.g. Baccalauréat (the A level equivalent). Some graduate entry programmes will require you to have a minimum grade on your degree. This is usually a non-negotiable requirement, and if you don't meet the employer's specific requirements then you might as well not apply. However, if you are intent on working for that particular organisation you can always look to enter via a different route, i.e. direct entry into one of their other jobs.

Relevant experience: young people by definition have less experience so you have to make the most of what you have. You can do this by highlighting prominently on your CV any work experience that is directly related to your target role (paid or unpaid), for example:

- student placements
- temporary jobs within the target field
- relevant voluntary work.

Other paid work (part-time or temporary): it does not matter how long you worked in each role, nor the job title. It is the transferable skills you acquired that are most important, for example:

- administrative work: accurate data entry
- working in a shop: customer service skills
- catering work: health and safety awareness
- helping at an event: dealing with the general public
- factory work: team work
- telesales: working to targets.

Voluntary work activities: these show your community spirit, energy, work ethic as well as potentially transferable skills, for example:

- any charity fundraising activities: organisational abilities
- visiting elderly people at a home: helpfulness
- involvement in charity campaigns: influencing and persuading
- writing articles for youth group newsletter: written communication skills.

Positions of responsibility which demonstrate that you have been trusted by others, can take charge of a task, show leadership, for example:

- student representative
- guide/scout leader/air cadet
- community responsibilities, e.g. church, youth groups
- student welfare volunteer.

Other activities which show your capabilities, for example:

- sports achievements and memberships
- any design projects
- any entrepreneurial activity, e.g. selling customised t-shirts
- public speaking/debating society
- amateur dramatics/music activities.

Relevant skills: you should itemise any specific skills you have which may be relevant, for example:

- your IT skills and capabilities, e.g. advanced user of Word
- specific communication skills, e.g. accurate message-taking, handling conflict, persuading
- language skills
- first aid
- clean driving licence
- research/report writing skills
- sales skills
- customer service skills.

Interests: it can be helpful for a young job-seeker to put down their hobbies and interests. Given that the employer is looking for potential as much as experience, try to choose leisure activities which show your personal qualities in a good light, e.g. helping at a charity.

Referees: two referees are the norm, one academic and one work-related, or a character referee if allowed. Do not include these on your CV but have them ready to give the employer following the interview.

CV example

This is the CV of someone whose experience in her target industry is relatively limited – just two work placements of a couple of weeks each. However, she has used these to their full potential and strengthened her case by including the transferable skills she obtained from the part-time and temporary jobs she worked in while a student to strengthen her case.

CV 1: Recent graduate CV

Sian Forrester

24 Green Street
Forreston
SV5 ABC
Tel: 0777 555 555

Career profile

Advertising graduate with sound knowledge and work experience within the industry. Undertook placements within an above-the-line advertising agency where I supported staff working on client briefs and assisted the planning team. Sales and customer service skills have been gained from working in a number of different retail environments where I achieved set targets. My ability to build strong relationships was demonstrated in the repeat business I encouraged from high-spending customers. I am looking to combine my advertising background with my sales abilities to work in an account management role with a creative agency.

Education

BSc (Hons) 2:i, Advertising   • Cartell University   • 2005–2008

- Course subjects include: Creative advertising, media, marketing and sales, e-marketing and consumer behaviour, communications psychology.
- Researched and devised our own advertising campaigns which were judged by industry professionals.
- Built own e-commerce website: www.sf.hotmail.com
- Financial management including budget-setting, cost control, forecasting, monitoring, etc.
- Advanced PowerPoint, Word, Excel and Publisher skills.
- Report writing on many advertising related tasks.

1997–2004   • St Augustine High School, Pelham

- 3 A Levels: English (B), Economics (B), French (C)
- 6 GCSEs English Language (A*), Economics (A*), French (A), Mathematics (B*), Chemistry (B*), Geography (C).

S Forrester 1/2

Experience

Placement • 2007 and 2008 • Deft Advertising Agency

First worked for Deft in 2007 but invited back for 2008. My activities included:

- Helping compile a research summary on a client's competitors for strategy discussion
- Verifying facts for a pitch to a prospective corporate client
- Providing administrative support for the team working on live client briefs including typing up notes and using Excel for contact lists. All work needed to be completed to the highest standards of presentation
- Liaising with the art directors and copy writers regarding the sending of documentation
- Working with the accounts function to understand their process and helping with the client billing records
- Supporting the planning team in organising a direct mail campaign to over 10,000 businesses
- Helping wherever required in the office, including welcoming visitors, refreshments and message-taking.

January 2006 to June 2007 • Amy's Boutique

Worked as sales assistant in this fashionable high-end dress store. This involved:

- Helping the team achieve monthly sales targets
- Keeping the store display immaculate to retain the store's particular image
- Assisting with stock-taking to ensure accurate records and identify any items to be put in the annual sales
- Asked for personally by a number of customers who I had advised in the past.

February 2005 to January 2006 • Grant Jason Shoes

Worked as sales assistant in shoe shop. This included:

- Keeping waiting times low by assisting customers quickly and efficiently
- Processing payments for purchases and notifying the manager of any payment issues
- Helping organise the stockroom to make it easier to find required shoes
- Increasing customer spend by recommending shoe accessories
- Assisting with store security to ensure stock was protected from potential theft or damage
- Working to group weekly sales targets.

Additional information

- Editor of the *Student Magazine*
- Run online forum for film buffs
- Mentor to student on my course
- French language skills

S Forrester 2/2

CVs for career changers

If you are looking to change your career, you need to be canny about how you market yourself on your CV. You are not going to be an obvious candidate. So grab the employer's attention early on to convince them of your suitability and commitment, before they become dissuaded by looking at your employment history.

Let's look at some of the practical tips that will help you.

Functional CV format
- Use a CV in the functional format to highlight your transferable skills and experience.
- Show on the first page how you meet the competencies required on the job description/person specification form.
- Include on the first page any voluntary work or extra-work activities that you have been involved in that are directly relevant to the role.
- Employment dates and job titles should go on second page.

Training
Some roles will require you to have undertaken specific training. If you have relevant or allied training, then include these on the first page. If you haven't then find out if there is specific training that you need, and if so, show in your CV that you are either currently undertaking or due to enrol on this course. However, don't expect the employer to pay for your training.

Considered decision
- Show that you know what the work realistically involves, e.g. by shadowing someone in the role, spending a day in a department or on a placement, talking with people currently working in these roles. You need to show your research has been thorough and appropriate and your decision to change career has been well thought through rather than a whim.
- Use a career profile and/or career objective statement to explain why you are looking for the new role and most importantly why you should be chosen for the role in question, i.e. why your background is an asset, how you can meet their requirements but also what you have to offer that is over and above the conventional candidate.
- Use key buzz words from the industry, show awareness of the industry's trends, specialist knowledge, etc. so that you can demonstrate that you are in the 'know'.

Here is an example of a CV of a service manager who wants to move into HR. He highlights his relevant knowledge and experience on the first page and states a commitment to undertaking professional training. He also shows that he was successful in his managerial role, is achievements orientated and not afraid of tackling uncomfortable or sensitive issues.

CV 2: Career change CV

Clive Gabel

1 Hamden Close, Greenways, Mardenham RL23 3AB
Tel: 07888 555 666
Email: cg@gmail.com

Career profile

Highly skilled people manager with over 8 years' experience of leading teams through periods of intense organisational change. Restructuring activities have included job and team redesign, recruitment and handling redundancies. Sound knowledge and experience in dealing with many aspects of employment law in relation to recruitment, disciplinary and grievance and managing diversity. Due to commence studies for a CIPD certificate course in September to build on my practical experience. Looking for an HR business partner role that can utilise my management expertise with my passion for people development and processes.

Relevant skills and experience

Recruitment and selection

- Fully trained in Recruitment and Selection best practice in respect of Employment Law and in-house company procedures.
- Experienced in writing job descriptions and person specifications, determining key competences, shortlisting candidates, chairing interview panels and salary negotiations.
- Dealt with a number of recruitment scenarios with equal opportunities implications including candidates with religious observances and those with disability needs.

Disciplinary and grievance

- Fully trained in Disciplinary and Grievance Handling both on in-house training and external 2-day course.
- Chaired disciplinary panels on several occasions for issues ranging from performance capability to gross misconduct. Sound knowledge of the process to be followed. Outcomes ranged from verbal warnings to summary dismissal.
- Appointed investigating officer for an allegation of harassment against a manager which was subsequently upheld. This required especially sensitive handling, both during the process and afterwards.

C Gabel 1/2

Performance management
- My team has been identified as one of the 'high-performing' teams in the organisation and held up by the CEO as a model of excellence.
- Conduct performance reviews with eight team members per year plus monthly individual and team meetings. Determine team and individual bonuses against business and personal targets.
- Mentor to two graduate trainees, both of whom are now on the internal fast-track programme.

Training and development
- Identified key competencies and behaviours required from team through conducting in-depth analysis in liaison with training manager and external HR specialist.
- Conducted skills diagnostic for individuals and team as a whole and set targets to bridge areas of gap.
- Organised a series of formal and informal training solutions ranging from classroom-based teaching to coaching, and work shadowing.

Career history
2000 – present • Service Manager • BRG Holdings

Joined this fast-paced technology organisation as a graduate trainee and was quickly promoted to manager. Current responsibilities include managing team of eight direct reports:

- Improved team productivity by 15% as a result of re-allocation of duties.
- Appointed project team leader on new Customer Service initiative, rolling out key messages through leading workshops, organising training, producing written materials, etc. As a result customer evaluations improved by 25%.
- Key liaison person for new £10 million service level agreement which, although initially unpopular, has weathered the earlier difficulties to deliver substantial cost savings and efficiencies.
- Created partnership agreements on technological contracts with leading players such as Jason White Group and Dales Consultants, which led the way for joint ventures worth £25 million.
- Reduced absence by 20% in my department as a result of tackling and resolving a particularly sensitive health issue that previously no-one had been willing to address.

Education

BA American Studies	Cartell University	1997–2000
CIPD, CPP	Central University	Commencing November 2008

Training

2-day coaching course	Recruitment and Selection	Objective setting
Disciplinary and Grievance	Appraisal Training	Influencing Skills
1st-line Management Course	Managing Absence	Handling conflict

C Gabel 2/2

CVs for people with career gaps

Few people have worked continuously from their first job to retirement and most people will have gaps somewhere in their career for all kinds of reasons including:

■ Being dismissed
■ Caring for a relative or other dependant
■ Ill-health or an accident
■ Maternity leave
■ Being in prison
■ Resigning and then looking for a new role
■ Travelling
■ Taking some time out for other reasons.

However, employers can be quite suspicious of career gaps and, depending on the length and frequency of the gaps, will want to be reassured that there is no hidden problem.

How do you deal with this?

Date format

Where the gap is only a few months, you can use the month to month or even year to year format for employment dates, e.g. January 2007–March 2008 (for gaps of a few weeks either end) and 2007–2008 (for gaps of a few months). You could even group together a few different past employments, e.g. 2006–2008: During this time, undertook varied administrative roles for organisations such as Jackson Foods and Dales Consultants in the telecommunications and retail sector.

Functional CV format

Use this CV format to highlight on the first page all of your key skills and experience. Put all past employer details and dates on the second page, which will serve to downplay their importance.

Give a positive explanation

If the gaps are still noticeable you may need to give an explanation. It is fine to put down career break for family reasons if you were raising a family or looking after a relative. Equally if you were travelling, studying, or on an interesting adventure, then these are also fine to state.

However, do not put down unemployment or redundancy as a reason for a career gap. Although it may be technically true, unfortunately it does give a negative image of a candidate who has struggled to find a buyer for their skills. Try instead to find some positive way to describe what you were doing at that time. Talk about any voluntary work you were undertaking, studying, writing, helping out with a friend's business, or working with a career coach to decide on your next move. Present an active, positive image of someone who may not have been in paid employment, but who was pursuing activities that added to their employability.

If the reason for the gap is a negative one such as illness or an accident then include this as an explanation on your CV only as a last resort. Any mention of poor health, even if it was a long time ago, will raise concerns over your fitness to work. If you do mention it, phrase the wording to make it clear that whatever medical problem there was, it is now fully resolved, for example 'Unable to work as broke my foot in accident. Now fully recovered.' If there is an on-going health issue that may affect your ability to work, or you are an ex-offender, see Chapter 1 for more information on how to handle these with an employer.

Prove you are ready to work

If you are looking to return to work after a career gap, then you will need to demonstrate to the employer that you have kept your skills fresh during your time away, that you are up to date, up to speed and willing and ready for the challenges of a full working life.

This could include:

- helping run a family/friend's business
- party planning
- reading professional journals
- re-training for a new career direction
- running your own small business
- taking a refresher course in your occupational field, e.g. teaching, nursing
- voluntary committee work
- voluntary work
- work placements.

You will also need good IT skills and so, if you have been away for a while, an IT course should probably be your first port of call. The above examples will all supply good evidence for your CV of your readiness to return to work.

The following CV is an example of someone wishing to return to paid employment following maternity leave. She also wants to change career direction and work in education rather than go back into her original field of market research. She has undertaken voluntary work at her local school to gain relevant experience and to check whether this is something that she enjoys. She has taken advantage of every training course available at the school. She sees the first step of classroom assistant as the means to helping her achieve a transition into the educational field.

CV 3: Returning to work following maternity leave and wanting to change career direction

Pat Jones

1 Gray's Court
Middletown BC5 678
Mobile: 0789 555 555
Email: pjones@gmail.co.uk

Career profile

Classroom assistant with experience of working with children in educational and informal settings at school and in the community. CRB checked and trained in first aid. Have attended workshops on how to deal with children with special needs and used this to good effect while assisting a pupil with mobility challenges. Excellent numeracy and written skills gained from market research background. Strong IT skills. Have great interest and passion in helping children to develop their potential. Looking for a classroom assistant role to pursue this aim. Due to attend classroom assistant training in January 2009.

Relevant skills and experience

- Knowledge and experience of classroom work through working as teacher's helper for Reception and Year 1 at local primary school.
- Assisted teacher in Year 1 in helping to manage particular pupils with challenging behaviour in line with school policy.
- Supported primary school children with their reading and helped in the library, encouraging the children to have fun with books.
- Took care of the younger children in helping them with their lunch and toileting arrangements.
- Supervised the children in the cookery class, helping them learn about healthy eating and make snacks to take home.
- Have attended courses in health and safety, diversity and child protection.
- Involved in running of local toddler group including preparation for an inspection, which was highly complimentary regarding the resources available, the group's organisation and safety standards.
- Highly IT literate, so able to help pupils develop their computer skills and to support teachers with creative use of their electronic whiteboard.
- Ability to communicate effectively to wide range of people developed through previous experience as a market researcher.

P Jones 1/2

Work experience

Classroom helper   • Hays School, Gorton   • 2008 – present

- Supporting the teacher within the classroom by helping individual children with work activities, e.g. reading.
- Administrative duties, e.g. photocopying, making teachers resources, checking paperwork.
- Assisting a special needs child with mobility challenges to move around the school.
- Provided extra support on school visits to places such as the village library, a farm and the local museum.
- Helping the children look after the school garden, sowing seeds and watering plants.

Career break   • 2002–2008

During this time, I was involved in:

- Organising school events (PTA committee member)
- Helping run a voluntary community toddler playgroup that achieved superb feedback following an inspection.
- Administrative work for the family business including typing correspondence, spreadsheets, etc.
- Freelance market research project work.

Market researcher   • Jason White Group   • 1998–2002

- Devising and leading market research campaigns via customer focus groups, one-to-one interviews and street surveys.
- Designing and evaluating questionnaires to meet the client's objectives.
- Analysing information and producing statistical reports to enable clients to make informed decisions.
- Supervising and inducting other market researchers.
- Ensuring quality control through all aspects of the market research process.

Education and qualifications

BSc Biology (2:i)   • University of Greaterhampton   • 1993–1996

Three A levels, History (B), Geography (B) Economics (C), and eight GCSEs, including English and Maths.

IT skills

Excellent Word, Excel and PowerPoint Skills. Also experienced in working with a number of different databases to input data and produce detailed reports.

Interests

Reading, swimming and genealogy.

P Jones 2/2

Technical CVs

When an employer is looking for a candidate with specific technical skills, your first priority is to demonstrate you have the particular expertise they are looking for. Without this, your CV will not be considered. However, given that your CV is most likely to be viewed first by a non-technical person, usually a recruitment agent or HR officer, it also needs to appeal to and be easily understood by a non-technical person. You also need to remember that just as for any other CV, you also need to present an image of a candidate who has all the desirable personality behaviours, for example good communication skills, conscientiousness, etc.

Let's look at how you can achieve the balance between the hard technical skills in your CV and the softer skills.

Keywords

Keywords on your CV are essential if recruiters and employers are to find you on their candidate application database. You therefore need to list all of your technical skills, qualifications and relevant courses for the job. Put these on the first page of your CV and prioritise those that are of most relevance to the employer. Look through job descriptions, advertisements, etc. for a list of common keywords which appear for your target role and make sure they are all included.

Repetition

Be repetitive in regard to the technology, e.g. Java mentioned in several places in the CV confirms that you have a lot of Java experience, as opposed to it just being mentioned once.

Years of experience

Include the number of years of experience you have of a particular technology as a keyword search can be used to prioritise candidates with a specified amount of experience, e.g. more than 5 years' experience.

CV format

A functional CV format may be most helpful as it will prioritise the relevant skills on the first page of your CV. Length of CV is ideally still two pages. However, an experienced developer could have a longer CV as it lists all of the key projects with which they have been involved. IT professionals may also consider hosting their own CV website to show off their technical skills in the construction of the site as well as its content.

Bigger picture

Show your understanding of the bigger business picture and that you do not operate in an 'expert' ivory tower, by including achievements that talk about how your work helped increase organisational efficiency or quality, etc.

Soft skills

Emphasise your communication skills, something that technical people often neglect to mention but which are essential in any job. Include examples of communicating with technical teams and non-technical people, for example external consultants, end users and customers. Technical CVs are often so dry and full of functional detail about programming languages, etc. that they neglect to give a sense of the individual as someone who is easy to work with.

Project work

If you are working in interim or in-house projects, highlight the projects of most relevance to your target employer. Under each project include three to five sentences detailing:

- the company (or the type of company) if confidential
- reasons for hiring you, e.g. employed for my extensive expertise in XYZ
- scope of your project, size, budget, number of users affected, etc.
- the principal challenges or any obstacles faced
- what you did
- the benefit to the company.

Project management/technical management

- Focus on project size, value, number of staff, etc. Include project budget estimating, planning and preparation, requirements gathering and solicitation techniques, monitoring, risk assessment, quality control, etc.
- Demonstrate your ability to quickly build trusted relationships, establishing rapport and respect with business customers and other staff.
- Show your ability to manage and work with diverse teams of people, including actual and virtual teams if appropriate.
- Include examples of handling difficult projects and how you steered them back on course.
- State projects that were completed on schedule, to budget, etc.

- Include any favourable quality evaluations.
- Emphasise people and financial management skills, e.g. budgeting, monitoring finances, recruiting and developing staff, etc.

Starting a career in a technical field

You may have attended your course and obtained your technical qualifications but employers will want to see how you have applied your skills. This is of course more of a challenge when you are just starting your career and your experience is limited. If this is the case, consider offering free or low-cost technical services to family, friends, charitable organisations, etc. If you are a website developer perhaps you could devise one for your local community group, charity or a friend to enable you to build up a portfolio of your work.

In your CV use the career profile/objective statement to focus on your ability to learn quickly, your enthusiasm for this kind of work and your intention to pursue a career in this direction.

The CV example in this section is of a web-developer with three years' professional experience who is looking to specialise in e-commerce. He specifies the technical skills used for each project, and also demonstrates his understanding that his work needs to help his clients make money.

CV 4: Technical CV

Robert Ongwe

1 Canada Street, Greater Morton SL1 345
Mobile: 07777 555 555
Email: rongwe@gmail.co.uk

Career profile

Web-developer with 3 years' experience in developing and maintaining e-commerce websites for international businesses. Able to deliver a customer-friendly internet experience which provides sophisticated back-end management information systems using standard and bespoke packages. Enjoy advising and training non-technical staff on how to maximise the potential of their website. Extensive knowledge and interest in e-commerce marketing, an area in which I wish to specialise further.

Key skills

* Technical skills: MySQL, SQL Server, IIS, UNIX/LINUX, Microsoft Visual SourceSafe
* Languages: PHP, Java, ASP.Net, C#, HTML, DHTML, XML, XSLT, JavaScript, CSS

Education

BSc Computer Science (2:i)   • University of Crawford   • 2002–2005
Course included: web technology; computer architecture; Java, software systems; algorithms and data structures; advanced database systems; operating systems and networks graphical user interfaces.

Career history

Compuware Consultancy Services   • July 2006 – present   • e-Commerce Web-developer
Compuware provides IT consultancy services for organisations ranging from SMEs to multinational corporations.

* Designed and developed bespoke multicurrency e-shop for Bright Greeting Cards using SQL Server and ASP.Net, incorporating payment systems, customer account management, stock control and tracking information. This increased turnover by 45% in the first year.
* Used MySQL to re-vamp payment arrangements for online gaming website using a secure key-based system. Created facility for one-off and subscription payments, loyalty schemes, bonus item codes and special deals for referring a friend. This increased average customer spend by 15% per visit.

R Ongwe 1/2

- Devised stock control systems and Point of Sale (POS) interfaces using MS SQL Server to improve sales and delivery information for a high-volume retailer. This helped ease distribution log-jams which had previously caused difficulty.
- Designed bespoke shopping cart design for RST UK, a high-end fashion retailer using JavaScript. The aim was to complement the products by offering an attractive and unique interactive product browsing experience.
- Advised customers on search engine optimisation, generating reports using Google Analytics and Hitwise. Extensive liaison with SEO specialists to support marketing campaigns through organic campaigns and pay per click.
- Maintenance of several websites using HTML, CSS, PHP and browser-based content management systems to ensure fully functioning at all times.
- Initiated regular tests to benchmark conversion rates and as a result managed to increase click through rate by 10% for five clients within the first month of analysis.
- Have initiated extensive research on SEO, including in-depth reading, attendance at related forums, keeping up to date with latest developments in this field.
- Client evaluations have frequently rated my input to be of a high standard and commented on my helpfulness.

Maytec Solutions   • June 2005 – June 2006   • Web-developer
London-based IT consultancy offering a range of web-based services to corporate clients predominantly in the creative and media field.
- Experienced in the functional testing of both new and existing sites, usability, accessibility, interface and browser capability.
- Providing maintenance and answering queries from customers regarding existing sites and advising on enhancements.
- Designed and developed web-based survey builder using PHP to interactively create and display surveys online.

Dales Marketing Services   • December 2003–2005   • Telesales Adviser
Worked for this company throughout my student course where I was involved in telemarketing on behalf of local businesses.
- Contacting potential customers via cold-calling.
- Working to set targets regarding quantity and quality of telephone calls.
- Keeping accurate records and complying with Data Protection regulations.

Additional information
- Graduate member of British Computing Society.
- Hobbies include cycling, football and singing in a choir.
- My online profile: www.ongwe.com
- Examples of my e-commerce websites: www.xyz; www.def; www.jkl; www.abc; www.ghi; www.mno; www.pqr; www.tuv

R Ongwe 2/2

Creative CVs

If you are applying for a role as a creative professional, as a designer or to an organisation that delivers a creative product or service, for example a media company, then be careful of your assumptions about the kind of person you think they are looking to hire. Not all creative roles or organisations are alike. Some will look for high originality, others may prioritise speed and meeting deadlines. You need to know which you should be emphasising on your CV.

The layout of your CV is always being judged. However, for those applying for design roles there is an added challenge. The level of artistic skill, creative thinking and tastefulness that you display in your CV format will be a great influence when it comes to shortlisting.

However, before getting too carried away with the design, always remember that the most important thing on any CV is to demonstrate with examples how you match what the employer is looking for. So make sure the content is written first, before starting to work on the design.

- **Skills and experience:** establish your credibility early on. Prioritise relevant training skills and experience and highlight any required software training or qualifications
- **Enthusiasm:** employers will be looking for a sense of your passion for this type of work, so use lots of positive action words to communicate this. You may want to include how your work extends into your hobbies, e.g. teaching art classes.
- **Gimmicks:** gimmicky CVs can be fun and certainly grab attention but are not always practical. How can you photocopy a CV printed on a T-shirt? Make sure that your CV is readable and usable, otherwise it will end up in the reject pile.
- **Business-focused:** while they may appreciate your original thinking, like any other employer, they will also want to know that you work quickly, cost-effectively and to high-quality standards, so give examples of when you have done this.
- **Rave reviews:** include any examples where your work has been judged favourably by others, e.g. any awards won, commendations, repeat business.
- **Artist statement:** if you are a creative artist, you could also include a short and clear statement of your work and thoughts as an artist. Feel free to use relevant industry terminology as you will most likely be dealing with industry

professionals. Statements can include information on the themes of your work, the direction it is heading in, its meaning, etc. This can be tricky to get right, so it's helpful to get feedback from others on whether this is striking the right tone.

Designers

- Design students can create their CVs using a professional publishing package such as Quark or In Design. You can have fun using graphics, logos, photos, columns, shapes, watermarks, colour, etc. Just be careful not to over-design it and remember that if it is printed out, any colour will be irrelevant so make sure that it also looks good in black and white. Pay particular attention to font and typography. Your CV will need to be converted to Adobe PDF if it is to be emailed.
- You can try to create a CV that has a distinctive visual identity, rather like your own personal branding. Use it as a theme that works with your website, business cards, etc. in the same way that you would with a corporate client.
- Including examples of your work can personalise the CV. Label each image and be careful not to overcrowd. Lay these out tastefully and provide a link to other examples of your work on your website. Make sure the images on the CV are appropriate to the vacancy, that is don't include print work if you are going for a digital media role. You may choose not to include any images, and if so the impact of layout and typography becomes more crucial.
- Consider creating your own online CV, where you can include detailed examples of your portfolio. Include the link to the website on your CV.
- Print your CV on high-quality paper. The print finish must be impeccable.

Media CVs

Jobs in the media are desired by many but achieved by relatively few. In order to differentiate yourself from the many, you need to demonstrate that you are a serious candidate with the required technical background and knowledge, Although every role is different, you will also probably need boundless energy, stress tolerance and the ability to work with some fairly demanding personalities.

- Emphasise all courses, training and technical skills you have gained that qualify you for this role.
- Use positive action words throughout to show energy.

- Show how you are passionate about this work, perhaps through hobbies, e.g. running a community drama group or a film club.
- The media is a business that thrives on networking, so include as many well-known names in your CV as you can, to bolster your credibility by association.
- Write an achievement-based CV to present you as a 'go-getter'. Modesty does not work on media CVs.
- Include examples of ideas you generated that worked, problems solved – present yourself as an indispensable person.

Performer CVs

If you are an actor, singer or other performer, you need a very different type of CV.

- Use a one-page CV.
- Specify where your artistic training took place. Other educational qualifications are largely irrelevant unless it was a very prestigious educational establishment.
- Include a photo which has been professionally produced, to accompany your CV. Usually a 10' by 8' head shot in black and white for actors or a colour full-length photo for a presenter.
- State your height, colour of hair, eye colour, playing age and accents you can speak and sing in.
- List your experience by breaking down the productions and directors into film, television and theatre. Specifically name any prestigious directors, co-stars, etc. to build credibility by association.
- Singers should state their voice type and styles, e.g. soprano and musical styles.
- Always provide a professional portfolio with which you can demonstrate your abilities. Ideally this will be via a website where you can post photos, video, reviews.
- Include the name and contact details of your agent.
- Spotlight (www.spotlight.com/artists.html) is the photographic directory of all actors in the UK and is the first place directors look when casting, so your CV should be put in there.

The following CV is an example of a CV for a graphic designer, where the layout is as important as the content. The designer has personalised it with examples of his work but remembered that as in any business, employers are interested in employees who deliver the goods to a high standard and bring in the business.

CV 5: Creative CV for a graphic designer

8 Marsh Lane, Northwoods, SP1 888
0776 777 777
JSmith@email.com

CAREER PROFILE

Graphic designer interested in providing fun, memorable images that get
my clients noticed. Skilled in all aspects of print design, logos, posters,
leaflets and sales materials; my work combines functionality with a strong
brand image that communicates the client's message clearly and distinctively.
Many of my clients have been so happy with the work that they have commissioned
further work and/or recommended my company to others.

QUALIFICATIONS AND TRAINING

BA (Hons) 2:1 Graphic Design
Grant University 1999–2002

Expert software skills: Illustrator, Photoshop, Quark, InDesign, Macromedia,
Adobe, Quark Xpress, Corel

WORK EXPERIENCE

The Graphic Design Company   2005–2008

- Won SE Design award for my work on the Grow Organic account.
- Provided the creative input to the sales pitches that successfully brought
- over £100,000 worth of business to the company from high-profile
  clients such as Grant and Thornton, Vista Software Solutions and Global
  Marketing Group.
  Led design team on production of suite of sales literature for Dales
- Consultants which involved complete re-branding in line with new
  corporate mission statement.
  Designed logo and corporate literature for a new legal organisation
- (Formant and Jones) following merger of two separate companies
  Commissioned by Wright Stationery Ltd. to produce corporate brochure in
- line with corporate social responsibility guidelines, e.g. recycled paper.
  Created innovative promotional pack for Harris Clothing sales staff using
- three-dimensional models.
  Devised fun direct-mailing pack for Go for It! advertising campaign.
- Developed advertising campaign for Falstaff Organic Farm for the local
- paper.
  Created poster advertising campaign for launch of new
- lifestyle service rolled-out via banners and posters on buses, tube and taxis.
- Created exhibition materials including posters, leaflets, banners, T-shirts for
  Best Job Recruiters attendance at trade fairs.
  Designed business cards, leaflets and advertisements for Inkwell
  Consultants Ltd.

Elderflower Design   2003–2005

- Quickly promoted to work on larger projects because of the feedback the
  company received from customers.
- Designed leaflets for Youth Outreach and was then commissioned to
  produce a whole suite of other marketing materials worth over £50,000.
- Developed sales literature for Shardwell Electronics sales representatives.
- Devised a three-dimensional calendar for promotional use.
- Produced exhibition materials for Shardwell Electronics for prestigious
  conference event.
- Devised T-shirts for fun run charity event sponsored by The Women's Group.

INTERESTS

Film, art galleries, cycling, scuba-diving, painting

CV advice for managers and executives

A managerial role is generally one which has responsibilities for planning and directing the work of others. They usually work at an operational level in the business, responsible for a particular department or function. If you are applying for managerial-type roles, then in addition to job-specific information there will be some generic skills and competencies that are likely to be required.

Examples of these are outlined below:

- staff management experience
- financial management
- commercial acumen and business awareness
- strategic planning, conceptualising, forecasting
- relationship management upwards, downwards, sidewards, externally
- planning, scheduling and resourcing activities
- defining and setting targets for team
- problem-solving, objective decision-making
- self-confidence and stress tolerance
- ability to drive change
- high-level verbal skills, including presentation skills, influencing, negotiating, conflict management
- high-level written skills: presentation of complex information, setting out business sector or job knowledge as appropriate.

An executive has a role which encompasses organisation-wide responsibilities and the strategic side of the business. In addition to the competencies required by managers, an executive will also need to demonstrate in their CV that they have acted on a larger stage, for example:

- strategic planning for the whole organisation rather than just one department
- setting budgets for others rather than just for their own department
- increasing profitability and efficiency for the whole organisation
- external focus to the larger business environment
- setting targets and goals for others.

Executive CVs should therefore focus on achievements and should give examples of activities which:

- increase profitability and efficiency
- introduce and implement change
- demonstrate astute financial management
- help the business grow
- manage adverse conditions
- manage relationships internal and external to organisation
- improve quality of operations under your remit
- research and make informed decisions on complex matters
- produce reports or presentations to support a business case
- set and achieve targets for team, department, or organisation
- specify the size and scope of your responsibilities, e.g. size of budget managed, number of staff.

Here is an example of a director's CV that highlights the professional qualifications required for the job and the input they have made to the success of the organisation as a whole.

CV 6: Director's/manager's CV

Jo Chapman

Address: 22 High End Road, Galston AB9 XYZ
Telephone No: 01555 555 555
Mobile: 07755 444 444
Email: jc@yahoo.co.uk

Career profile

Finance Director with 20 years' experience working within the advertising business. Highly experienced in contract negotiation, preparing and winning contracts worth over £15 million in the past 2 years alone. Facilitated a number of strategic changes which improved the financial stability and income potential for the organisation. Used to working in fast-paced environments with high sensitivity to market conditions. Track record of identifying profitable growth opportunities while ensuring very careful risk management.

Career history

Finance Director   • J G Howard Advertising Group   • 2000–2008
J G Howard is a leading advertising agency with turnover of £100 million and 200 staff. Major clients include blue-chip companies such as Formant and Jones, Dales Consultants and Berkshire Construction Group. Responsible for leading finance team of seven and responsible for another five in the property and legal teams.

- Won Dales Consultants contract worth £15 million in 2007. Responsible for preparing and delivering the financial bid that has opened up a brand new business opportunity within the transport sector with substantial growth potential.
- Project-managed the implementation of the Dales Consultants contract, including organising staff, technology and financial requirements to achieve launch within only 4 months of agreeing the contract.
- Doubled the profit from advertising revenues for major client by negotiating preferred supplier deal on massively advantageous terms.
- Introduced new financial management system to facilitate improved financial modelling capabilities. Linked this with training of finance and operational managers to show how this information could be used at departmental level to improve monitoring of financial performance.
- Identified business opportunity to partner with academic institutions such as universities, which enhanced credibility on certain 'blue-sky' projects.
- Achieved necessary cost-savings of over £2 million in 2006 as a result of difficult market conditions. Redundancies were minimised as a result of careful cost control, natural staff attrition and a recruitment freeze.

J Chapman 1/2

- Reworked presentation of our costing proposals to improve transparency and avoid re-negotiations further down the line.
- As Board Director, helped devise and resource organisational strategy to achieve financial robustness, move towards a more diverse client base, and grow the business opportunities within a tight market.

Financial Controller • Wright Stationery Limited • 1995–2000
Reporting to Finance Director and responsible for 10 staff and the operational management of the Finance function.
- Identified business opportunity for York Design to partner with Wright Stationery to achieve cost savings of over £200,000 per annum on resource costs, premises and shared support functions.
- Project-managed the sale of sister company Celtic Document Supplies, which mitigated closure costs of more than £5 million had a sale not been agreed. All staff retained their jobs, which had been at risk.
- Improved departmental efficiency as a result of conducting work-flow assessment which highlighted log-jams. Reorganised staff roles to move to new more streamlined work processes.
- Facilitated greater liaison between finance and front-line managers by arranging for finance staff to each spend some time in different areas of the business to increase understanding and enhance relationships. This led to managers involving Finance at an earlier stage in the budget-setting process which subsequently improved the quality of the information being received.

Head of Management Accounts • Clarkson Toys • 1990–1995
Managing team of two for this international manufacturing company with turnover of £50 million.
- Spotted discrepancies in financial information which uncovered fraudulent practices in a geographically remote part of the business.
- Developed new way of presenting financial information for non-financial managers that helped them to understand more easily the financial performance of their department.
- Trained and developed three new members of the Finance Department in the new financial management software.

Corporate Cost Analyst • W and H Atkins Limited • 1988–1990
- Produced complex costing reports for senior management presentations.
- Advised department heads on financial performance against targets with recommendations where required.

Education and qualifications
Member of CIMA since 1990
BA Business Studies (2:i) University of Colchestershire

J Chapman 2/2

CVs for internal promotions

If you are applying for an internal post, perhaps a promotion, you need to undertake the same degree of research, preparation and hard business sell that you would use for an external vacancy.

- Fully research the role. Do not make assumptions as to what you think the role is. You simply have no excuse for ignorance. Go speak to the manager, HR, other people who have key relationships with the post-holder to find out what the ideal candidate will offer.
- Do not assume that the interview panel, even if it is your current manager, will know everything about you and your achievements. Spell these out on your CV. They need reminding of your good points.
- Emphasise that you are an easy person to hire as you know the organisation so can 'hit the ground running'. This gives you an advantage over an external hire.
- If you are in competition with another internal candidate never criticise or try to undermine them either subtly or overtly. Focus on the positives that you have to offer.
- Your CV will need to be truthful as it will be examined by people who can contest any claims you make that are unsubstantiated. Be careful as to what you claim as your achievements or abilities – just make sure that you provide plenty of examples to prove them.
- The most common fault of candidates applying for internal promotions is modesty. They assume their current performance will be enough to convince the shortlisting panel. It won't be. Be confident, realistic and show your enthusiasm and capabilities for the new role.

Using the format guidelines and the content you have collated, it is now time to sit and write your version of your CV. Use the checklist in Table 12 to help you.

TABLE 12: CHECKLIST FOR YOUR CV

Contact details are complete and fully functioning	☐
Career profile/objective matches target role	☐
All factual information is accurate	☐
Positive action words used throughout	☐
Gives examples of achievements	☐
Gives examples of key skills in action	☐
All relevant qualifications including training are included	☐
Gives examples which show your positive personal qualities	☐
Presentation of CV is smart and professional	☐
No more than two pages	☐
Format of CV is checked for compatibility with recipient software	☐
Spelling and grammar is perfect	☐
CV is always accompanied by covering letter/email	☐
Feedback obtained from at least three people to check that it is error free and conveys desired impression	☐

IN A NUTSHELL

This chapter has looked at some situations where CV content and layout requires slightly different treatment in order to help you present as a strong candidate. However, always remember that the same three rules will apply regardless of your particular CV challenge:

- tailor the content to provide examples that you have exactly what the employer is looking for
- use a format that right on the first page enables you to prove you are the ideal candidate
- pay attention to the professional layout of the CV, which will be taken as an indication of your approach to your work.

11 AND FINALLY...

As you have been reading Part I, completing the activities and devising your CV, you have also been acquiring some of the essential skills of career management, that is:

- knowing what you have to offer an employer
- understanding how to research and target the role you want
- the ability to articulate the above to an employer and show them how you can meet their needs.

This means that when you go to an interview and they ask 'Why should we employ you?' you will genuinely know why.

It will also be of immense help to you when you are networking for your next role, looking for promotion or planning a future career change; in fact throughout your career.

The truth is, in a competitive recruitment marketplace, it is not always those who are most capable who get the job – it is those who understand and apply those principles of career management. You are on your way!

Wishing you success!

Corinne Mills
www.personalcareermanagement.com

INTERVIEW ANSWERS

INTRODUCTION

The prospect of going for any interview can be pretty daunting, even more so if it is a process that is billed as a 'tough' interview. Images of being grilled by a relentless interviewer come to mind, but in fact, when they are done well, interviews are not intended to be deliberately intimidating, or designed to trip you up; they are simply designed to be very thorough. The plus side is that if you handle them well they give you the best opportunity to show yourself in a good light. Part II is designed to make sure that you do handle them well, and by following our guidance and tips you'll be well armed to face the toughest of interviews.

We have deliberately aimed this part at graduates, middle and senior management roles, as people in this bracket are most likely to experience this type of interview. Overall, it will be of use to anybody seeking a professional role in an organisation.

Part II is about a very particular type of interview – the structured competency-based interview. Experienced recruiters use them a lot, and they are probably the toughest interviews you will come across. With the right knowledge, preparation and work experience, though, you can actually turn the situation around and make it the most straightforward interview you have. We'll explain how in more detail later, but for now rest assured that if you follow the guidance in these pages and you have the appropriate experience, then going for this type of interview is not going to be intimidating. On the contrary, you're more likely to do well and get the job you want.

So, this part will provide you a rich resource to help you prepare for that job-winning interview. Whilst it will introduce you to a very specific type of interview, the approaches and techniques presented here will stand you in good stead in any interview situation, giving you the chance to manage it in a way that demonstrates your skills and abilities.

Ceri Roderick and Stephan Lucks
www.pearnkandola.com

12 WHAT IS A COMPETENCY AND WHAT IS A COMPETENCY-BASED INTERVIEW?

This chapter is going to be a vital starting point if you have no knowledge or previous experience of this type of interview. In it you'll discover:

- what competencies are

- what the interview process is and how an interviewer will structure the interview

- how competencies can be grouped into three easy-to-remember categories that will help you in your preparation.

Exploring competencies

You may well have come across the term 'competencies' before. Most organisations refer to competencies, but what exactly are they and how are they useful? Understanding how and why competencies are used will help you to focus your preparation and perform your best at interview.

Put simply, competencies are the way that organisations define the qualities that they need (and that you need) to be excellent at a job. Not to be confused with skills, competencies are usually concerned with *how* we do things, whereas skills are usually about *what* we do. Think of competencies as the adjectives of skills. To give you a concrete example:

- 'Producing accounts' is a skill. It is a specific set of steps and procedures.
- 'Providing information in a timely and accurate manner' is a competency. The 'timely' and 'accurate' descriptors – the *how* bit – make this a competency. So, competencies are the behaviours which are used to exercise a skill.

Competencies are usually concerned with how *we do things; skills are usually about* what *we do.*

When using them for recruitment and performance measurement, businesses need competencies to be specific enough to be recognisable by people, but general enough that they can be applied across a range of jobs in the organisation. So, coming back to our example above, 'Producing accounts in a timely and accurate manner' is very specific; it applies only to people working in an accounts role, and would be inappropriate in, say, a research and development role. However, 'Providing information in a timely and accurate manner' can apply to both roles – and probably a lot of others as well.

Competencies are typically drawn together in what is known as a 'competency model'. A competency model is simply a collection of competencies which define what outstanding performance would look like. Typically, organisations have between seven to nine competencies, although of course some organisations have many more.

Let's take a look at some competencies:

- planning and organising
- creativity and innovation
- team leadership
- achievement orientation
- analytical thinking
- influencing and persuading
- energy and drive
- judgement and decision making
- motivating others.

The nine competencies listed above are typical of those that organisations use and could be applied to a wide range of different jobs. Competencies that you may have come across may well have different names to those listed above, because competencies in part describe the nature and culture of an organisation and, quite rightly, organisations hone the wording to reflect their specific needs. In this sense, the competency framework is an important way in which an organisation differentiates itself and makes clear – for itself and for others – 'what it is you have to do to be effective around here'. So, while specific wording will vary, the nine competencies outlined above are a good generic 'average' of the kinds of competency you will see, and they fit a lot of organisations.

A lot of work has been done on job analysis and on statistically analysing organisational behaviours to identify what it is that differentiates good performance in any specific job. Look at most competency models, and they can be collapsed (or clustered) into three broad areas. This gives you a very useful shorthand for understanding the competencies of an organisation. The three areas are:

- **Task competencies:** these are about delivering/completing tasks, setting objectives, getting things done.
- **Thought competencies:** these are typically about direction, strategy, creativity, problem solving, change, innovation, judgement, decision making.
- **People competencies:** these are about the people things, communicating, motivating, developing.

As you can see from this list, almost all jobs will require elements from each of these three areas. For example, very few jobs are purely about task delivery – there are bound to be 'people' and 'thought' elements involved. In the same way, very few jobs would allow you to focus on 'thought' to the exclusion of all else; it's highly likely you will have to talk to people and deliver something too!

We have clustered the example competencies here into the task, thought and people categories:

Task	Thought	People
Energy and drive	Judgement and decision making	Motivating others
Achievement orientation	Analytical thinking	Influencing and persuading
Planning and organising	Creativity and innovation	Team leadership

We call this model the Leadership Radar™, because, like steering a ship or flying a plane, you need to keep your eye on all the radar screens if you want to navigate a safe course. Sometimes you'll need to focus on just one screen, at other times all three screens need to be taken into account. We'll return to this model in Chapter 13 and show you how you can use it to make a success of interviews, for example by using it to simplify your preparation.

Structured competency-based interviews

Not all interviews are the same, and not all interviews are equally effective in uncovering relevant information on which to base a selection decision. For a long time – and for some organisations this includes the present – interviews focused on work history, some general questions about what you were interested in, why you wanted to work for the organisation and so on. Such unstructured interviews, often conducted without there being any clear criteria in mind, did little more than give the interviewer some general idea about your social confidence and verbal fluency and 'whether they liked the look of you'. Research showed that such interviews operated at little better than chance levels in terms of picking the right person for the job. In a lot of cases, the organisation would have done just as well by selecting CVs at random. There is a joke in the HR profession that you could just throw the pile of CVs in the air, and the ones that landed face up got invited to interview. (It *is* a joke, and we know of no one actually doing this!)

A structured, competency-based interview is intended to counter this impressionistic approach and is designed around three core premises:

- past behaviour is a good predictor of future behaviour
- competencies are a good indicator of success at a job
- maintaining a structure and asking each candidate the same questions ensures that you can more systematically differentiate between candidates in terms of relevant criteria.

Let's look at each of these in turn.

Past behaviour is a good predictor of future behaviour

Research has indeed shown that what people do and how they do it is relatively consistent over time. Past behaviour is therefore a good predictor of future behaviour. That is not to say that people cannot learn and develop over time, and a good interview will explore your learning as well – particularly when the job represents a step up from previous roles or involves different kinds of work. In general terms, however, if you can provide lots of rich examples of how you have structured and planned tasks, the interviewer can increase their confidence that this is an approach that you regularly adopt and that you will therefore bring it to this job as well.

Competencies are a good indicator of success at a job

Again, research has shown a relationship between how well somebody's competencies are developed and how successfully they perform their role. So, for example, people who score poorly on 'focusing on customers' in an interview also tend not to perform well on this in a job. The interviewer's task is to explore each competency thoroughly enough to be able to give a confident rating of your likely performance in relation to that competency. So, what you are good at is a fairly obvious indicator of your performance in a job that involves that skill, but at the same time the interviewer has to be satisfied that you really do have that competency.

Maintaining a structure and asking each candidate the same questions ensures that you can more systematically differentiate between candidates

This one is quite logical really. If you do not ask questions about the same competencies of all candidates that are being interviewed, you will not have all of the information that is needed to make a good hiring decision. There is no point exploring one person's people management skills and another person's organisational skills only. You won't be able to differentiate between the two. The structure also ensures that nothing is left out and that all areas are explored in sufficient depth. Once again, the interviewer's job is to pursue a particular line of enquiry until they are satisfied that they can give you an accurate rating.

IDENTIFYING COMPETENCY-BASED QUESTIONS

Have a look at the questions below and see if you can identify the structured competency-based questions:

1. 'Describe to me a time where you helped a member of your team to improve their performance.'
2. 'What sort of people management experience do you have?'
3. 'One of your team is not performing as well as they need to be. What would you do?'

Of the three questions above, only 1 is a true, structured competency-based question.

Question 2 is quite generic and is not designed to elicit specific past behaviour. It invites the candidate to describe their approach, and of course has the risk that they will decide to describe only the positive aspects of their style, or give you a textbook answer that does not represent what they are actually capable of doing.

Question 3 is what we would call a situational question. It presents you with a situation and asks what you would do. Again, it does not test what you have actually done – it asks what you would do, hypothetically. People who are quick witted, and fast on their feet can answer this kind of question well; the trouble is, you are then measuring how well they can answer questions and not how well they can actually deliver the competency. We could give you a very plausible theoretical answer to a question about how we would resuscitate someone after a heart attack – we've watched enough episodes of *Casualty* – but we have never done it, nor would you want us practising on you!

What is the structure and process of the interview?

There are two key components to a well conducted interview: the structure/ process and the questioning technique. The interviewer will often use a process called the funnel technique, where, essentially, he or she will funnel and probe more and more to gather very specific details about what you did in a particular situation.

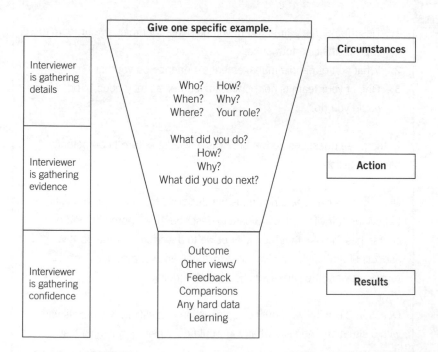

Give one specific example.

| Interviewer is gathering details | Who? How? When? Why? Where? Your role? | Circumstances |

What did you do?
How?
Why?
What did you do next?

Interviewer is gathering evidence — Action

Outcome
Other views/
Feedback
Comparisons
Any hard data
Learning

Interviewer is gathering confidence — Results

As you can see from the funnel technique diagram, the interviewer will start with a broad question designed to elicit a specific example. E.g. 'Describe to me a time where you helped a member of your team to improve their performance.'

Following this, the interviewer will gather further details, such as the circumstances, who was involved, when this was, where, what your role was and why were you involved. The interviewer will then move on to gathering information about what you did – your actions, why you did them, and what other options you considered. They will want a step-by-step run-through of what you did.

Finally, the interviewer will want to know about the outcome or results of the situation. What sort of feedback did you get, what hard data have you got about the outcome, what did you learn, would you do anything differently if faced with a similar situation?

All of this is summarised by the **CAR** acronym on the right of the diagram. It's important to remember this and to have it at the back of your mind for every interview. Framing your answers in these terms will help the interviewer to focus more quickly on the positive attributes you want to get across.

- **C**ircumstances
- **A**ction
- **R**esults

You can imagine that with this level of questioning and probing, it's going to be difficult to make something up in the spur of the moment. And with all of this probing, the interviewer is not only collecting details of what you have done, they are also building confidence that you are being truthful in your responses.

It is this structure, the probing and the seeking of real examples of activity, that differentiates the competency-based approach from the more traditional interview process. Please believe us, that it is very difficult to invent answers in this situation – it shows! What you can do, based on familiarity with the structure, is prepare and present your examples in a way which helps the interviewer. This will also help you!

THE RECRUITMENT PROCESS

You can encounter an interview at various stages of the recruitment process:

- as an initial screening method before being asked to come back for another form of assessment
- as part of a longer day where different tools are used, e.g. psychometric tests, written exercises, or a role-play
- during an assessment centre – similar to above, but typically more in depth and making use of group discussions, simulated meetings and written exercises
- as the very last stage before a final decision is made.

How will the interview be conducted?

Some companies will have a single interviewer, whilst others are likely to use two. Whilst this may at first seem intimidating, it is actually doing you a favour. Best practice is to use two interviewers, as it is a demanding job and taking notes whilst interviewing can be very difficult. Splitting the workload, therefore, makes it a more accurate and reliable process and reduces the chance of error creeping in.

Other organisations use a panel of interviewers. This is particularly popular in public sector organisations. Panels are typically made up of between three and five people representing different departments or interested parties. There may also be an HR representative in the interview. In a panel, there will usually be one person who chairs the process and the others will ask the questions. It is usually a very formal process and from that point of view can be more intimidating, but the intention is the same as with a non-panel format.

A final way that an interview may be conducted is over the telephone or using technology such as video conferencing. This approach is likely to be used if a role requires a lot of telephone interaction, such as a telesales position, or if, for logistical reasons, it is not possible to have a face-to-face interview. If applying for a role that has an international dimension, for example, you may well have an interview using video conferencing technology with interested parties who are unable to attend in person.

Finally, of course, the number of interviews you face may vary. Some organisations will use several interviews to start filtering down from many applicants to just a preferred few. Yet others will conduct several interviews, with each interview focusing on just one or two competencies rather than on all at one go. This is becoming more popular with more senior roles, as the complexity of the job being applied for can make it difficult to explore everything at once – unless of course they were to interview you for several hours at a time!

Whatever the format of the interview, or whatever stage of the selection process it is being used, the same principles apply in terms of how to conduct yourself and make sure that you present yourself as well as possible.

Why are competency-based interviews used at all?

Competency-based interviews work better for the organisation, even though they require more effort, training and preparation on the part of the interviewer. Businesses wouldn't bother if there wasn't a pay-off – and there is one. At the same time there is also a pay-off for you as the candidate.

The table below shows how well different types of assessment methods are able to predict later job performance. For those who are not statistically minded, the numbers in the second column are what are known as correlation coefficients and they are a measure, in this instance, of the validity of a selection process. In other words, they show the relationship between performance in one situation and performance in another. Correlation coefficients can range between -1 and +1, with a value of 0 indicating no correlation, a value of -1 meaning perfect negative correlation and +1 meaning perfect positive correlation. The higher the number, therefore, the better the validity or predictive power of the tool. (To illustrate the significance of this we've included tossing a coin, which has a correlation of 0.)

Method	Validity
Psychometric (ability) tests	0.5
Assessment centres	0.5
Structured interview	0.4
Competency interview (past behaviour)	0.4
Situational interview	0.3
Unstructured Interview	0.3
Graphology	0.02
Tossing a coin	0

Structured interviews and competency-based interviews are among those with the highest correlations. So, competency-based interviews are used because they let an employer make a better prediction of how well someone is likely to perform in a job.

However, their ability to facilitate better selection decisions is not the only reason why organisations use structured competency-based interviews. Employment legislation is now such that it is incumbent on the employer to be able to demonstrate that their processes are fair, should an applicant call them into question. Structured competency-based interviews are fairer for a number of reasons.

■ The competencies tested are relevant to the role – asking questions about your people-management skills is clearly relevant to a managerial position. Asking you how you would build a tower with three pieces of rope, a few straws and some sticky tape is not.
■ The process follows the same structure, so all applicants are treated the same – it will generate comparable data.
■ The process creates a clear audit trail that is evidence based.
■ The structure and training reduce the impact of bias and stereotypes – the process is therefore fairer. Again, research has shown that the differences between how different groups of people e.g. men and women, Black and Minority Ethnic (BME) or non-BME perform in this type of interview are fewer than in other types of interview.

The combination of the thoroughness, fairness and validity of the interview is the reason why organisations use them. To put it bluntly, it reduces the chances of making a poor hiring decision (the cost of which is usually about

1.5 times salary, when you consider having to re-advertise and reselect a more suitable person) and reduces the risk of being taken to a tribunal on the grounds of discrimination.

Why should you care about any of this? The answer is that the benefits to the organisation actually hold benefits for you too, as shown in the table below.

Features of the interview	Benefits to you
Valid, it is a good predictor of job performance.	You are being selected on the basis of relevant attributes. Getting a job for which you have the right characteristics will result in higher job satisfaction than if you are accidently selected for one that you are not so good at.
Competencies are linked clearly to the role.	You can see the relevance of the questions, there is no dark art involved – perceived fairness is thus higher.
There is a clear audit trail, notes are taken.	Evidence is available to enable the organisation to provide you with feedback, whether you are successful or not.
Structure ensures all candidates are treated the same.	The process is fair, chances of discrimination are reduced.

So whilst these interviews are tough, in that they really test your capabilities, it's better to be on the receiving end of one of these than of some other, unstructured, open-ended interview. Handled well, they give you a better chance to get your relevant abilities across.

The feedback we get is that people much prefer to get a job after having gone through a tough interview that was conducted professionally, clearly related to the role and fair, than to go through an interview that seemed less thorough, less related to the role and unfair. In the latter, you may end up in a job that you are ill-suited to, or worse, be discriminated against in some way. From our experience we know that job applicants, whilst finding structured interviews tough, are more likely to buy into the decision that is made, be it positive or negative for them. Those who get a job feel that they really have earned it, whilst those who are rejected understand why. The feedback that is given, which is linked to the competencies and therefore to the role, helps them to recognise why they were not suitable and, importantly, provides information that they can use for development purposes. Although you may not feel it at the time, you should, therefore, be pleased if you have been invited to this type of interview, rather than feel daunted by it!

What is the interviewer looking for?

So you now know what a competency is, what a competency-based interview is and why they are a good thing. But what is an interviewer looking for when they ask you all those questions?

Simply, they are exploring your competence to carry out the job/role you have applied for. The interviewer is interested in the evidence that you can provide as to your suitability and, specifically, is looking for concrete examples of things that you have done. They will be asking you to illustrate your experience and skills by talking them through real examples of work activity in your career to date – thus eliciting that evidence of past behaviour that we now know is a good predictor of future performance.

People much prefer to get a job having gone through a tough interview that was conducted professionally.

Remember **CAR**? (See page 179 if you've forgotten.) The interviewer is asking you to provide information about the context of the situation, what you did and what the results were. They are looking for a comprehensive answer that illustrates what you actually did. They are not looking for general answers that illustrate what you might do in theory.

IN A NUTSHELL

In this chapter we have looked at the idea of the competency-based interview and how it differs from a more traditional interview. In summary:

- Competencies are the qualities that are needed to perform effectively in an organisation.
- Competencies can be grouped into three broad headings of task-related, thought-related and people-related activities.
- In its assessment processes, an organisation may use a structured, competency-based interview as a means to assessing whether you have the experience necessary to demonstrate these competencies. Research has shown that this is a good method of assessing competencies – performance in the interview is related to job performance.

13 PREPARING FOR THE INTERVIEW

'Can't I just be myself: I'm qualified for a sales job and surely they will see that?'

We've heard candidates say this, and while 'be yourself' is very good advice, trusting to your native cunning rather than some proper preparation is leaving a lot to chance, especially when you are competing with candidates who have done their homework – and believe us, a lot of them will. In this chapter we will:

■ show you how to research the organisation you are applying to

■ show you how to understand its competencies and selection criteria

■ give you tips on researching the interview situation

■ show you how to prepare yourself.

Perfecting your preparation

Preparing for your interview is essential if you are to have the best chance of giving your best. Not only does preparation help you to anticipate some of the questions you are likely to be asked, it also ensures that you have gathered some basic information about the organisation that you are hoping to join. After all, if you are planning to work for it, you should at least aim to find out if its reputation, its operating style and the way it is likely to use you matches your requirements. From its side, you are unlikely to impress if you can't talk with some understanding about the business, its operating environment and competitors (if private sector) or its main purposes, objectives and services (if public sector). In an ideal world – and particularly for senior level roles – the recruitment process should be one where both parties are trying to make an informed decision about how good the 'match' is. You are only going to be able to take part in this assessment of mutual 'fit' if you have done some homework.

The good news is that it has never been easier – thanks to the internet – to research organisations; the bad news is that you have to assume that all the other interview candidates will do diligent preparation and research as well. So, how do you make yourself stand out?

As a minimum, your preparation should include:

- researching the organisation and/or the department that you are applying to
- finding out as much as you can about its selection criteria/competencies
- finding out as much as you can about the interview process (timing, structure, location, interviewers)
- personal preparation – understanding your assets and risks in relation to the job and preparing yourself mentally.

Researching the organisation/ department

There are several very good reasons for researching the organisation you are seeking to join.

- So that you know exactly what you are getting into – is this the kind of organisation in which you can prosper; how do your talents match its advertised needs?
- So that you can ask sensible questions at the end of the interview – you will usually be given the chance, and it is a final opportunity to impress.
- So that you can anticipate some of the questions you will be asked – what are the key things the organisation is likely to be looking for?
- So that you can show you are interested in the organisation, motivated to join it and that you have been proactive in investigating its requirements.

It's worth emphasising that most organisations will expect you to have done this research and will be disappointed if it becomes clear that you haven't. Imagine these questions being asked:

- 'So how much do you know about us?'
- 'What makes you interested in working for us in particular?'
- 'What do you see as the main challenges in the role you are applying for?'
- 'What do you think about our recent press coverage?'

Giving a decent answer to questions like these depends on the research you have done. Even when applying for an internal position, perhaps in a different department, you should still do your basic homework. You have to assume that the person or people interviewing you are enthusiastic, passionate and committed to their business. You need to mirror this if you want to 'get on their wavelength' and impress.

Where to find information
Company website
Clearly, the internet and the organisation's own website should be your first port of call. This will usually give you valuable information about the structure of the organisation, its stated values, its markets and services and the kinds of people it employs in different roles. You may also find reference to the specific job you have applied for; if you do, you should read this very thoroughly, making a note of how the job fits into the wider organisation and any other information about the job role.

Job and person specifications
It is worth being clear about some of the different terminology organisations use to define jobs and the people who do them. Typically, there are two main distinctions to be aware of:

- **Job/role specification**: this usually describes the nature of the role in terms of duties and responsibilities. In other words, regardless of the specific individual doing the job, this is what any job holder would be expected to deliver. A typical example might be 'monitor and control expenditure against department budget'. This doesn't say anything about the attributes needed to do this, it simply describes the duty. If the job/role description is all that is available to you, you need to take the extra step and think about 'what kind of person would they be looking for to do this well'. In other words, you need to produce your own 'person specification'.
- **Person specification**: this goes further than the job specification, to describe the kinds of attributes and skills required to do the job well. A typical example might be 'detail-conscious and accurate in checking figures'.

Sometimes organisations muddle these up and you may need to do some reading between the lines in order to better understand the kind of person the organisation is likely to be looking for, and not just the duties involved in the job. The table below gives some examples.

Job specification	Person specification
Monitor and control expenditure against department budget.	Detail-conscious and accurate in checking figures.
Produce plans for staff allocation to projects against tight timescales.	Structured thinker who does not become flustered when under pressure.
Implement team objectives in line with department priorities.	Clear communicator who can brief people about what is required and when.
Answer customer calls and deal with any complaints that arise.	Even-tempered and calm when dealing with irate people.

JOB AND PERSON SPECIFICATIONS

Here are some job specifications for you to interpret yourself. Think about the kind of person who would do that part of the job well; what kind of personal characteristics would they have?

Job specification	Person specification
Analyse monthly sales figures and produce summary reports	
Represent the firm at conferences and trade shows	
Conduct annual appraisals and agree annual bonuses	

Remember, this part of your research is all about understanding the job and what it will take to do it well!

Most large organisations will provide a wealth of information online. Typical website headings include:

- **About us**: always read this, it typically contains some company history, information about structure, key people, recent news coverage.
- **Careers**: clearly important, you should read all the relevant information under headings like 'Meet our people', 'Why join us?' as well as looking for definitions of different job roles, job specifications and any overall company values and competencies they provide.
- **Publications**: it is well worth looking at the company report, not just in terms of the organisation's performance (remember, the company report is a PR document!) but also in terms of values, objectives and company culture.

Even small organisations will have websites that include a lot of relevant information.

Other websites

If you put the name of your target organisation into any of the main search engines you will get a lot of other hits in addition to the company's own website. It's worth exploring some of these because they will give you a view of how the business is seen by outsiders. Organisations are all keenly interested in their reputation. By having a sense of how the world sees them you will be much better equipped to give intelligent answers (and ask intelligent questions) during your interview. Wikipedia, market intelligence websites, newspaper sites, consumer sites and profession/trade sites can all provide very useful background. Be nosey, try to understand what makes the organisation tick!

Newspapers and magazines

While these are most likely to be useful for direct information about large organisations, they can also tell you a lot about what is going on in a particular market or sector. So, while a small retailer you are applying to may not get much in the way of regular coverage, the financial pages of the main papers will tell you a lot about the retail climate, which parts of the sector are doing relatively well or badly, and so on. If you are applying to a listed company it is also well worth knowing the current share price and whether its trend is up or down – while you might not drop this information into the interview directly, it will tell you something about the likely mood in the business.

For broad information about trends and wider market factors, *The Economist* is a particularly good source. It conducts regular sector reviews that can give you a strong insight into what is keeping the directors of your target organisation awake at night! A quick look at the trade press section in any large newsagent's can also pay off in terms of background information. An hour spent reading *The Grocer* (retail), *Oil and Gas* (energy sector), *Accountancy Today* (business consulting) and similar journals can go a long way to acquainting you with the issues, the players and the jargon, particularly if you are applying for a job in a sector that is unfamiliar to you.

The organisation itself

Don't hesitate to be pushy in terms of accessing any information that the organisation itself can provide. Check to see if it is willing to send you the competencies or criteria it will be interviewing against; ask if there is anyone you can talk to in order to get a better insight into the job; take advantage of any offer of a visit or a pre-interview briefing. Asking for these things shows that you are keen, and the worst that can happen is that they say no!

Do you already know anyone who works for your target organisation? An informal discussion with an insider can tell you a lot. Failing that, explore any contacts you have with suppliers of your target organisation, or even with its competitors. Again, such people can give you a relatively objective view of the business. For example, a candidate we worked with used a personal contact in a competitor organisation to get just such a 'heads up' on a prospective employer. The insight they gained included the backgrounds of some key members of staff, information about their reputation in the sector and details about a key project that they were currently struggling to deliver. Most of this information was directly applicable to the interview.

At the end of your research, the questions you should be able to answer include the following.

■ What are the main business priorities at the moment?
■ How are they seen by the competition; by the staff; by the industry?
■ What are they famous/infamous for?
■ What do they hold up as their big successes or failures?
■ What kinds of people get ahead in the organisation?
■ How do they compare to or differ from similar organisations?

The more you can find out, the better. As we will see later, this information is not intended to enable you to be a smart alec during the interview; rather, it puts you in a much better position to understand the questions you are being asked and, as a result, to frame better answers.

Understanding their competencies/ criteria: what are they looking for?

In Chapter 12 we looked at a model for understanding and simplifying any organisation's competencies – the 'task, thought, people' model. We can now apply this in order to prepare for different kinds of interview approach and different kinds of questions.

'Task, thought, people'

You will encounter some interviews that are less structured and where the criteria are much less clear. With preparation, you can be in the best possible position to get your strengths across even when the interview process is less than ideal. Your homework in terms of 'what are they looking for' is even more important in this situation, as you may not be able to rely on being questioned in the relevant areas. The 'task, thought, people' model is particularly powerful here. Even if the organisation does not have (or is not willing to share) its competencies/criteria, it will be looking for attributes that cluster under these headings. Using the 'task, thought, people' model as part of your preparation, you can present information in a way that they will find easy to identify and digest. By using the model, you will give more rounded, more complete answers, even when questions are not particularly well framed. For more on this, see Chapter 18, on 'non-competency-based questions'.

Remember:

■ **Task competencies**: typically about operational delivery, results, implementation, plans, targets, getting things done.
■ **Thought competencies**: typically about direction, strategy, creativity, problem solving, change, innovation, judgement, decision making.
■ **People competencies**: typically about teams, collaboration, empathy, interpersonal skills, influencing, communication, personal development, motivation, coaching.

Here is a typical list of competencies used by an organisation as part of its selection process. The organisation has not clustered them in terms of task, thought, people but, as you can see, it is quite simple to do this:

Planning to achieve results	TASK
Broad-based commercial thinking	THOUGHT
Innovation and change	THOUGHT
Team leadership	PEOPLE
Analytical thinking	THOUGHT
Developing self and others	PEOPLE
Operational implementation	TASK

If you have access to the competencies in advance, you can prepare by doing this clustering yourself. This will pay off during the interview in terms of your ability to quickly identify the focus of the question. Once you have clustered the competencies you can start to think about your best examples and illustrations to get across the relevant attributes.

The table below gives some examples of organisational competencies that we have clustered for you.

Task	Thought	People
Sales focus	Change orientated	Team leadership
Planning and organising	Creativity and innovation	Collaborative working
Commitment to results	Strategic thinking	Engaging others
Energy and drive	Broad-based business thinking	Networking and communicating
Achievement orientated	Provides vision and direction	Emotional intelligence
Commercially driven	Creative problem solving	Empathy / developing rapport
Delivering results	Analytical thinking	Motivating others
Project planning	Thinks outside the box	Building and developing teams
Project management	Exploring new ideas	Influencing and persuading
Resource management	Inventive and imaginative	Team working
Target orientated	Judgement and decision making	Interpersonal skills

Having the model in your head, you can shape your answers more effectively. Holding on to three ideas – task, thought, people – is a lot easier than trying to memorise and then reference a whole competency framework in 'real time'! The model lets you quickly identify that 'this is a *task* question' and pinpoint the key aspects of your style that you want to put across in your answer.

Take the following example:

'Can you tell us about a time when you had to plan something in detail; how did you go about it?'

This is a 'task' question; it is about operational delivery and the competency being explored is 'planning to achieve results', so your answer should play to this expectation, as follows:

"OK, well a recent example is my coordination of the Birmingham exhibition: when I'm planning I like to make sure that all factors are considered, so I drew up a detailed checklist which I then turned into a project plan. It contained all the key dependencies and resources mapped against the time line. The deadline was quite tight so I did daily checking to make sure that the exhibition design team, the sales team and the venue team were all talking to each other and that they were all operating to the same plan."

The emphasis in the answer is on the implementation steps taken – the *tasks* that were performed (I considered all factors; I drew up a checklist; I turned it into a project plan; I checked daily) – so that the questioner is reassured about your approach to planning.

Holding on to three ideas – task, thought, people – is a lot easier than trying to memorise and then reference a whole competency framework in 'real time'!

Suppose that you had given the following answer to the same question, this time giving a people-based answer:

"OK, well a recent example is my coordination of the Birmingham exhibition: when I'm planning I like to get the team together early, so we had a number of meetings where we agreed who was doing what. Everyone enjoys this process; it gets the creative juices flowing and it gives everyone a chance to contribute early on; I also made sure that I got the right people on the team with representatives from design, sales and from the venue. That way everyone knew what everyone else was doing."

On the face of it, this is not a particularly poor answer, but it does not fit the model that the interviewer has in his/her head; this makes it more difficult for them to quickly identify you as someone who knows how to go about detailed planning. Your answer tells them that you give emphasis to collaborative, team-based work, that you are interested in whether people are enjoying their work and that you see the importance of communication; but that is not what they were exploring in their 'task' question. At the very least this means that they will have to refocus you and ask follow-up questions – if they are good at their job. If they are not, you will simply have missed the chance to tick this particular box.

Researching the interview situation

Nervousness is an inevitable part of interviews for most of us, and anything we can do to minimise it is likely to be helpful. Once again, the more you can find out in advance about the actual interview situation, the better. If you can, you should at least find out the following:

■ The timing of the interview: how long will it last? This will give you a sense of how expansive you can afford to be with your answers.
■ The interview format: will it be a structured, competency-based interview? What, if any, other components will there be to the interview, for example, a biographical interview or an element based on your CV and work history?
■ Who will be interviewing you: will it be one person or a panel of two or more?
■ Details of venue: the last thing you need is to be in a panic about finding the right location!

A lot of this information should be contained in your invitation to the interview, but don't hesitate to contact the organisation to clarify any of the above points about which you are not clear.

Dealing with more than one interviewer

Most structured, competency-based interviews will take at least one hour and it is common for them to be conducted by two people so that they can share the job of taking notes. Knowing this in advance can help you to visualise the interview situation and minimise any apprehension you may feel. There are some points to bear in mind if you are going to be interviewed by more than one person.

■ While your attention should be mainly directed to the person who has asked you the question (about 70%), you should take time to 'include' the whole panel as you answer questions. This can be a matter of simply taking the trouble to make eye contact naturally with the other panel members, or of referring to them as you give your answers. For example 'Yes, I think I am pretty detail conscious – the example I gave Peter earlier was one where I had to be right on top of the detail.'

■ Make sure you don't accidentally ignore anyone, for example because they are sitting at the end of the panel table or because they are quieter.

■ In panel interviews it is common for the interviewers to take one competency area each; this makes it easier for you to identify the topic area under consideration.

Dealing with questions on CVs and work history

It is also quite common, especially for more senior-level jobs, for your CV and work history to be explored in detail – often as a separate part of the interview. You should be ready for this – think through the key points you want to get across in relation to the experience you have described in your application or CV. Make sure, if there are any gaps in your work record, that you have a clear explanation of what you were doing. Trying to gloss over any periods of unemployment or hoping that they will not be noticed is very unwise; if the interviewer thinks you are prevaricating or being less than honest this will colour their whole impression of you. It is much better to explain positively how you used any down time, so think this through in advance.

When the interview contains a biographical or work history element, it is common for the interviewer to ask about high points or low points of any particular experience and what you learned from them. As part of your preparation, go through your CV and ask yourself the same questions about the key experiences you have listed. For example:

■ What do I consider were my main successes in that role/situation?
■ What helped or hindered me?
■ What were the key skills/knowledge I brought to the situation?
■ What did I learn?

This is an important aspect of preparation because the interviewer will use your answers to assess things such as your objectivity, your self-awareness, your willingness to self-evaluate and your learning style. These are usually quite hard questions to answer 'off the cuff' because, even for the most quick-witted, they need some reflection time: so do your reflecting in advance. See Chapter 18 for more advice on answering non-competency-based questions.

Researching yourself: assets and risks

The final element of preparation that we will cover here is the time you should give to weighing yourself, your style and your assets/risks in relation to both the interview situation and the job. The details of how to make sure that your assets come across in terms of task, thought and people will be dealt with in detail in Chapters 15, 16 and 17, so here we will focus on other elements of self-awareness that are relevant to you as an interviewee.

Despite having conducted hundreds of interviews, it still surprises us how unaware people often are of their impact during the interview. So, how well do you know yourself? What do your friends/family/colleagues say about your impact when you are not around? Probably the only way you will find out is by asking them!

Your impact at interview

Part of your preparation should include a long, hard look in the mirror (metaphorically speaking), so as to make as objective an assessment as possible of people's likely first impression of you. Here are some questions you can ask of yourself – or of others – to help build self-awareness of your impact.

"How confident do I sound when talking about myself?"

Research shows that interviews often overemphasise – and thus tend to put too much weight on – social confidence and verbal fluency. Good interviewers will try to get beyond this so that they are not overly influenced by the 'spin' a candidate is putting on their achievements. Nevertheless, understanding how confident and fluent you typically sound is important. It's also worth remembering that for most people nervousness has a dampening effect on normal levels of confidence and fluency. Sources you can use to assess this include your friends, feedback from previous interviews and your own knowledge of whether, for example, people typically see you as thoughtful and quiet or expressive and extrovert.

Thinking about yourself objectively can be difficult, which is why you need to give time to this element of your preparation. You may even want to record yourself giving answers to some of the sample questions in this part.

There is no substitute for actually 'saying the words out loud' as part of your preparation. How does your voice sound? How quickly do you speak? Do the words you use make you sound confident? (Too many positives risk making you sound arrogant.) Do the words you use make you sound too modest? (Too many negatives will make you appear to be self-doubting and uncertain.) A lot of people find this balance hard to achieve, so do practise out loud.

It is worth visualising the interview situation, as a way of mentally preparing yourself.

"Are there any mannerisms or verbal 'ticks' I need to be aware of?"

Examples of verbal 'ticks' include 'ums', nervous coughs, nervous laughs, sighs etc. Other mannerisms may include fidgeting, an unusual posture or tooth tapping. Introspection can only take you so far with these; you need feedback from other people who know you well, and you need to ask them to be really honest and objective. Only worry about mannerisms if people tell you that they get in the way. Changing deeply ingrained mannerisms is not easy, and you don't want to end up looking self-consciously 'stiff' or uncomfortable.

If you need to change any of these things, give yourself plenty of time to work at them and practise. People tend to make the best impact at interview when they appear authentic and 'comfortable in their own skins' – so yes, do prepare, but don't change anything that will get in the way of 'you' coming across as a person.

"How formal or how open and friendly do I appear – particularly in the pressure of an interview situation?"

It is surprising how easy it is to appear overly stern at interview! It comes from concentration and from listening hard – the result being that we frown and our faces end up being less mobile than normal. Once again, care is needed in trying to modify this kind of behaviour – after all, sitting through an interview with a grin glued to one's face is less than helpful – but it does help to be aware of your 'natural' impact and whether it is likely to be an asset or a potential risk. Once again, this kind of preparation needs to be done well in advance.

Assets and risks in terms of the job

Your research into the competencies needed for the role comes into its own here; again, we would suggest using the 'task, thought, people' model as a way of checking – in broad terms – how your experience, skills, competencies and personal attributes map onto the organisation's requirements. We have already talked about how to use this model during the interview, but it is also worth using it as a way of getting a broad picture of where you are likely to be perceived as relatively strong or weak in terms of their criteria. So ask yourself:

- Am I likely to come over as a TASK person? Is a lot of my experience about operational delivery; are my best examples about driving things through against deadlines; do I find it easiest to talk about delivery, plans and targets?
- Am I likely to come over as a THOUGHT person? Is a lot of my experience about developing ideas or strategy; are my best examples about creativity and innovation; do I find it easiest to talk about analysis, judgement and insight?
- Am I likely to come over as a PEOPLE person? Is a lot of my experience about getting results through others and developing people; are my best examples about communication and engagement; do I find it easiest to talk about influencing, coaching and collaborating?

For most of us, as we have seen, one or two of these areas tend to be more highly developed than the others, often because of our natural preferences or our experience. But it is worth giving some thought to how your natural preferences are likely to come to the fore during the interview. If, for example, your analysis tells you that you are most likely to impress interviewers as a *thought* person, with a strong second preference in terms of *people*, then you can shape your preparation to ensure that you are able to call up examples of detailed implementation, meeting deadlines and delivering against obstacles so as to reinforce your 'task' credentials if required. The risk, otherwise, is that you will find yourself less able to tackle questions based in one or more of these domains.

More guidance on how to develop your answers in each of the three areas of the 'task, thought, people' model is provided in Chapters 15, 16 and 17.

IN A NUTSHELL

Doing some basic homework is essential if you are to show off your many talents to best advantage. Key preparation steps to remember are:

■ Research the organisation and/or department; you don't need to be an expert, but you should be able to demonstrate that you are interested in them.

■ Find out as much as you can about the selection criteria; knowing what they are likely to be looking for makes it much easier for you to focus your preparation.

■ Research the interview process itself: who, how and when.

■ Prepare yourself; understand your assets and risks in relation to the job, get yourself in the right frame of mind and work on your personal impact.

14 DURING THE INTERVIEW

Another book in this series, *You're Hired! Interview*, gives a lot of excellent coverage on how best to conduct yourself during an interview, but we felt a short guide here would be useful (we advise you to read the other book if you want more detail). Most of the points are reiterated throughout Part II at appropriate points, but this chapter is your one-stop reference on how to present yourself to best advantage during the interview. This chapter will cover:

■ the interview situation

■ building rapport

■ being authentic and credible

■ the way you answer questions – how to help the interviewer

■ closing the interview.

Arriving for the interview

We are going to assume that you have done your homework about the organisation, the competencies and the specific role you have applied for, and that you also know what the format of the interview will be. We are also assuming that:

■ you know where the interview is being held (do a dry run if you can so that you are sure about travel time and location)
■ you will arrive with time to spare (give yourself time to relax and catch your breath)
■ you are well turned out and set to impress!

All of the above will have an impact on how comfortable you feel, and therefore on how you conduct yourself during the interview.

The interview situation

An interview can feel like a contest, a situation where you are in the dentist's chair and the interviewer is trying to extract information from you or catch you out in some way. The best interviews should not be like this. A better way to think about it is as a meeting where both sides are going to share information and come to a mutual decision about suitability or 'fit' with a particular organisation or role. The more you can think about the interview in these terms, the better able you will be to 'be yourself' and benefit from the guidance that follows in this chapter. Most of what you will read below is focused on removing any barriers between you and the interviewer, thus letting them go away with the feeling that they know the 'real you' – as well as having heard about your many positive attributes!

Professional but 'human' is the ideal impact you should be seeking to achieve.

Building rapport

A well-trained interviewer will be working hard to establish rapport, setting you at your ease so that you can perform at your best, but you too have some responsibilities in this regard. Interviews – and interviewers – will vary in terms of the amount of formality or relaxation that is encouraged, and in the first few minutes of entering the interview room and meeting the person (or people) you should be gauging the tone of the interview. Meeting the expectations of the interviewer – in terms of your behaviour – is an important part of rapport building because it helps to put *them* at ease.

FIRST IMPRESSIONS

In practice, most interview situations are about two strangers meeting each other for the first time. The more you can do to make these first few minutes relaxed, the better. If you look and act tense, it is likely that the interviewer will also feel a degree of tension. At the same time – even though they will work hard to put you at ease – they will form an impression of you that will take some time to shift.

In general, match your behaviour and conversation to that of the interviewer; if they are brisk and businesslike, then be polite and respond accordingly – don't try to have a conversation about the weather or the traffic if they are clearly not interested. At the same time if they – and they often will – ask you about your journey, then respond in kind; ask them how their day is going, how far they have to travel to work and so on. You need to be alert to the fact that the interviewer will need to get down to business at some point, so be guided by them.

Think of an interview as a meeting where both sides share information and come to a mutual decision about 'fit'.

Other ways in which you can make a good impression on the interviewer include:

■ Being sensitive to the fact they need to manage time: be guided by their hints – or indeed instructions – to move the conversation on.
■ Showing interest in the questions that are being asked: you can indicate this both verbally and non-verbally, for example by head nodding in

response to the relevance of the question or by actually saying that you recognise the merit of the question. Examples include:

- *"That's a good question"*
- *"Yes, I think that's a very relevant point"*
- *"I can see that you're trying to focus in on my planning skills here"*
- *"That's an interesting question"*

Using these phrases can also buy you precious thinking time!

■ Signalling what is going on: for example, if you lose the thread of the point you are making, don't just plough on regardless but say, 'I'm sorry, I've lost the thread here, can you remind me of the original question?' This helps the interviewer to 'manage' you.

■ Being alert to the interviewer's tone, while not assuming from the interviewer's demeanour that you can assess the impact you are having or how well you are doing. They have a professional job to do, which often means they will be quite focused. Don't let this put you off. The interviewer will get annoyed if you are continually seeking approval for your answers with phrases like *'was that the right answer?'*, or *'is that OK, you look a bit worried?'*

Things that will definitely get in the way of rapport include:

■ Too much questioning of the intent of a question or of the purpose of the process. Phrases like *'why are you asking that question?'* or *'why do you keep asking me for examples?'* will not go down well. It will make you sound suspicious and cagey. It's fine to clarify if you are unsure about a particular question, but don't make it sound as if you are questioning the interviewer's professionalism or motives.

■ Too much challenging of the basis of the question, or telling the interviewer what they should be asking. For example, *'I'm not sure that your question is relevant, given my experience'* or *'I think a more relevant question would have been ...'* are not likely to help the interviewer warm to you.

■ Referring to preparation notes. During the interview itself, it is very hard to maintain rapport if you are trying to read notes. It also looks as if you are trotting out a prepared answer rather than answering in real time. If you must refer to notes, you need to position their use very carefully, for example by explaining that you just want to make sure you are accurate about numbers, or that you want to make sure you have remembered events in the right order. Our advice would be to avoid using notes if at all possible.

■ Inappropriate use of humour. You need to be very sure of your ground – and your talent in positioning jokes – before you risk throwing in the odd funny story or pun. You cannot know the interviewer's sense of humour and you are as likely to get it wrong as to get it right. An interview is no place to be taking this kind of risk.

Being authentic and credible

The interviewer will be more reassured about your answers, and therefore your capabilities, if they feel they are dealing with the 'real' you. In other words, the more authentic and credible you can be, the better. What does this mean in practice?

■ Try to avoid putting on an act. The more you can let your natural style of interaction come through, the better. The interviewer won't feel that they are having to see behind a mask.

■ Use self-disclosure. Share information about yourself (appropriately!) as a way of demonstrating that you are open and honest. Volunteering information in this way has a powerful impact in terms of authenticity and credibility; not only does it show that you are not trying to hide anything, but it also shows that you have the confidence to recognise some (hopefully minor) flaws. Self-disclosure, when well used, also gives you the chance to demonstrate self-awareness; this always impresses, because if you can show a degree of objectivity about yourself, the interviewer is likely to get the impression that you can apply this same skill more broadly in their business.

■ Build trust. Even the most affable interviewer is constantly monitoring how much trust they can have in your answers, how much you are exaggerating your attributes, how honest you are being. Once you lose trust it is almost impossible to win it back in the short time you have available, so don't put it at risk! Don't lay claim to experience that you don't have, and don't pretend to have knowledge that you don't have. Remember that the interviewer doesn't have to catch you out in an untruth – all they have to do is be unsure – for it to have an impact on their assessment of you – and not for the better.

■ Be interesting. As part of your preparation you will have recalled some relevant examples of your experience to illustrate your capabilities. Some of us are much more factual in our ways of describing things, while others tend to be more colourful, painting a picture of what happened. Clearly there is a balance to be found here, but it is worth going over your examples and 'stories' to assess their interest level. If necessary, think of ways to add richness (while sticking to the truth) to the story, people, places, events that make your description more vivid (but not more long-winded!).

■ Be interested. All interviewers will be concerned to assess your motivation to come and work in their organisation. You need to signal your interest, both in response to specific questions and when you get the chance to ask some of your own at the end of the interview (see below).

■ Protect your credibility. In Chapter 13 we suggested that as part of your preparation you should 'take a look at yourself in the mirror' to see if you need to be aware of any quirks or mannerisms that are likely to affect an interview situation. The same holds true for what you say. If you have led an outrageous and bohemian youth, then you may want to consider what effect sharing information about it will have on the interviewer. Remember that they will have very little other information about you to go on – you don't want to scare them with stories about your riotous behaviour when they have no context for interpreting it! In the same way, you should mention unusual hobbies or pastimes carefully. Highly colourful examples will stick in the interviewer's mind, so be sure that they are the images you want them to have.

The interviewer will be more reassured about your answers, and therefore your capabilities, if they feel they are dealing with the 'real' you.

LASTING IMPRESSIONS

At a practice interview session we staged some years ago, the young woman being interviewed was asked 'What do you do in your spare time?' She answered – with great enthusiasm – 'I breed rats'. With the years that have passed we doubt that the interview panel can remember anything of the woman in question – but we bet they remember that she bred rats!

The way you answer questions

In the coming chapters we provide a lot of guidance and examples of the best ways of answering questions, but it is worth making some general points here. A good interviewer will give you a lot of guidance about their expectations – particularly in the context of a competency-based interview, where they will have a clear structure that they want to follow.

From your point of view, you are likely to leave the best impression if you are focused, professional but conversational in your style of answering. You will get a lot of guidance on this later, but here are some specific 'dos' and 'don'ts'.

DO

- Listen carefully to the questions you are asked. As well as noting whether the interviewer is expecting an answer about task, thought or people, you should pay particular attention to phrases like 'can you give me an example?' This means that the interviewer wants you to describe something that really happened.
- Make it clear what your role was in any situation you are describing. Try to find a balance between using inclusive terms like 'we' did something (shows team orientation and modesty) and 'I' did something (shows much more clearly what your personal role was). Overuse of 'we' will leave the interviewer unsure about your personal involvement.
- Avoid using too much jargon in your answers. Don't assume that the interviewer will be impressed – or indeed will know what you are talking about – if you pepper your answers with too many technical terms or business acronyms.
- Aim to be thorough but concise in the answers you give. Interviewers' hearts tend to sink when they hear phrases like *'OK I need to give you some background first'*, followed by a 10-minute description of the history of ABC Ltd. Aim to produce answers that are no more than 2 minutes in length – as you practise this you will realise that 2 minutes is quite a long time to keep talking. (Two minutes is about the time it would take you to read a closely typed A4 page out loud.) If the interviewer wants more information, they will ask for it.
- Be aware of the speed at which you talk. It is hard to monitor this in 'real time' during the interview, so it needs to be part of your preparation. Get

some feedback, or listen to a recording of yourself. Talking too quickly when under pressure and when the adrenalin is flowing is a common fault which needs to be remedied before the interview.

DON'T

- Be long winded. Try to assess in the early stages of the interview how much detail the interviewer is after. Are they interrupting you and trying to move you on, or are they pausing and asking you to 'say a bit more'. Be alert to this and try to modify your answers accordingly.
- Be too terse. If you are asked a specific 'closed' question such as 'how many people were in your team at that point?', then a short answer is fine, but most of the interviewer's questions will be 'open', asking you to describe or explain something, and one-sentence answers to these questions will make it hard work for the interviewer.
- Focus on negatives during your answers. 'Difficult' situations tend to stick in our minds and are often easier to recall. While they will show that you can overcome obstacles and persevere, too many will start to make your working life sound like a horror story! This is why we recommend recalling examples of things you have done well, projects that had a good result, as part of your preparation.

Closing the interview

Research shows that what we say in the first 2 minutes of meeting someone and what we say in the last 2 minutes have a disproportionate effect on the impression we give. For this reason it is well worth thinking about what your closing remarks will be.

At the end of the interview you will nearly always be asked if you have any questions you would like to ask. It is worth giving this exchange some thought. You should be aiming to ask a question – or a couple of questions – that show you are thoughtful about and interested in the role or the organisation. This is not the time to produce a list of ten detailed queries about aspects of the job. The interviewer will usually be trying to manage time, so it is worth assessing whether they have allowed 5 minutes, or 15 minutes, for this closing stage of the discussion. At the same time, asking no questions risks sounding as though you are not really interested and motivated to join them.

It sounds obvious, but the best questions to ask are ones that you genuinely want to know the answer to – they will sound authentic and relevant. It is certainly OK to ask questions about 'next steps', or when the organisation is planning to make a decision about the appointment; it is also quite appropriate to ask questions of a more general kind, such as *'Do you know the size of the new team yet?'* or *'When is the move to the new site planned?'* or *'How are customers responding to the new branding?'*

Avoid questions that sound too 'needy', such as *'Are you interviewing a lot of people for this job?'* or that are naive and should have been answered by your preparation, for example *'So how many stores do you have?'* or *'Are you based here in Leeds?'* or *'Do you have a manufacturing and a sales department?'* You should really know the answers to these questions in advance, and asking them at the end of the interview risks sounding as though you haven't done your homework or are not really interested in their business.

The parting shot

How you close the conversation is nearly as important as how you start it. It is your final chance to leave a good impression in the mind of the interviewer. Here are some final tips:

- Leave on a positive note. Signal that you have found the conversation really interesting or very informative, or that you have really valued the chance to learn a bit more about the business.
- Encourage continued contact. Depending on the nature of the interview, it may be appropriate for you to ask if there is any more information they need, to check that they have your contact details or to ask if it would be appropriate for you to seek some general feedback on the interview at some future date. Asking for feedback in this way is a final signal that you are developmentally orientated and keen to build your self-awareness.
- Leave purposefully. Don't bolt from the room, but don't shuffle out either!

IN A NUTSHELL

Manage the impression you make by avoiding barriers that may get in the way of establishing a positive relationship with the interviewer, and by knowing the signals that will create a good impression. In summary:

- Think about and work to build rapport with the interviewer.
- Be yourself as much as you can: the more authentic you are, the less the interviewer will feel that they have to 'get behind the mask'.
- Manage the way you answer questions: professional, human, not too terse, not too long-winded.
- Close the interview positively – leave a good last impression.

15 TASK-BASED QUESTIONS

Example Answers

How you get things done is an obvious area of interest for a prospective employer and task-based questions aim to get at just this. The 'task' arena is about how you organise yourself and others to deliver; how you coordinate people and resources to achieve something; how you structure, implement and execute projects/ assignments in order to achieve objectives. In this chapter we will:

- show you how to recognise task-based questions

- show you how to prepare

- give you examples of questions and of poor and better answers.

Putting the **CAR** model to work

In Chapter 13 we showed how the 'task, thought, people' model can be used to prepare yourself for interview; now is the time to put this preparation to work. This section looks at how to recognise questions that are trying to get at your 'task' skills and competencies, as well as showing you a range of questions and answers. The example questions and answers will be pitched at different levels and we will go through to identify the main 'dos' and 'don'ts' of framing strong answers to these tough questions.

THE **CAR** MODEL

Remember the **CAR** model from Chapter 12? The acronym will help you to structure answers in a way that gives the interviewer a clear picture of what you did in a particular situation. It stands for:

- **C**ircumstances (or Context)
- **A**ction (what you did)
- **R**esults (what happened as a result of what you did).

We will use this model to critique the answers to all the example questions that follow.

Recognising task-based questions

What should you quickly look out for in an interview question to tell you that the interviewer is looking for a task-based answer? From our experience, questions containing a combination of the following words should trigger your recognition of a task focused question. Words like:

organise	goal	objective	delivery	targets	deadlines
budget	system	process	steps	stages	project
manage	implement	execution	monitoring	controlling	measure

Questions containing words or phrases built around these 'task' words are likely to require a clear, structured answer from you, showing what you actually did.

Task-based questions are trying to reveal your approach to getting things done. Are you methodical and systematic in your delivery style – or are you a more creative implementer? How do you go about prioritising or project management? How do you track and monitor progress to ensure delivery to target, budget or quality standards?

More than for other kinds of questioning, it is important that the medium and the message line up in the way that you build your answers. In other words, if your answers are poorly structured and all over the place, it will be hard to convince the interviewer that you are systematic and organised in the way that you implement tasks!

Task-based questions are trying to reveal your approach to getting things done.

Preparing to respond to task-based questions

We are not suggesting that you should memorise answers in advance of an interview – you should always frame your answers based on the question you are actually asked. However, it does help to have in your mind some good examples of pieces of work you have delivered – or have been closely involved with – that showcase your delivery and 'task' competencies. It can be surprisingly difficult to come up with your best examples in the heat of the interview moment.

Have in mind some good examples of work you have delivered that showcases your delivery and 'task' competencies.

ACTIVITY 16

PRACTISE USING *CAR*

Spend a few minutes considering the following. Try to recall examples of situations where you have had to:

- organise something relatively complex
- deliver something to a tough deadline
- implement a new process or system
- overcome significant obstacles to achieving an objective
- coordinate resources to achieve a goal.

Use the **CAR** process to frame a short description of each example, making sure that you cover the **circumstances**, the **action** you took and the **result**.

EXAMPLE ANSWERS

The remainder of this chapter contains example interview questions and answers to give you a feel for how to interpret and respond in the best way. We will help you to explore what not to say, by reviewing poor answers, and will show you better answers on which you can model your own responses.

Levels of question

We have split our examples into three broad sections to differentiate between different levels of role:

■ Graduate/trainee management
■ Middle management
■ Senior management.

At entry and middle levels of recruitment, the task domain is mostly about self-organisation, planning and personal delivery style and how you meet deadlines and quality standards; at more senior levels it is about mustering resources and lining them up to deliver the required goal.

We suggest that you use the examples from all levels as part of your practice: the intent of the question will be relevant, only the expected scope of the answer will change.

Graduate/trainee management level

At graduate level it is all the more important to have thought through the examples you are planning to use – most obviously because you may not have a wealth of work-based examples that you can call on. Interviewers will be realistic in their expectation in this regard, so don't be put off. It will help, however, if you can make your examples as concrete as possible and, ideally, related to something that they, in turn, can relate to the job. For instance, using an example of how you planned your work study and revision would not be as strong as using an example of how you planned a meeting or an event.

Remember what the interviewer is looking for; they want to see signs that you can organise yourself to deliver, that you think through the steps and stages needed to accomplish something, that you met deadlines and/or achieved a successful result. If you only have limited work experience to call on, try to choose examples that involve some or all of these elements. Examples that we have seen used successfully include:

- the organisation of a visit or field trip
- contributing to running a one day conference
- plans or processes you have used to ensure that you met a deadline
- planning and organising a holiday
- your approach to delivering results in a part time or vacation job.

Here come the examples.

Interviewer: Can you tell me about a situation where you had to organise something in detail?

✗ Poor answer:

"*Yes, well, when I was working in the supermarket over Christmas I redid the Saturday work roster because so many people were off sick; I had a chat with all the Saturday team and we agreed that something had to be done because we were all working too much overtime. It had got to the point that one more person going sick would have meant that we were seriously understaffed, we wouldn't be able to restock shelves or even fully staff all the tills.*"

Why is this a poor response?

Mainly because the interviewer is going to have to ask a lot of follow-up questions to find out what actually went on. The circumstances have been partially described, but not in enough detail; the action taken is very woolly – 'I had a chat with the team' – and the outcome or result is not covered at all. The clue is in the question: the interviewer wants to know how you organise, so explain the process that you went through.

✓ Better answer:

"*Yes, well, when I was working in the supermarket at Christmas we had a staffing problem because so many people were off sick. I took on the job of redoing the work roster because it was clear that we were going to be understaffed if nothing was done. I checked availability with all the existing staff, matched this with the staffing requirement and then built in an allowance for temps in case anyone else should fall sick. I showed the new roster to the team and got them to agree where they were willing to put in extra hours. Everyone was very cooperative and the end result was that we kept to full staffing for the whole period.*"

This is still a relatively short answer, but it does cover the **CAR** format:

- **Circumstances** are covered: 'it was Christmas and we had a staffing problem'.
- **Action** is explained: 'I checked availability and matched it with the staff requirement'.
- **Result** is described: 'we kept to full staffing for the whole period'.

This answer is likely to tell the interviewer that you are purposeful and structured in tackling this kind of challenge.

Can you think of any ways in which this answer could have been still stronger? Here are some suggestions:

- A little more detail would have made the answer richer, for example, how many staff were involved, how big was the shortfall, how did you identify the problem?

- Make your own role clear: 'I took on the job' does not make it clear whether you were being proactive or were responding to someone else's request.
- Timing: over what period did this all happen – hours, days? Putting in some of this detail makes the example more vivid and convincing.

Interviewer: Tell me about your experience of managing or monitoring expenditure against a budget – give me an example if you can.

✗ Poor answer:

"*Well, when I was secretary of the sports and leisure committee I was responsible for looking after the amenities budget – basically the budget for any minor repairs or refurbishments that were needed to the sports hall and changing facilities. It was really a matter of checking that we could afford any proposed repairs, that we got the cheapest quote and that the trades people got paid at the end of the work.*"

Why is this a poor response?

As well as missing out the **CAR** structure, the example described does not give the interviewer any clear evidence about your approach to monitoring and controlling and this is probably what they are after. The intent behind this task based question is likely to be as follows:

- Can this person control things?
- Does this person monitor what is going on so that they can control things?
- How does this person monitor what is going on so that they can control things?
- Does this person measure and check the right things to ensure that the flow (be it money, time, electricity or project days) is predictable and that the resource won't run out unexpectedly?

The answer above does not cover any of these points.

✓ Better answer:

"*Well, when I was secretary of the sports and leisure committee I was responsible for looking after the amenities budget – basically the budget for any minor repairs or refurbishments that were needed to the sports hall and changing facilities. At the start of the year I asked all the committee members for their predictions for expenditure and for their spending priorities. I matched these to the budget and then made an allowance for unexpected repair bills – the previous secretary told me that about 20% of the budget was a sensible contingency fund. I then made a prediction for our quarterly spend so that I could keep tabs on the budget throughout the year. In fact we had very few unexpected repairs that year so we finished with a small surplus."*

Here the **CAR** format is much more clearly followed:

- **Circumstances**: managing the budget for minor repairs
- **Action**: predicting spend, checking spend
- **Result**: a small budget surplus showing that the spend had been effectively controlled.

At the same time this answer shows that a systematic approach has been taken to measuring, monitoring and thus controlling the relevant resource – in this case money. The interviewer will be reassured that this person is diligent in ensuring that they have the right processes and the right information to manage (or control) the outcome.

Interviewer: Can you give me an example of a time when you had to deliver something to a tight deadline?

✗ Poor answer:

"In my first job I had a role in a small marketing department. We were under a lot of pressure because of three exhibitions that were coming up over the next 3 months. We decided that we had to make some decisions in terms of priorities otherwise we would risk failing to have all the stands ready in time. The key to hitting the deadlines was recognising that we had to outsource some of the design work so that we could concentrate on the Excom exhibition, which was by far the most important. I was never convinced that the other two exhibitions were relevant to us at all – in fact I think we should have pulled them – and I'd have been really unhappy about putting Excom at risk so I think it was the right decision."

This is a task-based question; the key terms are 'deliver' and 'tight deadline'. The answer above does not give a convincing picture in these terms. All we discover from this answer is that 'some decisions were made about priorities' and that 'some work was outsourced'; we can't be sure about this person's role in the process because of the use of 'we'. The rest of the answer focuses on negative aspects and tells us nothing about the result. The upshot is that the interviewer has not learned much about this person's approach to delivering under pressure, which is the purpose of the question.

✓ Better answer:

"*We were under a lot of pressure in marketing because we had to prepare for three exhibitions all with tight deadlines. The exhibitions were all in mid-May and we were already in April. The lead time was five weeks, which is very tight to get all the design work done and I could see we had a problem. I decided to prioritise the Excom work and to outsource the design of the other two exhibitions, which were less critical in terms of our marketing plan. I made it clear to the team that the Excom material had to be ready for proofing in 3 weeks and I built a daily checklist to make sure we were on target. I used the same approach with the outsourced design, getting daily updates from the design agencies to track progress and to make sure there would be no surprises in terms of the costs. In the end we hit the target for all three exhibitions and I was very happy with the design quality we achieved.*"

Hopefully you can see why this is better. Think of **CAR** again:

- **Circumstances**: the nature and timing of the deadline are explained.
- **Action**: we now know what was done, how progress was monitored and what objectives were imposed.
- **Result**: we have a clear statement that the deadline was met to the right quality standards.

More broadly, the interviewee has understood what the interviewer is looking for, namely, a description of what was done to meet a difficult target. From this the interviewer can reasonably surmise that this person is willing to take action – and knows what action to take – in order to deliver an objective. Notice as well that the interviewee has used language that is appropriate to the question area: terms like 'lead time', 'prioritise', 'critical', 'checklist', 'target', 'updates' and 'track progress' all help to show that you understand what the question is getting at.

There is one additional step you can take to impress, and that is *framing* your answer to show that you have understood the questioner's intent and that you have a systematic approach to this kind of situation.

Starting your answer:

"I try to take broadly the same approach to delivering against tough deadlines; what I usually do is work back from the delivery date, build in some margin for error and then schedule accordingly. For example, we were under a lot of pressure in marketing ..."

Closing your answer:

"... and I was very happy with the design quality we achieved. This is pretty much the approach I take when I'm faced with challenging deadlines."

It is important not to dwell on your broad approach for too long – remember that the interviewer wants to know what you actually did – but some 'topping and tailing' of your answer, as in the example above, helps the interviewer to be confident that your general approach to this kind of challenge is also consistent and systematic.

Dealing with follow-up questions
Structured interviews involve follow-up and probe questions, so let's take this example one stage further.

For task-based questions, try to give your answers using 'tasky' language. For example, use terms:

- prioritise
- checklist
- plans
- targets
- measures/metrics
- schedule

Interviewer: I see, so what were the main obstacles you had to overcome?

✗ Poor answer:

"*Well a lot of stuff got in the way really. The team wanted to try and do all three exhibitions in-house and a lot of time was wasted convincing them that we had to outsource, but I managed this in the end. Once it was clear that I couldn't win the argument to pull the other exhibitions, I concentrated on convincing them that Excom was the important one and that we had to work flat out on it. Another problem was the design agencies. We hadn't used either agency before and I was really worried that they wouldn't be up to our quality standards, especially given the timescale, so I had to spend a lot of time with them getting them up to speed; I was on their backs a lot but it paid off in the end.*"

This answer manages to be both vague and very negative in its tone: sounding negative is a risk when you are asked to describe 'obstacles' or problems that occurred. What is needed is a much more structured and positively oriented answer, as we show next.

✓ Better answer:

"*There were three main challenges in this situation. First was putting all the evidence in front of the team to make it clear that we had to outsource; once I showed them the work schedule and the key dates they agreed that we had to go to an agency. Second was the challenge of getting the agencies up to speed; I got them to come in for a briefing, meeting our team and setting up the review meetings so that we could check progress. Third, I wanted to make sure that we avoided the same situation in the future, so I set up a working group to make sure that we had better scheduling in place to anticipate workflow problems like this.*"

This follow-up answer is structured, it is clear in describing the steps that were taken and it emphasises positive aspects of the situation, rather than dwelling on negatives. In this case the interviewee has also taken the opportunity to show that they have learned from the experience and done something about it.

WHAT DID YOU LEARN?

Interviewers will often ask 'what did you learn from the situation?'
Anticipating this question in your answer is a good way of helping the
interviewer out, and it always impresses.

Middle management level

At this level you can anticipate that the questioner will be probing still more
and be expecting you to be more 'managerial' in your answers – in other
words, to consider the wider consequences of your actions and multiple
factors/resources that had to be organised to deliver the result.

Here are some examples.

✓ **Interviewer: One of the competencies we are interested
in is monitoring and controlling; can you give me an
example of a situation where your approach to monitoring
was important to achieving an objective?** _STAR_

✗ Poor answer:

"*Yes, I think that in operational situations such as the one you have here in
the dispatch department it's really important that you have a good feel for
how everything is running. I use the PRIME 2 system; I think it does a really
good job of monitoring batch delivery. If you set it up right you can get instant
progress reports, for example relating to particular consignments or to any
delays in the system. I relied on it a lot in my last job because it took a lot of
the guesswork out of work scheduling. So my approach is to make sure that
there is a reliable system in place and I think PRIME 2 is hard to beat.*"

There is not much evidence of **CAR** being applied here. While the answer
might be OK as an advert for PRIME 2 (whatever that is!), it doesn't give the
interviewer much information about this person's approach to monitoring
and controlling. In particular, it fails to give the required concrete example.
The mistake here is to 'hear' the last part of the question, 'your approach to
monitoring', but to miss the all-important 'give me an example'.

✓ Better answer:

"Yes, I think the key part of having the right controls is understanding the pressure points in the system and making sure that the monitoring system lets you anticipate problems. Let me use an example from my last job; we had a dispatch department that was consistently overloaded because of unpredictable production. They would be quiet for several hours, then working like crazy because production had released several batches at the same time. I got the dispatch supervisors to monitor throughput for a month to see if there was any way of predicting the workflow, and sure enough there was. I then implemented a system where dispatch could monitor orders coming in; I worked out that the lead time for particular products was predictable. In the short term this was more work for the supervisors – using the order book to predict workload 2 weeks in advance – but in the longer term it smoothed out the peaks and troughs and made everyone's life easier. It also meant that dispatch was much more efficient and that customers got their orders on average a whole day earlier."

While there is scope for adding more detail to this answer, it does follow the **CAR** principles.

- **Circumstances**: 'we had a dispatch department that was consistently overloaded'.
- **Action**: 'I implemented a system where dispatch could monitor orders coming in'.
- **Result**: 'dispatch was much more efficient'.

The interviewer can tell what the issue was, what the person did and what the result was. Overall, the answer gives the interviewer relevant information to assess whether this person understands the competency 'monitoring and controlling'.

Interviewer: Can you give me an example of a time when you had to overcome significant obstacles in order to achieve a result or deliver something? STAR

✗ Poor answer:

"*I suppose the best example I can think of is when we had to merge the Bradford and Leeds offices. We had about 30 people in each office – I was managing Leeds – and I was asked to bring the Leeds people over and combine the two sales departments. As you can imagine, there was a lot of resistance but I persevered and managed to get it all done within 3 months. People don't like change so it was never going to be easy; the main thing is to be crystal clear right from the start so people know what to expect. I spent a week in the Bradford office explaining the situation – there was a lot of resistance, especially from the sales managers but some straight talking drove the change through in the end.*"

What's wrong with this answer?

You have probably noted that the basics of **CAR** are present but there just isn't enough information about the obstacles or what was done to overcome them. There are also some sweeping generalisations in the answer – 'people don't like change' – and these are best avoided, since they may contradict the organisation's competencies or the interviewer's preferences!

Let's follow this question through with some probes.

Interviewer: So what were the key obstacles?

✗ Poor answer:

"*Well it was the fact that the sales managers didn't want to change their territories, they were very possessive about them.*"

...mpromised; a bit of shuffling of territories meant that
...about the same revenue potential as they had had before."

...starting to feel a bit like getting blood from a stone. Remember that this is a task-based question; the interviewer wants to know the person's approach to overcoming obstacles. The answers so far do not suggest a systematic approach to meeting these challenges; for example, 'a bit of shuffling of territories' sounds far too offhand. Now this may just be the interviewee's shorthand for a rigorous process of analysis and reallocation, but you can't tell that from the answer. Think what the interviewer is looking for in asking this question – it probably includes:

- *Does this person persist when the going gets tough?*
- *Can this person use alternative methods if plan A is not working?*
- *Does this person have a structured approach to implementation?*
- *Did the person have a clear objective in mind?*
- *How did they ensure that things were happening to time and to budget?*

None of these is adequately dealt with in the answers so far, and the interviewer is going to have to do a lot more probing to get to the facts. The answers below come much closer to dealing with the question well.

✓ Better answer:

"*I suppose the best example I can think of is when we had to merge the Bradford and Leeds offices. We had about 30 people in each office – I was managing Leeds – and I was asked to bring the Leeds people over and combine the two sales departments. The first thing I did was set a 'go live' date by which the merger had to be completed. I set out a time line – 2 months – and developed a project plan so that nothing would be missed – there was a surprising amount of detail to consider, everything from terminating leases to transferring customer contact numbers. The second thing I did was to spend a week in the Bradford office to clearly communicate the change and its implications. I had one-to-one meetings with all the sales managers, explaining the situation and asking them to buy into the plan. There was a lot of resistance initially; they were worried about the implications for their bonuses if their territories changed too much. So, plan B was to sit them all down and agree how territories would be shared. The third step was to create a transition team and to allocate all the tasks from the project plan so that everyone knew who was responsible for what. The result was that everything got done on time and we were all co-located in the Leeds office by the start of May."*

Interviewer: So what were the key obstacles?

✓ Better answer:

"Apart from winning the sales managers over, the biggest challenge was the sheer amount of detail involved. Everything from telephone numbers to getting the sales reps' cards reprinted; strong project management was essential to keeping track of it all. The scariest moment was when it looked as if the lease on the extension to the Leeds office would not come through in time. I had to call a special meeting with our contracts people to make the seriousness of the situation clear – I wasn't prepared to accept any delay in the merger – and, in fairness, they pulled out all the stops and got the contracts signed."

Look back at the list of interviewer's objectives we gave at the end of the 'poor answer' section above. These answers cover all the relevant ground and would leave the interviewer pretty clear about the interviewee's style of delivering this kind of task. Key things to note are:

■ *the answer itself is structured – 'firstly', 'secondly', etc.*
■ *the question asks about obstacles; a specific obstacle is described, together with how it was overcome*
■ *timescales and objectives are described*
■ *there is sufficient detail that you can tell what the person actually did.*

Senior management level

At more senior levels of recruitment you can expect the scope of the questions to be wide, with the interviewer looking for answers that are pitched at the right level. For example, if the job you are applying for is head of training in a large, multi-site organisation, the interviewer is going to want to be reassured that you recognise the scope of the job and that your competencies are up to it. This means that you should try to use examples that reflect the challenges the job will hold. You are unlikely to impress if you limit yourself to examples based on running a small training department in one location. You will need to think of those things that you have been involved in that show you can deliver companywide.

At more senior levels, the interviewer will also be expecting to see that you can deliver through other people, and not just through your own task focus. At department or functional head level (or higher) the interviewer will want to know things like:

- whether you can win and coordinate resources
- the scale of your objective setting
- that you measure and monitor the right things
- that you can create the conditions that let people deliver
- that you are able to initiate, to make things happen.

Interviewer: Quality is a key issue for us at the moment; can you give me an example of a significant quality issue you have had to deal with and tell me how you went about it?

✗ Poor answer:

" *I've always felt that quality has to be at the heart of business culture, my personal approach is to try and set an example, getting things right first time and avoiding doing the same job twice. I don't think anyone sets out to do a bad job but sometimes management doesn't set the right example. There was a time when I was with ABC Ltd, when customer service levels had dropped off to an unacceptable level. It was a staff turnover issue so I got our recruitment people to change the agencies we were using so as to get a better level of applicant. It didn't happen overnight, but the better-quality staff has started to drive the complaints levels down. I think quality is all about people taking personal responsibility for their actions, it's hard to control quality, you have to build it in.* "

This is a limited answer, too brief on the detail, preceded and followed by a lot of waffle. No sign of **CAR** here. Depending on the seniority of the job, this example might also be too local.

✓ Better answer:

"*To my mind, quality is often a matter of training people well and letting them know what is needed from them. When I was General Manager at ABC Ltd our customer research began to show that customer satisfaction had started to fall. Now, there are lots of potential reasons for this and I wanted to know in more detail what was going wrong. I brought in some customer service specialists to look at the issue across all our call centres, because if it was affecting one region, chances were it would be affecting the others. The research showed that the main issue was staff turnover; because of the need to get frontline call handlers working quickly we had cut back on the training time and this was showing in terms of how effectively customers were being dealt with – waiting times were too long. I asked the call centre managers to come up with a solution – quickly! I told them that we needed to get the satisfaction figures heading in the right direction in weeks, not months!*"

Interviewer: So what was the outcome?

✓ Better answer:

"*Their first reaction was to ask for a bigger training budget, but finances just didn't allow this so I asked them to think again. The eventual solution was to improve the recruitment process – we changed to a recruitment agency rather than doing it in-house and this actually ended up saving us money. Better recruits and a better system for supervising them in the first 3 months made a significant difference.*"

Interviewer: How much difference?

✓ Better answer:

"*Waiting times are now down to below our competitors' average and the last customer survey showed that we had edged up two full points in terms of customer satisfaction. It was too easy to forget that the call handler was our key contact with the customer, a fall in quality here could affect the whole business; it's too easy to think of it as an administrative activity rather than something that adds real value to the business. My job was to recognise this and get the right people to do something about it.*"

This sequence of Q and A shows a much fuller and wide-reaching approach to quality. The reference is to a companywide issue, there is emphasis on taking action, it is clear what was done and the outcome is clearly described. The interviewee has also taken the opportunity to show business-wide consideration of this issue. The interviewer is likely to be convinced that here is a person who recognises a delivery problem and knows how to take the right action to fix it. At senior level, task focus is usually about *initiating* and not just about personal execution, and this answer demonstrates this well.

Interviewer: The proposed merging of our four divisions down to two represents a significant change; can you give me an example of when you have implemented a major initiative or change programme?

✗ Poor answer:

"*Well I've never done anything on the scale of what you are proposing here, but my first reaction is to focus on communication. People are likely to be unhappy, you always get competitiveness in this kind of situation and I would want to get all the key players together and set some ground rules at the outset. It's likely that some jobs are going to be at risk, so we would need to start consultations early. Incidentally, I noticed that XYZ Ltd are talking about consolidation as well – I know that they are in a different market to you but I think it's interesting that so many of the big players are making similar decisions at about the same time. Where was I? I'd probably want to set up a change team as well, made up of people from all the divisions so that we could avoid any duplication of effort. I had to do something similar at ABC Ltd when two sales teams had to be merged; communication was the key, I made sure that people were talking to each other throughout.*"

Here we have a negative, followed by a lot of hypothetical solutions, followed by an irrelevant digression, followed by a poor example; not likely to impress!

✓ Better answer:

"*Yes, you have a significant challenge on your hands. My experience of this kind of merger is that people are at their best when they are clear about what the intention is rather than working in an atmosphere of rumour and suspicion. At ABC Ltd the Board gave me the role of merger coordinator, the job was to bring the sales teams from all the product lines together into a unified sales function. I gave myself the target of achieving an integrated department within 3 months and I pulled together a team to do this. I appointed a head of communications and a head of coordination. They reported to me weekly in terms of the various work streams that were necessary to bring about the change. I separated the coordination and communication roles because my experience is that conflicts arise if the same person is trying to implement and time communication as well – I saw this done badly when I was at XYZ Ltd and I learned the lesson!"*

Interviewer: What did you do in practice, how did you see your role?

✓ Better answer:

"My job was to keep everyone focused on the target and to provide the support and resources they needed. For example, by working with the two heads I had appointed, the weekly project meetings were a forum where we could anticipate any obstacles and take action to tackle them. There was one point where there was an issue to do with redrafting all the employment contracts to bring them into line. The coordination head pointed this out and I took it on myself to get our legal department to focus on this, bringing them into the project plan and giving them clear timescales for delivering the work. They had their own priorities to worry about, but I made it clear that I wouldn't allow the contracts issue to slow everything down and that other matters they were working on would have to be reprioritised."

Once again, this answer makes the interviewee sound structured, clear about what they did and, just as importantly, attentive to the questioner's need for detail – that's why they asked the follow-up question.

None of the examples given above is perfect, nor are they meant to be 'model answers' that you can paraphrase or memorise. What they do illustrate is the kind of answer that is most likely to impress if you follow the tips we have given.

IN A NUTSHELL

Task-based questions need a structured, task-based answer. The interviewer wants to know what you did and how you did it. To summarise:

- Think through some good, task-based examples of your work in advance.
- Look out for the key words that tell you if the interviewer is expecting a task-based answer.
- Follow the **CAR** structure as you give your answer – **Circumstances, Action, Result**.
- It's OK to top and tail your answers with more general points, but not at the expense of a clear, concrete example.
- Structure your answer, tell the interviewer what you did first, second, third.
- Be succinct and avoid too many digressions or side issues.

16 THOUGHT-BASED QUESTIONS

Example Answers

This chapter focuses on questions that are trying to get at your thinking style; how you plan, prioritise, innovate and consider the bigger picture. As before, it gives you a chance to understand and practise this kind of question, and it is vital reading in preparing for a competency-based interview. In it we:

■ define the competency domain of thought leadership

■ explain how it relates to all roles, irrespective of the level of the role you are applying for

■ give you example interview questions

■ provide example responses.

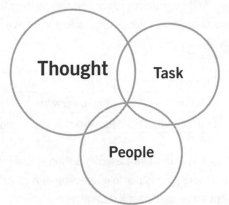

Thought-based questions

There are not many roles that don't require an element of thought leadership. Even the most basic administrative role will require the ability to explore and analyse a problem, identify potential solutions and then implement them. Where solutions do not exist, then creative responses and new ideas are required. Some of the best administrators that we have worked with are those who have been able to discuss with us what we wanted to achieve and then find a way of implementing it by generating new ideas.

For more senior or complex roles, the dimension of thought leadership is about more complex problem solving, involving many variables, longer-term thinking and scenario building, right up to visioning and strategy.

It's an important aspect of most jobs, then, and in this chapter we'll explore how to recognise a 'thought leadership' question, and we'll give you some example questions and answers for different levels of role.

Recognising a 'thought-based' interview question

What are the key ingredients of a 'thought-based' question? What will alert you that the interview is trying to explore aspects of your thinking and problem-solving style? As a rule of thumb, the words below are likely (but not always), to relate to thought leadership, and should therefore trigger your thinking about aspects of your previous roles where you have had to problem-solve in some capacity.

creative	problem	new	strategy
develop	identify	come up with	complex
plan	opportunity	analyse	idea

Another way to recognise a 'thought-based' question is when it does not obviously relate to delivering a task or to interacting with other people; this can be quite hard to spot and sometimes it depends on where the emphasis is in the question. So, for example:

'Tell me about a time where you worked with others to develop a new concept'

is likely to be a 'people' question, rather than a 'thought' question.

Whereas:

'Tell me about a time when you developed a new concept'

is clearly a 'thought' question.

Preparing to respond to thought-based questions

This very simple exercise will help you to prepare and respond to most of the example interview questions that we'll present in this chapter. Where it does not fit directly, there will usually be a way of doing so – finding an angle that makes it relevant to the question being asked.

GATHERING YOUR THOUGHTS ON THE FOLLOWING:

- an example of where you came up with an idea
- an example of where you had to solve a problem
- an example of where you had to set longer-term direction
- an example of where you had to plan something.

On a sheet of paper just jot down a very broad outline of each issue against the **CAR** model that we introduced in Chapter 12.

If you really struggle to think of examples in one of the four broad areas above, it is likely that it is a potential weakness for you. Equally, it may simply be that you underestimate what you have done to demonstrate competency in that area. One way to address the latter is to speak to a colleague or friend. They may be aware of instances where you have demonstrated this and be able to remind you.

IDENTIFY THE COMPETENCIES TO DEMONSTRATE

As part of your interview preparation you should have identified the organisation's competencies. Once you have these, you can better prepare potential examples to respond to questions.

EXAMPLE ANSWERS

The remainder of this chapter is given over to example interview questions and answers to give you a feel for how to interpret and respond to the question. It's split into three broad sections to differentiate between different levels of role:

- Graduate/trainee management
- Middle management
- Senior management

Moving up these three levels, responses to questions need to increase in their complexity and level of focus. An easy-to-use general rule is that for a trainee management role the focus is likely to be at the individual level (although not exclusively); at the middle management level, the focus is at team or departmental level; and at senior management level the focus will increasingly be heading towards business unit or even organisational level. Remember, these are generalities and there will always be exceptions, as you will see in some of the examples we provide. When deciding on which level of question to look at, think about the remit of the role rather than exclusively about the level. You may find, for instance, that some of the middle-management level questions will be equally applicable to a more junior role.

Graduate/trainee management level

Interviewer: Please describe a time where you have had to solve a difficult problem.

✗ Poor answer:

"Oh yes, there was this time when I had a summer job when there was a clash on the rota. Someone needed to free up a day to enable them to attend a medical appointment, so we needed to sort that out. We looked at the rotas to see who might be able to substitute and obviously needed to take legislation into account to ensure that the shifts were adequately staffed. In the end, someone did 2 hours' overtime to cover for him during his appointment."

First of all, this example is very similar to the one provided in Chapter 15 on task-based questions, but it does not adequately differentiate between 'task' and 'thought'. When you use the same or a similar example to respond to two different questions it's important to clearly illustrate how the example relates to the question being asked, and how it differs from your earlier use.

Also, the response lacks structure. Although we know what happened, we don't really know the context, and the credibility is limited. A clearer response would follow **CAR** (Circumstances, Action, Results) and would have given a better insight into the circumstances leading to the situation, the action taken, and the results.

Another problem with this response is that we do not really know what role the interviewee took. What did they contribute to resolving the problem, what data did they draw on, how did they reach a conclusion? Again, the response has limited credibility as a result.

✓ Better answer:

"*Yes, for a summer job I worked in a place where they operate a shift pattern, with three shifts in a 24-hour period: 7 'till 2, 2 'till 10 and 10 'till 7. I had been asked by the manager to look at the rota for what hours staff were due to be working. One of the other members of staff had requested to be released from a shift as they had an important medical appointment that they needed to attend. The difficulty was that overall, we were slightly short staffed anyway, so finding a way of releasing this person and still being able to adequately staff the shift was going to be difficult. I therefore needed to look at all the information available to me and provide some options for how it might be possible to grant the request.*

I looked at the previous 3 weeks' rotas to get a feel for who had done what work; I checked the holiday requests to identify anybody who would definitely not be able to substitute and I looked at what activities had been scheduled which might require a particular staffing level. Finally, I looked at the guidelines which had been laid down for staffing levels in general to ensure that we were complying with legislation. Using all of this information, I generated three possible solutions. The first was to swap two people around, so that one of his off days would fall on the appointment day. The second was to run the shift with just one person fewer – but that meant we were not complying with guidelines. The final option was to ask somebody to cover the 2 hours that he would be away and to pay that person overtime. Even though that was the slightly costlier option, as we would have to pay one person 2 hours' overtime, this was my preferred option. I spoke to the manager and outlined to her the three options I had arrived at and which one I preferred. In the end, she went with my recommendation."

This is a well structured response, in the **CAR** format:

- **Circumstances**: working in a shift system, somebody needed time off for a medical appointment.
- **Action**: exploration of different sources of information, resulting in options being identified and proposed.
- **Result**: decision to offer somebody overtime for a couple of hours, which ensured everybody's needs were met.

The answer provides evidence of what the interviewee actually did – they used 'I' in their response. They also stated what data they looked at and what options they developed from their analysis. All this shows that they have understood the question as a 'thought' question rather than as a 'task' or a 'people' question.

The response could have been better still, there could have been a little more detail on how the decision was actually made, i.e. how the data was used and what the pros and cons of the options were. For example, the downside of running the shift with just one person less was not only that it did not comply with the established guidelines, it meant that if there were an emergency this could not be adequately dealt with. The downside of simply swapping people around was that it created problems with childcare arrangements for one person, and so the issue would not have been solved.

Interviewer: Give me an example of a time where you improved something.

✗ Poor answer:

"*As part of my role in the graduate recruitment team, I have responsibility for planning the campaign every year. This was a new responsibility that I had picked up, and I had heard many people complain that the campaigns were not very good. I therefore took it upon myself to improve them. So, I took the plans from last year and made some improvements, such as bringing the whole thing forward by two weeks, changing the booking system as well as the data capture. Overall, the whole thing worked better as a result."*

There is not much evidence of CAR here. We do know a little about the circumstance, and we have a very vague outline of the result in that overall the whole thing worked better. What this answer really lacks, though, is a clear explanation of the actions that were taken - we have no sense of the interviewee's thinking.

✓ Better answer:

"I was given then responsibility of managing our graduate recruitment campaign. Having heard from line managers in previous years that they did not think the process was as slick as it could be, I decided that as part of managing the process, I would try to introduce some improvements. Specifically, the two key complaints were that the booking system for assessors was "very messy" and that it took us too long to get back to applicants with a decision – this meant that some good candidates were lost as they took offers elsewhere. I therefore focused on improving these two aspects. With regards to the booking system, I worked with IT to introduce an online booking system. This was interactive, and when line managers logged in to book, it would tell them on which days we still needed assessors, thus making it impossible for some days to be oversubscribed and others to be undersubscribed. From the booking system they could also link directly to the online assessor training materials. With regards to us being late in getting back to applicants, I introduced an online tracking system of candidate performance, in conjunction with one of our suppliers. This enabled us to quickly gather information on candidate performance from across the different locations where we ran assessments and have an overall picture within 30 minutes of the last assessment day finishing. We could therefore make decisions much more quickly. Feedback from the different departments was very positive."

This answer follows the CAR principles far better than the previous response.

- **Circumstances**: There was negative feedback about two specific points.
- **Actions**: The interviewee addressed the two specific points of negative feedback and described the improvements made.

- **Result**: There was positive feedback from the different stakeholder departments.

There is scope to improve the response further still. On the actions front, there could be more detail about the options that were considered and how the interviewee finally decided between the options. On the results front, there could be more specific detail about the benefits as seen by the various stakeholders.

Interviewer: Tell me about a time where you encountered a significant problem with a system, process or procedure. How did you solve it?

✗ Poor answer:

"*I had felt for a while that our internal resourcing was not very effective. Being a consulting business, how we resourced obviously had implications on the quality of our work and bottom line performance. I therefore suggested that it would be better if one person took on overall responsibility for the resourcing of work. This would mean that one person had the overall, big picture view of how resource was being used.*"

Why is this a poor response? For a start, it is very brief and gives no depth around any aspects of CAR. It has the foundations of a good response, though, as it is clearly about an improvement. Let's look at a better response.

This time we'll give you two possible responses, based on different work scenarios.

✓ Better answer:

"*I used to work in a resourcing role in a small business where I was responsible for ensuring that our consultants were used in an equitable way. In reality what happened was that when a piece of work came in, project managers would speak to staff directly and allocate work to them. This came to my attention, as consultants would speak to me and complain that they felt work was not being allocated in an equitable way. Our staff survey had also shown a degree of favouritism occurring. So the current system was not working effectively. I made suggestions that all resourcing would need to go through a central person who would take account of availability, skills, performance and so on and discuss with project managers what the resourcing options would be. Rather than me dictating resourcing, it became a joint problem-solving exercise and ensured that project managers were still involved in the process. Feedback so far is that people feel resourcing is now more equitable."*

The above example demonstrates that a response need not be lengthy – it can be short and punchy. It is also a well structured response around **CAR**.

- **Circumstances**: The respondent worked in a resourcing role in a small business. Feedback about resourcing had not been positive.
- **Actions**: Suggestions were made to resource centrally based on skills, performance and project need.
- **Results**: There was positive feedback and staff survey results were better.

Clearly, there is more information to be gleaned here by an interviewer and there would be follow-up questions to probe about the detail and build confidence, but in essence, the example represents a solid response.

INTRODUCING CHANGE AND IMPROVEMENT

Think about the situations where you have introduced a change or made an improvement. Write down how what you suggested was different from what you did before. Note down what you based your idea/suggestion on and how you adapted it from what you knew or did previously. This will help you to distil what was different and how you used creative thinking in the workplace. You'll surprise yourself!

Let's look at another two responses to the same question. First a poor one, and then a better one.

✗ Poor answer:

"*My first training role was as a graduate in a bank. Part of my role required me to report on key financial indicators for the different business units. There was a very tight deadline for this which we never met as we were reliant on information coming in to us from the departments so that we could pull together the report. To get over this, we decided to send out reminder e-mails to all departments to remind them that we needed their input if we were to hit our deadlines. We also offered to support them in pulling the information together so long as they requested our support. Some departments did request support and one of us would see them, spend an hour talking to them to get the important information that we needed to enable us to put the report together.*"

There are several things that are wrong with this response. First of all, the interviewee uses "we" rather than "I". From an interviewer's perspective, they will not know who made the suggestions, or who was actually the driving force behind the improvements. Second, we have no information on the outcomes of this improvement. The response is also not very well structured and therefore difficult to follow. The interviewer's job is as a result, made more difficult so there would likely be many follow up questions.

Here's the second possible response to the question:

✓ Better answer:

"*Yes, working in the accounts department of the bank, we were responsible for drawing together the monthly management information for various parts of the business. We were a small team of three that were responsible for working on this. The real pressure points were always at the end of the month when we needed to quickly draw together all financial indicators and report back to the various business units. The problem was that we were reliant on them furnishing us with the raw data that we would then use to prepare our reports. This was not always delivered in a timely fashion, owing to the business pressure that they were under. We were therefore ourselves under pressure to deliver and frequently missed the deadlines, which was clearly not satisfactory. We were unable to put more resource into this, so a solution needed to be found that would enable us to deliver on time. The simple solution would have been to tell them that they just needed to deliver to us in time to enable us to*" *do our job, but the reality was that on, for example, a trading floor, the dealing always took priority over admin-related stuff. What I'd noticed was that part of the problem was the number of different reports that we were having to produce for the different business units which all essentially showed the same information, but just represented differently. The work was therefore repetitive and there was scope for changing this. I suggested that we speak to all BUs about this.*

To support this, I mocked up a report that contained all of the essential information that we provided in the different reports. With this, we were able to have a discussion with the heads of BUs, outlining our difficulties and that if we could agree on a common format then we would be able to meet our deadlines better without putting pressure on them to meet their deadlines with us. They were very amenable to this, and this is what we now do. The outcome is that we are now able to deliver all reports to them in a timely fashion even when they miss deadlines, and rather than having three people work on this we now do it with only two. This allows us to alternate between the three of us who does this on a monthly basis, and has provided more variety of work for us."

Not only does this response provide evidence of the interviewee making suggestions for changes, it also demonstrates them putting themselves in the shoes of another business area, a willingness to consult with and involve others and recognition of the commercial implications of their thinking. Whilst these areas might not be the ones being assessed by the interviewer in this question, the response provides additional information that either the interviewer or the interviewee can come to in other questions. In terms of **CAR**, the answer provides the following:

- **Circumstances**: preparation of financial reports in a bank where the team was overworked and producing duplicate reports.
- **Action**: suggestions for change to reports, and consultation with internal clients in order to achieve this.
- **Result**: development of a simplified report format that still met the needs of all parties while reducing the workload for the finance team.

USING AN EXAMPLE MORE THAN ONCE

Whilst an interview question is designed to elicit information about a specific competency, most work activities actually involve more than one competency. You'll therefore find it impossible to restrict your answer to only that competency. You do need to emphasise the relevant competency, but you can also come back to the same example and use it differently. A word of warning, though – don't use the same example more than twice. The danger is that you will not demonstrate sufficient breadth of experience.

Middle management level

For a middle management role, the interviewer will be seeking more complexity in the issues that you talk about. Either your examples will need to have a higher level of focus or the issues will need to be more complex and more interrelated, requiring more careful consideration and balancing of implications.

Interviewer: Tell me about a time where you had to anticipate potential problems and how you went about developing contingencies.

✗ Poor answer:

"*Well, that's part of a manager's job really. It's important that I keep on top of what is going on in our market place. I do this by regularly speaking to my contacts and reading the trade press. I have also instigated regular weekly meetings with the team, where we all report back what is happening in the market and this allows us to take corrective action at an early stage. For example, I recently completely restructured my sales team as our competitors were beginning to catch up with us and I needed to take corrective action quickly. The restructure made us more nimble and better placed to beat the competition.*"

Why is this a poor answer?

The answer starts at a general level. When eventually an example is cited, it is not very detailed or specific. Remember, this is for a middle management role, so an interviewer would be expecting more depth to the response. Had the interviewee followed the CAR principles more closely, we would have a more in depth and detailed response.

✓ Better answer:

"*Yes, as manager of a sales team of ten people, I was becoming increasingly aware of a competitor that was beginning to encroach on our territory. To date, we had not lost sales – our clients were buying both products – but we obviously needed to ensure that in future this didn't change. The way we were set up as a client team at the time was that different sales people were specialised in different products, and between them covered a very large geographical area. I could see that our competitors were more nimble and I needed to find a way to match this. What I did was to split the big area into five smaller ones and restructure the team such that two sales execs were responsible for each of the smaller areas. This meant that they would also need product training so that they could speak to their clients in a knowledgeable fashion and provide continued good client care. The overall impact of this was that the sales execs developed a more intimate relationship with their customers – they had fewer, and more time with them, and were able to offer them a wider choice of product. They were also more nimble in their response to client needs. This approach counteracted what our competitors were doing and we were able to continue to grow sales.*"

Whilst this is a short and succinct response, it encapsulates the sort of thought leadership that is expected at this level. It demonstrates an awareness of the need to look outside of the organisation, to be aware of competitors and to position the business, at team level, to respond to a threat.

Clearly, there is much more information for an interviewer to elicit here. Other aspects to be probed could include: the data that was used to drive decision making, who was consulted, the options that were considered, the strengths and weaknesses of those options and the risks that were being taken.

Interviewer: Tell me about a business opportunity that you became aware of and what you did to capitalise on it.

✗ Poor answer:

"*One of my key clients called one day to speak to me about a need that he had. Basically, he needed some support with advice around a redundancy situation that he potentially had to deal with. This is an area of specialism for us, and we were able to support him in both the legal aspects of this to ensure that he did it right, as well as providing some training interventions to support managers who might be losing some of their staff. Finally, there was scope to provide support on the outplacement work. I wrote a proposal outlining our approaches to all three and sent this to him.*"

For a middle management level, this is a very basic response. In any business development situation, you would expect a response that might include a written proposal. The example does not demonstrate any originality of thought, proactive action or any lasting change. In short it does not demonstrate sufficient thought leadership.

✓ Better answer:

"*I took a call from a client one day with whom I had a really good relationship. We had been working with them for a number of years and providing them with HR services. This was our area of specialism, and he respected our responsiveness and integrity. He also mentioned to me that what he missed was some of the technology that he knew that some of the bigger players in the market were providing, although at much higher cost than us. This led to a discussion around his technology needs. Given that we were not a software house, I started to explore the market to see if there was a potential small IT firm that we could partner with so as to meet the needs of this long-standing client. I sourced a potential partner and worked with them to put together a profit-share model. Armed with this, we were able to meet with my client and discuss how we might be able to support them. This was the first time we had done something like this and the result was that it allowed us to start offering more sophisticated solutions to our clients.*"

Although this is not an example of proactive action, it demonstrates a willingness to look at a situation and to problem-solve, resulting in more business that later translated into an overall organisational impact. From this perspective it demonstrates leadership in creating a new way of doing things and driving business improvement. It also fits the **CAR** model:

- **Circumstances**: the example provides the context of a pre-existing, good client relationship that has been ongoing for a number of years. It also provides the reason for the client call.
- **Action**: the example then goes on to illustrate what actions the interviewee took in terms of trying to meet the client's needs by exploring possibilities with other technology suppliers.
- **Result**: the interviewee was able to provide more sophisticated IT-based HR solutions.

Interviewer: Can you give me an example of a time where you needed a solution to a problem where no precedent had been set?

✗ Poor answer:

"*We had no career break policy at all, and I knew that career breaks are becoming more popular. I therefore decided that one was needed and drafted out a broad policy that I presented to the senior management team. They thought it was a good idea and I therefore set about writing it in more detail. I put together a proposal outlining the business benefits, as well as outlining a financial model that would help us to better understand what the cost to the business was likely to be.*"

With a bit more detail, this could be a strong answer. There is evidence of proactive action, consultation with other people and a structured approach to introducing the change. The need for change was linked to potential business need and there was talk of an analytical approach. Were the response fuller and given in terms of CAR, it would be much stronger.

✓ Better answer:

"Yes, one of my team wanted to take a career break for six months. As a small business, nobody had requested this before and so we had no systems and processes in place to deal with it. It was Nigel, who had been with us for about 7 years and was a well regarded member of the team, so we wanted to retain him. I say this, because my first thought was he could just resign and then come back. Then I realised that we might not have any vacancies when he returned and we'd lose him. So I spoke to our head of HR, and with him, we drew up a career break policy that would allow people who had been with us for 5 years or more to be entitled to a maximum 6 months' break. Our commitment to them would be that we kept their job open, while their commitment to us would be to return for a minimum of one year after their break. The career break was unpaid. We arrived at this policy because I spoke to some contacts that I have in other organisations to see what they did, and our head of HR looked at it from the employment legislation perspective. The result is that we now have a policy that is popular and has been taken advantage of by a number of staff."

How well do you think this example answers the question? It is structured according to **CAR**:

■ **Circumstances**: the need for a new precedent was described.
■ **Action**: the interviewee worked with the head of HR to draft a career break policy.
■ **Result**: Nigel could take a career break and still be able to return to work afterwards. This action ensured that the business retained a good member of the team whilst at the same time meeting the needs of that team member.

In terms of quality of content, this example shows an ability to problem-solve at the level of looking outside and exploring. It does not provide evidence of starting from a completely blank slate, nor does it show originality or ingenuity in solving a particularly difficult issue, and thus defining precedent on a much broader level. If the interviewee had wanted to demonstrate originality of thought or approach, a different example should have been used, perhaps one where they had researched something for themselves rather than working with somebody else.

CREATIVITY AND INNOVATION IN THE THOUGHT DOMAIN

Interviewees often assume that a response relating to change or problem solving needs to demonstrate innovation or creativity. Indeed, creativity and imagination are two things that interviewees often find difficult and intimidating to respond to. This doesn't need to be the case; the sorts of innovation and creativity that interviewees assume are needed are not what the interviewer is necessarily looking for. Many interviewees place themselves in the 'uncreative box'. This actually limits their thinking and makes responding to such interview questions difficult.

In the workplace, creativity is also about using an existing process in a new way or in a different setting – it does not need to be a totally original idea.

Senior management level

For senior management roles, the examples that you give in an interview will need to demonstrate breadth of thinking with a broader focus. At this level, it is likely that decisions will have an impact on a whole business area or even on the organisation as a whole, and that it will be longer lasting. The financial implications are also likely to be bigger. An interviewer will be looking for evidence that issues have been well thought through, that they demonstrate awareness not only of the internal organisational environment but also of external factors, including other organisations, the industry as a whole, the economy and, potentially, the political agenda. As you can see, many factors need to be drawn into the 'thought' domain at this level.

REVIEW YOUR THOUGHT LEADERSHIP EXPERIENCE

Think of examples that you could give in response to these three questions, based on your experience.

- Describe an occasion when you have initiated significant change in the workplace for the benefit of the organisation.
- Tell me about a time when you have used recent developments in your area to inform your decision making.
- Can you give me an example of where you had to develop a new strategy?

Interviewer: Describe an occasion when you have initiated significant change in the workplace for the benefit of the organisation.

✗ Poor answer:

"The most recent example would be changes to our pay and remuneration system. It had not been looked at for a number of years, so it was about time that it had an overhaul. I asked HR to carry out a benchmarking exercise for me so that we could get a sense of how we were remunerating our staff compared to our competitors. The analysis showed that many of our competitors were paying more, so obviously we needed to keep up with them. I therefore recommended that we find ways of equalising our pay to the current market conditions. When we evaluated this in our next staff survey we found that staff satisfaction and engagement had increased from the previous year, so it seems to have worked."

This is not at all a strong answer. On the surface, decisions and actions seem to be data driven and the results seem to have benefitted the business. The problem, though, is that the thinking is not joined up and the conclusions drawn do not follow from the original premise. The interviewee has not been able to provide an example of a clear antecedent, action and outcome.

Changing salaries as a result of a benchmarking exercise is fine, but the increased engagement cannot be linked to this. An interviewer will be looking for clear, rational and data driven decision making, together with an evaluation and outcomes that make sense in the whole context.

✓ Better answer:

"*The most recent example that I can think of is in our pay and remuneration process. We conduct an annual staff survey and I had noticed a trend in the feedback with regard to how people perceived remuneration in the business. This was a tricky one, as people didn't openly discuss it, but the survey indicated that there was a general sense of inequity and a bit of a 'black box' approach to it. It obviously needed addressing, and at one of the senior team meetings I raised this and volunteered to look into it. It was outside of my area as I'm not HR, but I recognised that as someone that was dealing with the commercial realities of the business on a daily basis I could work with the HR director to implement some change. The consequences of not doing so could potentially have been a steady stream from our doors to our competitors. So, to cut a long story short, I did some research into what approaches to remuneration were commonplace in our industry, what the perceived upsides and downsides of the different systems were, and with this information worked with our head of HR and some remuneration specialists to devise a new scheme. Our most recent staff survey has shown better results in this area, and our business has continued to grow, despite some difficult trading times.*"

The above example demonstrates succinctly the initiation of some change that had an impact at the organisational level.

- **Circumstances**: review of staff survey indicated dissatisfaction with remuneration.
- **Action**: the interviewee then describes, in broad terms, what he did, i.e. becoming involved and researching approaches to remuneration.
- **Result**: implementation of a changed process, and staff survey results with more positive feedback from staff.

More generally, the interviewee has demonstrated awareness of internal issues, looking outside the business and using that as a basis for driving change within the business. Overall, the initiative seems to have had a positive impact. More detail is clearly needed in this answer. For example, there is no detail about what changes were actually made and how they were introduced. Information on this would give the interviewer more confidence, as well as providing subsidiary evidence on task- and people-based issues.

Interviewer: Tell me about a time where you have used recent developments in your area to inform your decision making.

✗ Poor answer:

"*It's always important to keep on top of new developments in the field. We actually have a department that deals with this and I often work in close collaboration with them to introduce new products and services. For example, I recently suggested to them that they look at improving our online discussion forums that we host to support some of our products as I felt there must be more we could do to make them interesting and engaging.*"

This response really lacks depth at this level. There is some indication of change, but it is presented in a way that suggests it happened as an aside. There is also no real sense of ownership – it's implied that this actually sits with another department and that the interviewee has limited exposure as a result. This may well be the case, but as an interviewee, you need to think about how to make the best of the limited experience that you may have, whilst obviously staying truthful.

Let's look at a better response:

✓ Better answer:

"*Sure, as an IT and internet business, we need to keep on top of the latest developments in the marketplace and ensure that our customers are also kept up to date. As part of our customer service commitment, we run several discussion forums that allow users of our products to keep in touch with not just us, but also each other, and thus discuss their experiences. Our support staff also read these and will from time to time contribute to them. Now, discussion forums are a bit dry and they're not really like a proper discussion at all because everything is completely sequential. Recently, there has been a new development that combines different web communication methods into one allowing both chatroom- and forum-style communication. It has made the process of communicating far more collaborative. Now clearly, this was going to be an entirely different form of keeping in touch with our customers, and from a change perspective, we had to plan both internal and external aspects of this change very carefully. On a broader level, it needed changes in skills and attitude from both our staff and customers and as such was not without its problems."*

Again, this response is short, and there is scope for exploring it in much more detail. However, the outlines of a senior management-level response are there. It demonstrates proactive introduction of change, based on an awareness of what is going on outside the business, to drive improvement. The change had both internal and external impact and required the need to address attitudes and skills – a complicated change initiative by anyone's standards.

The response also suggests more involvement and drive from the interviewee than the previous, poorer, answer.

Interviewer: Tell me about a time when you recognised that the current strategy was no longer appropriate.

✗ Poor answer:

"As an organisation in business for over 20 years, we had developed an excellent name in the marketplace and frequently our reputation preceded us. As a result, there was relatively little that we needed to do in the form of sales and marketing activity. However, the recession of 2008/2009 put a stop to that. Our order book very quickly began to dry up and there were fewer prospects in our pipeline. Our reliance on having developed intimate relationships with our clients and keeping close to them was, on its own, not going to see us through this difficult period. We needed to become more proactive and we needed to grow a stronger market awareness beyond those clients that we regularly worked with. Fundamentally, we needed a change in strategy. So I suggested to my fellow directors that we needed to re-examine the strategy, as I felt it was no longer effective in the prevailing economic climate."

The example is not very strong, it is a little reactive – strategy was changed in response to a drying-up pipeline. At this level, a good candidate needs to be off the mark more quickly and recognise, for example, at the onset of the economic downturn, that current strategy would not be sufficient. Whilst responding differently to the question and indicating that the actions were spontaneous might improve the answer, it is likely that an interviewer would discover this through their probing. A better response would be one that demonstrated proactively addressing a strategic issue.

The interviewer will also be looking for more detail as to exactly how the respondent became aware of the situation, for example, what key indicators they were looking at, and how this compared not just to the previous year, but to other times of economic downturn.

✓ Better answer:

"*As a business, we are over 20 years old, and in that time have developed a really good reputation in the market place, to the extent that we did not have to actively market ourselves. In the recession of 2000, things did slow down a bit but we were still able to meet our targets. When the recession hit in 2008 though, I recognised that we needed to change the way we go to market. It was clear from what was happening in the markets that this recession was going to be much deeper and longer. All the reports were pointing to the fact that a wider sector of industry was going to be affected and it was unlikely that we would escape unharmed. It was obvious that we could not afford to rely on our reputation alone. A rethink of our strategy was therefore needed, so this is what I suggested to the board. I supported this recommendation with some "what if" analyses that showed potential recommendations of not doing anything. These indicated that we would be able to maintain our position for approximately 2 months, but that after that, sales volume would shrink and costs would increase owing to the weakness of sterling to such an extent that we would need to try to look to drastic ways of managing our costs – potentially even redundancies.*"

Why is this response stronger? Action was proactive as well as showing learning from the experience of the previous recession. The respondent also provided evidence of some analysis that was carried out to support the recommendation made.

In terms of CAR, we have evidence for C and A. It is too soon to have any results, but the answer could have been strengthened by providing information on the indicators that would be looked at to evaluate the outcome in the strategy change.

Interviewer: Tell me about a time when you recognised that change was needed.

"*One of our production facilities was not meeting its expected targets. When I explored the underlying reasons for this, it became apparent that the production unit manager hadn't adopted the new ways of working that we had introduced the previous year as part of a general drive to increase production. At the time, she had been hesitant but had agreed to buy into the change and try to make it work. In fairness to her, she was managing a difficult site that had a history of disagreement with senior management. In my discussion with her, though, it had become apparent that she hadn't succeeded in implementing the changes we had discussed and so the facility was falling behind its production targets. This clearly needed to be addressed quickly because it was having an overall impact on the business plan. What we decided to do was to identify those employees that would be supportive of the change and only with them, on certain lines, introduce these new changes. We changed our implementation plan, with the overall aim still being that we would ultimately convert the whole facility. My thinking was that by showing it could work on a small scale in the facility, alongside the successes in other facilities, we might be able to get them on board with what we were proposing.*"

This example addresses an aspect of organisational change. It demonstrates the respondent's awareness of the change not having lived up to expectations and their willingness to alter the implementation approach so as to make it work.

- **Circumstances**: a change had been introduced which had not yet taken hold in a production facility. Consequently, the facility was underperforming.
- **Action**: identify a small cohort of supportive individuals and introduce the change to them, in the hope that this would then cascade through the unit.
- **Result**: is not provided, as it is too early.

However, do you notice something else about this response?

It's actually an example of a piece of change implementation that has not gone particularly well and, as such, the response shows some negative indicators against managing change. In other words, had the change been managed better from the outset, and in particular given the history of that particular production facility, the challenges encountered might have been avoidable. The interviewee would therefore have been better off choosing an alternative example.

Further practice questions

Look at the questions below and sketch out on paper a broad framework response. Try to make this align with the **CAR** model. The questions are suitable for all levels of role, but you may want to adjust them to provide a better fit for the role you are applying for.

- Give me an example of a time when you had to analyse a complex (business) problem and make some recommendations.
- Do you have an example of a time when you analysed some information in order to help you make a decision?
- Describe an occasion when you have initiated significant change in the workplace for the benefit of the organisation. *Or, for a less senior role:* Describe an occasion when you have made changes to a system or process in order to bring about an improvement.
- Tell me about a time where you needed to find a solution to a new problem.
- How do you think the current economic change is impacting our industry, and what changes have you put in place to address those threats? (This question is for senior roles).

ACTIVITY 20

MOCK INTERVIEW

Ask a friend to conduct a mock interview with you and provide you with feedback. Give them some questions – the ones from this section if you struggle to write your own – and practise. Key things to watch out for:
- Are your responses clear and easy to understand?
- Was your response full and comprehensive, without rambling or drifting?
- Did you structure your response according to **CAR**?
- Were your examples as recent and as varied as possible, to demonstrate breadth of experience?

IN A NUTSHELL

Thought leadership is important at all levels; its importance increases with seniority. A solid response gives the interviewer confidence that you can deal with the intellectual challenges of the role.

■ The 'thought' domain is about direction, strategy, creativity, problem solving, change, innovation, judgement and decision making.

■ Depending on the seniority of the role, you need to think about the focus of your responses: is it mainly at the individual, team or organisational level?

■ Creativity is not always about originality. Creativity can also be demonstrated by applying existing approaches to a new situation.

17 PEOPLE-BASED QUESTIONS

Example Answers

People competencies are often weighted especially highly by organisations' selection processes. References, CV and track record will say a lot about your 'task' and 'thought' competencies without revealing much about your style when it comes to working with and managing people. For this reason you can expect a tough interview to focus strongly on this aspect of your performance. In this chapter we will:

- remind you how to use the **CAR** model to frame your answers

- cover how to recognise people-based questions

- show you how to prepare examples of your people skills

- give you a range of examples of poor and better answers to help you prepare for the 'people' skills part of a competency-based interview.

What are employers looking for in terms of people skills?

Businesses know that your 'people' skills are often the key to success, so it is no surprise that they will be particularly interested in how well you work in teams, how well you manage and lead people, how confident and credible you are with customers and how well you develop people.

Interviewers want to know how well you work in teams, manage, lead and develop people, and how credible you are with customers.

At entry and middle levels of recruitment the interviewer will be most interested in your interpersonal skills; at higher levels they will want to see that you think strategically about people issues and that you can build strong teams around you. At all levels they will be interested in issues such as:

- ■ how well you handle conflict
- ■ how you consult, engage and bring people in
- ■ how good you are at influencing
- ■ what your management/leadership style is like
- ■ how self-aware you are

■ how flexible your style is – whether can you be democratic or more directive, as the situation needs.

As in the earlier sections, we will use the **CAR** model (Circumstances, Action, Results) as a way of encouraging you to build good answers, so you may want to refer back to Chapter 12 for a quick reminder of how to use this approach. As before, questions and answers will be pitched at different levels and we will go through them to identify the main 'dos' and 'don'ts' of framing strong answers to these tough questions.

Employers will be looking for a range of people skills and balance in your interpersonal style. Choose your examples accordingly.

Recognising people-based questions

Look out for words or phrases like these to help you recognise that the interviewer is looking for a people-based answer:

influence	persuade	inspire	motivate	team
challenge	disagreement	engagement	culture	succession
talent	cooperation	performance management	appraisal	communication
team building	attitudes	personality	personal impact	rapport
credibility	trust			

Questions containing words or phrases like these are likely to require an answer based on your perceptions of people and on your own awareness of your style with other people. People-based questions are trying to get at things such as:

■ do you recognise your own impact on other people?
■ are you typically cooperative – a team player – or are you more independent?
■ perhaps most importantly – will you fit in?

Preparing to respond to people-based questions

We are highly evolved social animals, skilled in making judgements about other people – based, sometimes, on pretty flimsy evidence – so the interviewer will also be interested in your self-awareness and self-presentation during the interview (see Chapter 14). Once again, the words you say and the way you say them will need to join up if you want to leave the interviewer with the best possible impression.

ARE YOU A PEOPLE PERSON?

As well as the preparation already covered in Chapter 13, try to recall examples of situations where you have had to:

- get people to buy in to an idea or process
- pass on a difficult message
- handle interpersonal conflict
- develop/coach a person or a group
- make 'people' decisions, such as who to put in a team
- 'sell' an idea or a product
- plan communication across a wide group of people.

Once again, use the **CAR** process to frame a short description of the example, making sure that you cover the circumstances, the action you took and the results.

EXAMPLE ANSWERS

Graduate/trainee management level

Interviewer: Can you give me an example of a time when you have had to deal with an interpersonal conflict or disagreement in a team?

✗ Poor answer:

"There was a time in the design team when one of the senior designers was causing a real problem. It was his attitude really; he was very critical of everyone else's work – even if it had nothing to do with him – but was very unwilling to take any criticism of his own stuff. The juniors were getting very de-motivated. In the end we had to get the head of marketing to have a word and he did improve a bit. I think he was insecure, basically, he still doesn't share his own ideas but at least he has stopped criticising everyone else."

This is not a good example of a people-based answer. There is no sign of what interpersonal skills were brought to bear to tackle the situation, nor is there any evidence relating to this person's approach to dealing with conflict. Indeed, what evidence there is, is negative! For example:

- the outcome is hardly positive
- the action was to get someone else to tackle the issue
- there is no evidence of getting to the root of the problem
- there is some evidence of avoiding the difficult conversation rather than tackling it.

By asking a 'people' question the interviewer is looking for evidence that you can deal with difficult conversations; they will not be reassured by this answer.

✓ Better answer:

"*There was a time in the design team when one of the senior designers was causing a real problem. His style was quite abrasive; he was very critical of the work of some of the junior designers, to the point that they had started avoiding him. It was bad for team morale and it meant that they weren't getting the benefit of his design expertise. While I wasn't his manager, I decided to have a quiet word with him – I wanted to see if he was aware of the impact he was having on people. It turned out that he was under a lot of pressure himself and that a lot of his criticism was the result of his not having time to think through the feedback properly. He really didn't seem to be aware of just how rude he sounded when he was under this kind of time pressure. I think making him aware of it was half the battle, and while he was a bit 'off' about my feedback initially, he agreed that team morale was really important. What he now does is to set aside review time with the juniors rather than them just firing designs at him as they are completed. This seems to be working and the team seems a lot happier.*"

Circumstances, action and result are much more clearly explained here.

- **Circumstances**: a problem individual who was causing friction.
- **Action**: taking the initiative in speaking to the individual.
- **Result**: the individual changed his behaviour.

As a result, the interviewer will be in a much better position to judge this person's people skills. In particular:

- the person recognised that there was a people problem
- they didn't shy away from a potentially difficult conversation
- the people issue was tackled in a professional way
- the issue was viewed from both sides – the manager's and the juniors'
- the good of the team was a clear motivation for action
- the result seems to have been good.

People-based questions are often trying to get an assessment of your emotional intelligence. In other words, how well you understand yourself, how well you understand other people and how well you can flex your style to have the impact you want in a particular situation. This answer ticks a lot of these boxes.

Interviewer: Can you tell me about a time when you had to 'sell' an idea or new concept to a group of people?

(This example is one that is frequently asked as a part of structured interviews).

✗ Poor answer:

"*There was a time when the team I was supervising in the call centre were very resistant to a new shift pattern that was being introduced. It didn't affect their overall hours but the start and finish times were slightly different – only by half an hour. Call centre staff are notorious for being picky about any change in routine and I knew there would be a lot of moaning. What I did was to get them all together in their shift teams and let them sound off before I explained that this change applied to everyone and that they would soon get used to it. It took a couple of weeks but they soon settled in to the new routine.*"

Not much sign of emotional intelligence or interpersonal sensitivity here! A particular problem with this answer (amongst many) is the tone used to describe people and their feelings. Phrases like – 'I let them sound off' and 'a lot of moaning' do not sound respectful or sensitive to their issues. 'Notorious for being picky' also sends out the wrong signal, suggesting that all staff are the same and that it is OK to stereotype them. In short, the answer again provides negative evidence about people skills. Remember – a people question demands a people-based answer. This answer is very task focused – it doesn't tell the interviewer much about how you sell ideas or influence people; in fact, it sends out a message that the person is somewhat insensitive.

✓ Better answer:

"*When I was supervising the call centre team, the need arose to change the shift pattern to bring it in line with other sections. I could see that this would need discussing with the team because it might have an impact on their domestic arrangements, pick-up times and so on. Once the memo explaining the change had come through from HR, I spoke to everyone in turn, picking them up during their breaks. I wanted to hear of any concerns from them personally – better than doing it in a group where some people might be nervous about speaking up. There were some worries, but I tried to reassure them on a case-by-case basis. I made it clear that they still had flexi-time*" *available as a way of smoothing out anything that was particularly difficult in terms of hours. I also tried to sell the positives; the new shift pattern would help people to avoid peak travel periods. Doing it this way seemed to work, because no one raised any grievances and the new pattern was in place without too much trouble."*

You can see **CAR** at work in this answer.

■ **Circumstances**: a problematic change of shift pattern in a call centre.
■ **Action**: deciding to speak to each person individually.
■ **Result**: no grievances and the new pattern was in place with little trouble.

Just as importantly, you can see the person responding to the 'human' side of the question. The answer shows recognition of concerns, a well thought-through approach to how to sell the idea (one to one rather than in a group), and emphasis on the positives as a way of gaining agreement. From this answer the interviewer can tell that this person is thinking through the 'people' implications of the change and has exercised sound judgement as to the best way of communicating the change.

Middle management level

As the level of the interview goes up, so will the interviewer's expectations about the scope of your 'people' competencies. At middle management level they will be interested in questions such as:

■ Can this person balance and resolve competing interests or motives?
■ How does this person communicate/motivate across teams?
■ Do they think more widely about people issues, encompassing things like training and development and talent management?
■ How well do they manage 'upwards', how do they engage with different groups of people – peers, managers and subordinates?

Interviewer: Can you tell me about a time when you have had to communicate a tough decision about an individual or team? How did you go about it?

✗ Poor answer:

"OK, well after the merger at my last job, it was clear that the marketing department was overstaffed and that we would have to make some redundancies. I have always believed that 'clean and fast' is the best way of communicating this kind of news so I took a lot of time to draft a letter to each individual explaining that jobs were at risk and describing the process we were going to go through in detail. I got a lot of help from HR because it's so important to get the details right. I made sure that everyone got the letter on their desks at the same time and I made it clear that HR would be available to deal with any questions that they had."

This is a task-based answer – it says what the person did but it does not pick up on the subtleties of human communication and behaviour that the interviewer is really interested in. Interpersonal style does not come through and the interviewer is going to have to ask a lot of follow-up questions to get at this detail. There is also a risk that, having noted the task-based approach to the issue, the interviewer will be looking for evidence that this is indeed the emphasis of this person's style and that the more subtle emotional intelligence skills are missing; in other words, the interviewer will now check for still more negative evidence. Let's see what happens with the probe questions.

Interviewer: So how did people respond?

✗ Poor answer:

"Well, clearly people were concerned; I could see a lot of worried faces around the office but at least everyone knew where they stood."

Interviewer: Did this affect performance?

✗ Poor answer:

"I don't think so; HR did a good job of explaining the timing and that the process would be fair and transparent."

Interviewer: So how many people did you lose, what was the reaction of those who stayed?

✗ Poor answer:

"We lost five in the end and the four who stayed have reallocated the workload so that the marketing plan is still pretty much on track."

At this point the interviewer is likely to give up on trying to get this person to describe the human elements of the situation. They will conclude that the person is task focused but is not showing any signs of recognising the motivational issues or the personal sensitivities of the individuals in the team. So what does the interviewer actually want to hear in this situation? Some of the key elements they need to hear in the answer include:

■ recognition that people's feelings and apprehensions matter in this situation

■ recognition that a 'people' response has been made to a 'people' problem; for example communicating, talking, understanding, engaging, supporting

■ that different options have been considered based on an understanding of people's likely reactions and recognising the need to keep the marketing function running smoothly

■ that there is some sign of interpersonal sensitivity, and awareness of how people will be feeling.

'People' answers do not have to be 'soft and fluffy' – the interviewer will want to hear a degree of objectivity being applied – but at the same time the answers do need to make reference to the issues listed above. Otherwise the risk is that the interviewer will come to the conclusion that this person does not 'do' people. As a result, scores on the people competencies are likely to be low.

✓ Better answer:

"OK, well after the merger at my last job it was clear that the marketing department was overstaffed and that we would have to make some redundancies. This is never easy, so I first spoke to HR to make sure that the process was crystal clear. We drafted a letter explaining all the details but I wanted to communicate the change personally, so I decided that I would call a meeting with the marketing team to tell them myself and then hand out the

letters to cover all the detail. I wanted to let them know that we recognised how difficult this would be and that we hadn't made the decision lightly."

Interviewer: So how did people respond?

"*I think telling them face to face paid off. Clearly they were concerned, but they were able to ask questions there and then – I didn't want bad information to start all kinds of rumours going – I had Brian from HR with me, so between us we were able to answer all their questions about the process and about timing. Interestingly, a lot of the concerns were about how ongoing projects could be finished. I thought that said a lot about the dedication of the team.*"

This sequence pushes a lot of important buttons in terms of 'people' answers and it is worth reviewing them.

- It recognises the importance of the 'personal touch'; communication in a difficult situation is handled face to face rather than impersonally. This is not to say that face to face is always better, but in the context of this question it shows that the person is not shying away from a challenging interpersonal situation.
- There is recognition of the 'human nature' aspects of the situation; people's fears and concerns are acknowledged and a rationale for dealing with them is explained – all provide signs of the emotional intelligence that the interviewer is looking for.
- Names are used; 'Brian' is referred to by name and this sends out an important signal that you are dealing with people and not with 'production units'. Using names makes your answer sound much more personal and suggests that you are interested in relationships.
- Good qualities of the team are referred to – 'dedication'; seeing the good in people is an important way of indicating that you are thoughtful about things like team dynamics, personal motivations – in other words, that you care about people issues.

When answering people questions you need to balance objectivity with evidence that you are thoughtful about the 'softer' issues. The best way of doing this is to make sure that your answers contain words relating to motivation, feelings, attitudes, concerns and all the stuff that makes people what they are.

If you are the kind of person who is naturally objective and tough minded, then review your examples with a view to taking the perspective of other people in the situation.

If you are the kind of person who naturally sees the human side of things, then make sure you do not sound too 'soft and fluffy'; the best way of doing this is to relate the people issues back to business performance.

Interviewer: Can you tell me how you go about managing your team in your current role? Give me an example of how you run your meetings.

✗ Poor answer:

"I'm really lucky in the current finance team; they are really motivated and enthusiastic so I don't have to do very much in terms of inspiring them. They are all very different characters but they get on really well. We have weekly meetings and I keep the agenda very open; anyone can raise anything they like – I find this encourages new ideas and problem solving – and I make sure that everyone has a chance to speak. I suppose you could summarise my management style by saying that I try to be very supportive; I can't remember the last time I had to throw my weight around – they know what needs doing, they gel, and the work gets done."

Superficially this looks like a very people-based answer, but there are some real risks with the 'I am a very nice person' approach. In most interviews, particularly at managerial level, the interviewer will be looking for evidence of *balance* in your managerial style. Earlier we mentioned the value of showing that you can flex your style to meet the needs of the situation, and this is not apparent in the answer above. The interviewer is going to have to ask a lot more questions to see if this person has anything other than a laissez-faire management style.

Interviewer: So how do you check that people know what they need to do?

✗ Poor answer:

"It's mostly a matter of having an open door so that people can check things with me; anything they are unsure about, I make sure I am available."

Interviewer: So what about when you have to be more directive, can you give me an example of how you handle this?

✗ Poor answer:

"*I suppose there are situations when the requirement is non-negotiable and obviously then I let people know what they have to do by when. I can remember times when it looked as if we were going to miss a deadline or where there was an urgent request for information, and in this kind of situation I can give clear instructions if I have to.*"

Eventually we get to some reference to a more directive style of management, but it still falls far short of being a concrete example and the whole sequence will leave the interviewer doubtful about this person's ability to behave in a more directive way when the situation requires it.

✓ Better answer:

"*I'm really lucky in my current finance team, they're motivated and there are no real weak links. They're all very different characters but they can all be relied on to deliver high quality work. I split my weekly meetings into two sections. First there is a progress and issues review where we all keep track of the current workload and look ahead to see what workload is coming. Second, I try to give at least half an hour to an 'open agenda' session where people can raise ideas or concerns. My broad approach to management is to make sure that the team are clear about their objectives and then to support them – keeping them on track when necessary – but generally I prefer a 'light touch' when possible. Clearly, if the pressure is on or if there is a problem I will intervene – pretty quickly, usually – because it doesn't help the team or me if we deliver late. The feedback we get is that we are the most efficient finance team in the business, so the approach seems to work.*"

This answer covers the ground in terms of **CAR**.

- **Circumstances**: a good team, different characters, but a need to manage them.
- **Action**: two activities are described – 'first', 'second'.
- **Result**: 'the feedback we get is that we are the most efficient finance team …'

There are still improvements that could be made, however (think back to our comments on earlier examples), to make this answer richer still.

- Describing what has been done to develop the team will give the interviewer insight into management style.
- An illustration of management style would be good, dropping in a 'for instance' to make the general comments more concrete.
- The interviewer asks for an example of a management meeting – picking a good example of such a meeting and describing it would answer the question.
- Naming and describing – briefly – some of the individuals in the team to make the answer more personal.
- Giving an example of 'intervening' would enable the interviewer to hear what the interviewee did and why.

As we noted in earlier sections, you will need to judge the level and scope of your answers, based on the interview situation you find yourself in. In general, however, mid-level managerial interviewers will expect to see that your people skills extend beyond your personal social skills, to include topics such as:

- cross-team communication
- succession planning
- developing talent
- building and harnessing the right skills
- influencing, persuading and selling.

Our final example looks at a question that explores people skills in the context of a customer-facing, selling situation.

Interviewer: Can you tell me about a time when you had to deal with a difficult conversation or a complaint from a customer?

✗ Poor answer:

"*Well obviously we work hard to avoid this kind of situation arising but occasionally we do have to sort out a customer problem. There was an issue on the Leeds project when it became clear that we were not going to meet the delivery deadline for the new phone system – not our fault, our suppliers had made a mistake. When the customer called I insisted on taking it because I knew it would be a tricky conversation. Sure enough, she was livid. I had to let her sound off for about 5 minutes – she was being completely unreasonable – before I could get a word in."*

Interviewer: So what did you do?

✗ Poor answer:

"I explained the situation – that our suppliers had let us down – and that we were chasing the order as hard as we could but that it would be another 5 days before we could deliver."

Interviewer: So why were they so upset?

✗ Poor answer:

"I'm not sure really, as far as I knew the delay didn't have much impact on their schedule, they weren't due to move into the building for another 3 weeks anyway."

Interviewer: So what was the outcome?

✗ Poor answer:

"She calmed down eventually; I promised that I was giving the matter my personal attention and that I'd see if I could offer some kind of discount to make up for the delay."

As well as some clear mistakes – which you should be practised at spotting by now ('I had to let her sound off') – the answer misses a lot of opportunities to show the people skills that the interviewer is looking for. For example:

- Where is the evidence of recognition of the customer's position?
- Where is the evidence of exploring, questioning or engaging with the customer to understand their position?
- Where is the evidence of using or building a relationship with the customer?

There are lots of missed opportunities here; the interviewer will only go so far in probing for the words they want to hear; words like 'understand', 'sympathise', or even 'sorry'. These are the words that would indicate that the 'human' aspects of the situation were understood. As it is, they are missing, and it is not the interviewer's job to give you the benefit of the doubt. Back to our mantra – a 'people' question needs a people-based answer, not a procedural or tasked-based response.

✓ Better answer:

"*Well obviously we work hard to avoid this kind of situation arising but occasionally we do have to sort out a customer problem. There was an issue on the Leeds project when it became clear that we were not going to meet the delivery deadline for the new phone system – not our fault, our suppliers had made a mistake. I took the decision to call the customer myself to apologise and explain – much better than waiting for them to call, and anyway it was the courteous thing to do. At first I was surprised at how upset she was, but when I explored the problem with her a bit it turned out that she had been hoping to bring the occupation deadline forward – it was going to embarrass her with her boss. I asked her if there was anything we could do to help – for example there was a system with a different spec that we could have made available sooner. We talked about putting this offer on the table with her boss so as to help manage her expectations. In the end we agreed to wait for the original equipment. The important thing was to keep the relationship on a good footing, rather than leaving the customer with a sense of having been let down by us.*"

Why is this a better answer? Apart from its being much fuller and richer, look at the words and the language being used: explain, apologise, courteous, upset, hoping, embarrass, help, expectations, relationship. 'People' words for a 'people' answer!

Senior management level

At this level of interview the scope will be wider still and the interviewer will want evidence that you can think about people issues across the organisation. Issues such as:

- communication between divisions
- strategies for establishing 'people' processes across a business

- high-level influencing
- establishing and retaining relationships with affected parties.

In our experience, interviewers at this level are particularly concerned about the kinds of relationships you will build with peers and other related parties, so your answers need to recognise the 'process' part of people leadership, while still retaining the sense of authenticity that comes from using personal examples.

Interviewer: Earlier you mentioned the merger with ABC Ltd. How did you go about building relationships across the new divisions?

✗ Poor answer:

"*My feeling is that the personal touch is essential here. We had a launch party for the new firm and as head of the legal function I made sure that I touched base with all my peers from across the business. I knew I probably wouldn't get a chance to meet them again for months, so I wanted to be sure that we had at least said 'hello'. I also made sure that I got 5 minutes with the MD, so that it would be easier to catch up again later – it's much easier to take a call from someone whose voice you recognise – and I got his agreement that the legal department would be at the top of the list when it came to the round of departmental meetings he was setting up. In the current situation he could see this made sense because of all the contract negotiations coming up. My aim was to get my credibility built early on so that he would feel he was in safe hands.*"

While there are some good things in this answer, for example the 'personal touch' in building credibility, it's just not systematic enough to 'sell' high-level people skills to the interviewer. As well as getting a fix on your ability to network at an 'event', the interviewer would have been hoping for a lot more evidence of a well thought-through approach to relationship building.

✓ Better answer:

"*Personal contact is clearly important – and I made full use of the launch party to introduce myself to some of the key individuals that I'd be working most closely with – but it was also important that I created some forums where the legal heads could get together – partly to get to know each other better but also to make sure that topics like continuing professional development and international standards were on the agenda. I wanted to quickly create a situation where there were no territorial barriers to our communicating flexibly and quickly when the situation needed it. We've had three legal heads meetings now and they're proving to be a valuable way of making sure that we're sending consistent messages into the business. I've always had a strong relationship with Alison, the MD, and I used this to let her know what I was doing so that she could use the forum to communicate with us as well.*"

This is a much more 'corporate' answer. The human touch is still here, but there is also a focus on organisation-wide people issues, such as communication and development.

We will take one more example, one where the question is more about interpersonal style.

Interviewer: The team you would be leading has been together for a long time now; can you give me an example of a situation where you have had to integrate yourself in this way?

✗ Poor answer:

"*My feeling is that you have to clear the air straight away so that people know exactly where you're coming from. When I was parachuted in as head of marketing at ABC Ltd I knew that it was going to be tough getting them to accept me. My remit was – quite frankly – to knock some heads together because business performance had been so poor. At my first meeting I decided that a 'hard but fair' approach was going to work best, so I made it clear that performance was going to be the only yardstick that I was interested in. I'm very open and honest in my style – I think it's the only way you can build trust at senior level – and I think they did find me quite blunt for the first 3 months, but it got results.*"

This is certainly an honest answer but it falls into a category of 'all or nothing' responses. What it does not show is any degree of subtlety or flexibility. The 'I am what I am' approach is courageous but risky, because its success depends on this person's style happening to fit the circumstances. What if the team to be led are already high performing? What if they are delivering great results under a lot of pressure and need support rather than 'hard but fair'?

✓ Better answer:

"*At ABC Ltd it was clear that I was entering a difficult situation; I had taken some soundings from other department heads and they told me that the team was having a tough time at the moment and that they were underperforming. My approach was to have one-to-one meetings with all the marketing directors to find out what the true situation was and get a sense for how people were feeling. I didn't want to go barging in without having some sense for the team's capability, and the meetings helped a lot. I didn't have a lot of time, given the pressure we were under but that original investment in getting to know them paid off, they were working in silos and I had to get them talking to each other. I eventually moved a couple of the directors to other roles, but because I had got to know the team, people could see the rationale for my decisions and it has helped to create a much more motivated group. I've taken the same approach with the new people I've brought in – encouraging them to have one-to-ones as well, and the result has been a much faster turnaround than if I hadn't invested that time.*"

The interviewer will get the following message from this answer:

- it takes account of both 'soft' and 'hard' factors
- the focus is on getting to know people before jumping to conclusions
- objective actions are taken, but on the basis of understanding people's capabilities
- expectations are set for how people should behave with each other
- time is invested in people.

At senior level in particular, where time is spent provides a very good measure of an individual's orientation in terms of task, thought and people, so signalling that you make time for people sends an important message.

IN A NUTSHELL

People competencies are highly prized and will be assessed by *what you say and how you say it* (see Chapter 14). Bear the following in mind as you prepare to respond to people-based questions:

- Make sure that you can recognise when the interviewer is focusing on the people domain.
- Showing high-level people competencies is about showing that you have the emotional intelligence to work well with and through people, getting the best from them.
- Think of examples of 'difficult' interpersonal situations or relationships you have encountered; this is a common area of questioning.
- Show that you can think companywide and long term, in terms of the people domain.

18 NON-COMPETENCY-BASED QUESTIONS – BUT STILL TOUGH!

Example Answers

You can't always rely on the interviewer to follow the professional processes we have described in Part II. Sometimes a 'favourite' question will slip in, or sometimes, especially in panel interviews, one of the interviewers will decide to go 'off piste' and test you with a question that is hard to relate to a specific competency. In this chapter we will:

■ explore the range of questions that might come up

■ show examples of specific questions

■ give you some 'dos' and 'don'ts' in terms of how to handle them.

Dealing with non-competency-based questions

Your best weapon in dealing with non-competency-based questions is still to identify what the question is trying to get at: is it task, thought or people, or a combination of the three?

■ You may be asked questions designed to test your specific knowledge or understanding of a topic or issue, or aimed at assessing how well you know a particular field or market.

■ You may be asked hypothetical questions – such as what you might do in a particular situation, or very vague, general questions such as 'Tell me about your leadership style'.

■ You may be asked self-disclosure or self-evaluation questions such as 'What is the biggest mistake you have made in the last 3 years, what did you learn from it?', or 'What is your proudest achievement over the last 3 years?'

All the principles we have covered so far still apply to this kind of questioning, specifically:

■ If they don't ask you for an example, try to illustrate your answer with real-life instances anyway.

■ Use **CAR** to frame your answers.

■ If you are asked a hypothetical question, respond by relating it to a real-life experience.

■ Get at the gist of the question by using 'task, thought, people' to analyse the questioner's intent.

■ Don't be afraid to clarify and reframe the question if appropriate, but check that you have understood their meaning. Answer their question, not the one you would like to answer.

Get at the gist of the question by using 'task, thought, people' to analyse the questioner's intent.

The examples that follow can't cover all the possible questions you might be asked, but they aim to illustrate some of the more common non-competency questions and give you some ideas about how to answer them well. The best advice we can give – experience tells us that it fits in with the interviewer's mindset – is to consider the 'task, thought, people' elements of the question and cover them all in your answer.

CV and chronology-based questions

While less common than used to be the case, interviewers will sometimes want to take you through your CV in some detail. This approach is often used by head hunters as part of their screening; they don't want to put you in front of their client if there are gaps or inconsistencies in your experience.

The interviewer will be trying to understand two things as part of this process; the first, as indicated above, is a straightforward accuracy check; the second is to understand the roles you have had in more detail.

CV checking

Before going for your interview, it obviously makes sense for you to have recently read your own CV! You do not want to sound unsure or uncertain about what you did and when. If there are any gaps or periods of unemployment in your work history, you should not sound embarrassed or defensive about them. Your best course is to show how you made positive use of the time.

Ideally, the interviewer will want to see a steady progression in your roles and responsibilities, but for most people careers are seldom so neat and linear. We all make bad choices occasionally and don't stay in a job for as long as we expected. Again, avoid sounding defensive and instead emphasise the positives that you took from any role, rather than sounding negative and full of regret.

If your CV contains a number of relatively short appointments you may be worried that the interviewer will see you as a 'job hopper' and take it as a sign of a lack of commitment or tenacity. The answer, again, is to be as honest as you can and to explain the situation and, most importantly, what you learned. The interviewer will not be impressed if you seem to have made the same mistake over and over again! Show that you have been thoughtful about what went wrong, that you have learned from it and that your approach is now different in some relevant way. For example:

"Yes, the two roles in marketing didn't work out as I had hoped. I think my mistake was to go for relatively small organisations where my experience of setting up marketing systems didn't fit their very reactive way of working. I think I managed to add value in both roles in the relatively short time I was there – I still have good relationships with those teams – but I did learn that a larger marketing function suits my skills better."

Chronology

Broader chronology questions aim to understand the choices you have made in your life, your achievements, your interests and enthusiasms, and how/why your experience has grown in the way it has. Interviewers will vary in terms of how far back they want you to go, but it is not uncommon for them to begin with your education, in order to understand how your interests and expertise got started. In all these questions it is better to sound purposeful rather than the victim of random circumstances. In fact, most of us have careers that have 'accidental' elements to them – we happened to meet someone or 'a friend suggested it' – the trick is to sound as if we exerted positive choices at key points.

More commonly, the interviewer will go through your jobs in chronological order, asking some or all of these questions about each role:

- Why did you decide to take this job?
- What were your main responsibilities/accountabilities?
- Who were your key customers/interested parties?
- What were your most significant achievements?
- What budget were you responsible for?
- How many people were in your team?
- Why did you decide to leave?

Now this can start to sound like a cross-examination, but your responses should be based on all the principles we have discussed so far:

- answer clearly and succinctly; avoid sounding vague about facts
- emphasise positives, not negatives; avoid 'I only had three people in the team' or 'the budget was much smaller than I would have liked'

■ prepare; you should at the very least think through what you regard as key achievements in the main roles you have had; phrase your answer using **CAR**.

These questions are designed to assess your experience and your past responsibilities in terms of how closely they fit the job you are applying for and it is worth considering, during your preparation, how good this fit is. Large mismatches will worry the interviewer – they won't necessarily rule you out, but they will reduce the interviewer's confidence in the decision they are making about you. For example, if the role you are applying for has responsibility for managing a budget in the millions and your previous experience has been for budgets in the thousands, you may want to think of ways in which you can plausibly close the gap. For example:

"*But I also sat on the finance committee and there we had oversight of turnover for the whole group, over £18 million when I left.*"

KNOWLEDGE-BASED QUESTIONS

We can't give you right and wrong answers to these questions, they will depend on your particular expertise but there are some general guidelines that should help you frame good answers.

Tell me what you think of the current state of the low-rental social housing market.

Clearly this is designed to assess how well you know this topic and, let's face it, either you do or you don't! Therefore there is little point giving you a model answer. But there are some simple tips you can follow as you build your answers to this kind of question.

- Your best response is to answer the question based on your knowledge of the subject area. These questions are often asked by a subject-matter expert who may not expect you to know as much as they do, but do avoid getting into a knowledge battle where you are disputing facts with the interviewer. These battles are hard to win in an interview situation. While it is OK to politely disagree with a point that has been put to you, avoid confrontation at all costs!
- In answering these more technical questions, start with general points and then work down to more specific details, but don't spend more than a couple of minutes on any one answer. If they want more detail they can drill down for it.
- Be honest about the boundaries of your knowledge, rather than trying to waffle. But rather than just give up and say 'I don't know', share what relevant knowledge you do have. So, for the example question above you might say: *'I haven't had a lot of experience of the social housing sector but my experience as an estate agent tells me that supply is likely to be a significant issue …'* Where you can, tell them what you do know rather than what you don't know, as long as this doesn't take you off the point.
- Be willing to take a few moments to pull your thoughts together, rather than blurt out an answer. Signal to the questioner that this is what you are doing by using phrases like *'That's an important question, let me think about it for a second'*, or *'There are a lot of factors to consider here, let me just collect my thoughts …'*

- If you have strong views on the subject raised, make sure that they are well thought through and that you can fully defend them. Avoid sounding too vehement or dogmatic. As a rule of thumb, the more strongly you feel about the topic, the more measured you need to be in the way you talk about it, in order to avoid sounding opinionated.
- Don't pretend that you know something that you don't. Being caught out on a technicality will leave a very bad impression.
- Aim to leave the impression that you are thoughtful and well informed about the subject area, rather than over-confident or even smug!

Hypothetical questions

There are a lot of reasons why these are not good questions for an interviewer to use, but they do still crop up. The main reasons why they are not very effective are that:

- they can assess only your intentions, not your actual behaviour
- they play into the hands of people who are verbally fluent but who may not actually possess the competencies under consideration.

So, what is the best way to handle this kind of question?

Tell me what you would do if you saw a customer abusing one of your staff.

The first step is to assess whether this is primarily a task-, thought- or people-based question; in this instance it is almost certainly a people-based question (though the intent of hypothetical questions can be hard to identify). A big temptation when faced with this kind of question is to say 'Well, it depends …', or to ask a lot of clarifying questions, such as:

- How angry are they?
- Are there other people around?
- What form is the abuse taking, is it verbal or physical?

These are all valid questions (and another good reason why hypothetical questions don't work very well – they are not clear enough), but they run the risk of your frustrating the interviewer. It is better to give your answer based on some sensible assumptions about the situation.

So you might answer as follows:

"*Well, assuming the abuse was verbal, I would intervene, probably saying something like 'is there a problem?' or 'can I help?' My aim would be to take any heat out of the situation once I knew what the problem was.*"

The very best way of tackling this kind of question is to then relate your answer to a real-life example, giving the interviewer concrete evidence – even though they were not professional enough to ask for it!

For example:

"*In fact something very similar to this happened to me when I was working at ABC Ltd; one of my colleagues was being shouted at by a customer so I went over and asked if I could help; the customer turned to me to explain, which gave my colleague a few moments to collect her thoughts. I didn't want the customer to think we were ganging up on him, so once things had calmed down I quietly withdrew. I spoke to my colleague afterwards and she said that the pause in the argument had made all the difference.*"

This answer, relating the question to real experience, gives a much more convincing illustration of your behaviour in this kind of situation. It also lets you apply the tried and tested **CAR** approach to building your answer. It is hard to do this if you are limited to the hypothetical scenario provided by the questioner.

There is a particular subset of hypothetical questions that focuses on the role you are applying for. It usually sounds something like this:

So tell me what you would aim to do in your first 3 months in this job.

It is well worth thinking through answers to this kind of question, depending on the role you are applying for. Make sure that you factor task, thought and people into the proposal you describe. You may have well researched views about what would be required and how you would make a difference, but the chances are that you will not know as much about the situation as the interviewer does. For this reason the following tips are likely to help in framing answers to the question in the above example:

- Emphasise learning, surveying the territory, getting an in-depth understanding, researching.
- Emphasise getting to know key involved parties, understanding roles and sensitivities.
- Emphasise using the above to quickly form a plan; if you have enough information, suggest tentative milestones or objectives for your first 3 months, 6 months and year.
- Sound purposeful but not arrogant in terms of your understanding of the situation.

Tips for hypothetical questions

- Do answer the question, but get the interviewer back to a concrete example as quickly as you can.
- Don't make your answer too elaborate; there is a risk of joining in with the fantasy and embellishing the scenario, giving answers to a whole range of possible outcomes. Keep your answer simple and then try to steer things back onto firmer ground.
- If the question is particularly vague, be willing to ask for some clarification, but don't sound as if you are trying to put the interviewer on the spot – this will not serve you well.
- For this kind of question it is particularly important to give yourself time to think; don't be afraid to buy yourself a few seconds by creating a pause, for example, *'That's an interesting situation, let me think for a second ...'*
- Bring your answer to a clear end, rather than letting it drift off; say something like *'Does that give you enough information?'* as a way of signalling that you have finished the story.

Vague or general questions

These can take many forms, but they are usually characterised by their sheer 'size' and the scope they give you for sounding vague. For example:

- 'Tell me about your approach to financial planning.'
- 'What do you think about change management?'
- 'What is your view about our proposed merger plans?'
- 'Describe your leadership style for me.'
- 'What do you think you would bring to the role you are applying for?'

Once again, we can't give you answers for all these questions, but there are some principles you can apply to add some clarity to your answers. We will use the last example – a too commonly asked question – to illustrate.

What do you think you would bring to the role you are applying for?

The temptation here is to launch into a long list of your personal attributes, for example:

"*Well, I'm proactive, I think I'm pretty good with people, my experience seems very relevant to your situation, I'm good at planning ... etc*"

This scattergun approach is unlikely to differentiate you from other applicants; a better approach is to stick to a few key themes based on your understanding of the competencies they are looking for. At the same time, try to make sure that you cover task, thought and people in your answer. Just because they have asked a very unstructured question does not mean that you cannot give a more focused answer. For example:

"*Well, my understanding of the role is that setting up the new department is the key objective and that you are very sensibly looking for competencies related to making this happen quickly. I believe my planning skills will be important – I've had a lot of experience in project management – I believe my broad awareness of the market will help me to shape the department and make it customer facing and I know the people management skills that I learned at ABC Ltd – during the merger – will be essential to developing the team and keeping their morale up in what is going to be a challenging situation.*"

Task, thought, people and a structure that relates your attributes to the job at hand.

This answer also makes use of the 'rule of three'. This is a rhetorical trick often used by politicians to give emphasis and weight to the point they are making, namely listing three ideas, or three actions or three attributes. In an interview, listing three is a good guide; listing more attributes than this risks losing impact. The rule of three also helps you to maintain your own focus and appear more focused to the interviewer as you give your answer.

Try to make sure that you use language that is as concrete as you can; 'I believe' or better still 'I know' has more impact than 'I think'.

Tips for vague or general questions

- Provide your own structure for your answer; use 'task, thought, people' both to interpret the question and to shape your answer.
- Use the 'rule of three' to add focus.
- Be willing to clarify if the question is particularly vague. For example: *'That's a big question, is there any particular element you would like me to focus on?'*

Self-evaluation, self-disclosure and motivation questions

Sometimes you will be asked to self-assess or to self-disclose as a means for the interviewer to discover how objective or how thoughtful you are about your own performance. They are often trying to assess your honesty with such questions, so an answer that is too glib or immodest risks leaving the wrong impression. Examples of these questions are given below, with poor and better answers.

Self-evaluation questions

- What do you see as your main strengths and weaknesses as far as leadership is concerned?
- Given what you know about this job, where do you see you have most to learn?
- Tell me what you are like at your worst.

✗ Poor answer:

"*Well I don't really think I have any 'worst days', my performance is pretty consistent!***"**

At best, this answer sounds arrogant; at worst, it risks sounding as if you have little self-insight.

✓ Better answer:

"Well, I try to make sure it doesn't happen often but when I am under a lot of pressure I do tend to be a bit less accessible to my team, it doesn't usually last for long and they know they have permission to tell me when I'm doing it!"

This answer admits to a human failing that the interviewer will recognise (and probably share), that is forgivable and that shows you have self-awareness.

Self-disclosure questions

■ What do you think is the biggest mistake you made in your last job, what did you learn from it?
■ What are you proudest of in what you have achieved in the last 2 years?
■ Where would you hope to be in 3 years' time?

✗ Poor answers:

"Well I'm not sure really, I want to see how I get on here first."

"I think by then I'll be ready for a role in a bigger organisation."

"Doing your job."

These are all awful responses, pretty much guaranteed to make you sound unfocused, uninterested or glib.

✓ Better answer:

"Hopefully making a strong contribution to the business in this role or an expanded role, depending on how quickly I progress. I'm ambitious, but clearly I'll need to establish myself first."

This answer manages to signal ambition and a desire to progress, without sounding arrogant; importantly, it also makes it clear that you want to grow in this business and you are not seeing it as just a stepping stone.

In terms of the impression you want to make, you should aim to create the impact of someone who:

- is thoughtful about their performance
- is confident about their strengths (not too modest!)
- is able to be objective about their own attributes
- has learned from their experiences
- is purposeful about what they want to achieve.

Motivation questions

It is not unusual for an interviewer to ask about your motivation. In other words:

So what is it that makes you want to come and work for us?

This non-competency-based question comes up sufficiently often that it is worth planning your response in advance. As before, the best answer is an authentic one, but there are some tips that are worth bearing in mind as you prepare and answer this kind of question.

- Avoid outrageous flattery: don't say *'Because you are recognised as the best IT employer in the region'* unless it is patently true.
- Avoid what they will see as trivial motives – they will want you to signal the same interest and enthusiasm that they (hopefully) have for the business. So avoid answers like:
  'Well the transport routes here are really convenient for me.'
  'You pay more than my current employer.'
  'I'm a bit bored where I am and I fancied a change.'
- Find some solid, positive reasons behind your application, for example:
  - a job with more scope or challenge
  - a chance to further develop your skills
  - reputation of the organisation
  - a chance to better use skills that you already have.

In general, it is better to find reasons for wanting to join that particular organisation rather than a particular profession or area of work. After all, the interviewer probably works for the organisation, and it helps if your enthusiasm validates the employment choices they have made!

Tips for self-evaluation, self-disclosure and motivation questions

■ Recognising some weaknesses or gaps in your portfolio of skills shows objectivity, but don't overdo it. If you can, show how you have recognised this deficit, what you have been doing about it and how it has improved.

■ Try to be objective in describing yourself 'on a good day' and 'on a bad day', but again, don't overdo it. Don't make any of your weaknesses sound fatal but do show how you manage them. For example *'I know I can be a bit of a perfectionist but I have learned to manage this so that I don't get hung up on detail any more'*.

■ Have at least one 'significant learning experience' up your sleeve. In other words, something that went wrong but that has left you a better person as a result. (In the Civil Service they used to say that no one got to be a Permanent Secretary without showing that they had survived – and learned from – at least one major crisis in their career.)

■ In the same way, have at least one 'significant success' available to be discussed. Analyse the situation in advance so that you can quickly describe the part you played in the success; if you can, break this down into task, thought and people and build your answer using **CAR**.

You will sometimes be asked about your ambitions or about the progression you expect to achieve. Your best guide here is to be honest; glib answers stand out like a sore thumb.

19 AND FINALLY...

We've covered a lot of ground in this part, our aim being to give you the best possible guidance to help you shine in a tough interview.

IN A NUTSHELL

Non-competency questions are hard to 'read' in terms of what they are trying to get at. Apply the same principles as you do to competency-based questions when framing your answers.

- Listen carefully and ask for clarification if you need to.
- Use **CAR** to frame your answer; describe the context, the action you took and the result in response to any question that gives you the chance to do so.
- Try to relate questions back to actual examples, where you can describe what you really did.
- Aim to be reasonably objective when asked to self-evaluate; present yourself as honest but confident in your abilities.
- Don't make things up or pretend to have knowledge or expertise when you don't; your credibility, once damaged, is extremely difficult to regain in an interview situation.

We've covered:

- the nature of competencies and how organisations use them
- how to prepare yourself
- some shorthand ways of assessing what a questioner is getting at – 'task, thought, people'
- some ways of building good answers – **CAR**
- above all, examples of poor and better answers to help you to practise framing your own impressive answers.

Throughout, we have tried to distil many years of experience (as interviewers and designers of interviews) into practical tips and guidance that will help you to do your best.

We have also made the point that, all too often, we tend to think of interviews as adversarial occasions, where one party is trying to catch the other out. Indeed, in giving you all this guidance we risk falling into the trap ourselves – by implying that there are specific ways to 'outwit' an interviewer. A final piece of advice, then, is to try to get out of this mindset!

In the great majority of interview situations that you will encounter you can – and should – assume professionalism and goodwill on both sides. To do otherwise is to risk turning the occasion into a game of hide and seek, rather than a meeting where two (or more) people are exploring mutual 'fit' in terms of a potential job or role. Our guidance in Part II has been focused on helping you to understand the kinds of process that interviewers use, so that you can help them to come to the best decision. Thankfully, this same guidance is also likely to enable you to present yourself in the best possible light.

Human social interaction is a highly evolved and sophisticated activity. Our ability to present ourselves well to others has evolved in parallel with our ability to detect characteristics such as trustworthiness, authenticity, credibility and so on. All of these highly developed interpersonal skills come into sharp focus in the interview situation, where the interviewer – whether explicitly or not – will be evaluating you in terms of some of these less definable characteristics, as well as in terms of specific competencies and job criteria.

Competency-based interviews – the focus of most of our examples – have been developed to help interviewers better focus on the attributes that matter, without being distracted by personal or irrelevant preferences – though, as mentioned above, it is difficult for anyone to fully 'switch off' the results of 60,000 years of social evolution! Our task has been to help you to recognise both the impression management and the more structured elements of tough interviews, and to prepare yourself accordingly.

Potentially, the greatest barrier is lack of understanding of the structured interview process and the characteristics the interviewer is looking for.

Our parting message, then, our best advice, is to be yourself – to be as authentic as you can and to use our tips to help remove any barriers that may prevent the interviewer from seeing you as the talented and valuable prospective employee that you are! Potentially, the greatest barrier is simple lack of understanding of the structured interview process and the characteristics that the interviewer is looking for. Armed with the information in this part you should be well prepared to avoid the barriers and ensure that the real you has the best chance of coming through at an interview. Coming through in a way that is professional and human helps the interviewer to see you at your best – and gives you the best chance of getting the job you want.

Good luck!

Ceri Roderick and Stephan Lucks
www.pearnkandola.com

PSYCHOMETRIC TESTS

INTRODUCTION

O n the basis that knowledge reduces fear and fear reduces performance, our aim is to give you expert guidance on how to approach
psychometric tests. Between us, we have over 30 years' experience in
designing, interpreting and using psychometric tests to help make employment
decisions for our client organisations. Over this time, we have used psychometric tests to recruit candidates for a diverse range of roles – from board directors
to shopfloor workers and everything in between. In doing so, we have worked
with many of the world's largest organisations as well as many smaller, regional
businesses.

In Part III we have distilled our knowledge and experience to help you to
maximise your ability to take, and pass, psychometric tests. The principles we
have outlined will be useful for any test taker, and the content of this part is
intended to be applicable to as wide a range of job applicants as possible.

As we take you through the world of psychometric tests we present examples
from a variety of test types, pitched at a wide range of difficulty levels. Whether
you are a first-time applicant looking to enter a graduate training scheme, or a
highly experienced executive exploring new avenues, we will guide you through
the process of test taking.

How to get the best from Part III

Do you know which types of psychometric test you will be asked to take the
next time you apply for a job? There are specific chapters dealing with each
of the major test types – numerical reasoning (Chapter 21), verbal reasoning

(Chapter 22), abstract reasoning (Chapter 23) and preference tests (Chapter 25). In addition, Chapter 24 covers the knowledge and skill tests that you might encounter. If you wish, dive straight in and read the chapter about the kind of test(s) that you will be taking. As well as very practical advice you will find example questions pitched at different levels of difficulty. Simply by getting more familiar with the test formats, your confidence will quickly increase and your performance will improve.

What about the other chapters? In our experience psychometric tests are often the least understood, and therefore the least comfortable part of the job application process. However, the fundamentals are surprisingly simple and we have outlined these in Chapter 20, 'What is a psychometric test?'. As with any discipline, once the basics have been demystified you will feel a great deal more confident in your own ability. Likewise, Chapter 26, 'Performing at your best', covers everything you will need to know about test preparation and test taking. This is crucial because, as our experience shows, although it takes a great deal of time to improve your true level of ability, there are many practical steps you can quickly take to ensure that you perform to the very best of your ability. As part of your becoming an informed and savvy test taker, we also tackle the common myths and misconceptions that surround psychometric tests and which are invariably unhelpful and often inaccurate. In Part III, we put these issues to rest by giving you a comprehensive low-down on how psychometric tests work and how they are used by employers to make hiring decisions.

Whichever psychometric tests you take in the future, the insight and advice in this part will ensure that you are as well prepared as you can be. We would wish you luck, but instead we offer the reminder that the harder you prepare, the luckier you will be.

20 WHAT IS A PSYCHOMETRIC TEST?

This chapter will help you to get to grips with the basics of psychometric testing, so that you become a more informed and confident test taker. As a candidate you will understand:

- The different types of psychometric test

- How psychometric tests work

- How employers use psychometric tests to make decisions

What is psychometric testing?

Psychometric tests provide a measure that employers can use to understand certain aspects of your mind. At first that might sound rather spooky. However, as you will see, there is no 'black magic' involved and, best of all, no invasive procedures are used!

In fact, far from the obscure old-world psychological tests involving ink blots, modern psychometric tests are transparent, objective measures, where each candidate has the same experience and opportunity to perform. Instead of vague interpretations, psychometric tests produce clear outcomes which give recruiters valuable information about you and your abilities.

How do psychometric tests 'measure' people?

If you want to know how tall someone is you would use a metric such as centimetres. Psychometric tests also use a metric to tell us 'how much' of a particular quality someone has. If we want to know who is taller out of the two, John or Chloe, we can measure both and compare the difference. In the same way, psychometric tests allow employers to make direct comparisons between candidates.

Psychometric tests allow employers to make direct comparisons between candidates

Psychometric tests work by comparing your responses with other people's answers – known as a comparison group. Each comparison group is usually made up of hundreds or thousands of people who are in a particular country and have reached a certain educational or occupational level. The information about comparison groups is provided to hiring organisations by the publisher.

How does this work in practice? See the case studies over the page.

Case study – Comparison groups
German graduates

Michael is based in Germany and is applying for his first job with a graduate recruiter. The company compares Michael's scores on a psychometric test he took with other German graduates. Michael's score is expressed as a 'percentile'. If Michael's score is on the 50th percentile, the employer knows that he is exactly average in comparison with his German peers, i.e. 50% score lower than him and 50% score higher. In fact, Michael is on the 65th percentile, so he has performed better than 64% of his fellow German graduates.

UK senior managers and professionals

Sophie is based in the UK and is applying for a role as the head of research and development at a pharmaceutical company. Sophie's test scores are compared with those of a group of senior managers and professionals within the UK. Notice that this comparison group is at a similar level of seniority to Sophie, although it is not industry specific. This is the most common approach in psychometric testing, although some employers, in highly specialised sectors such as investment banking, will use very specific comparison groups based on their own sector or organisation.

In essence, remember that psychometric tests work by comparing your answers with the answers given by other, similar people.

What do psychometric tests measure?

In principle, a psychometric test could be designed to measure almost any aspect of your mind. But that's a lot of ground to cover, so let's keep this simple. Employers use psychometric tests to measure two broad categories of qualities – abilities and preferences. The main differences between ability tests and preference tests are shown in the following table.

Ability tests	Preference tests
Include reasoning with numbers, words or diagrams	Include personality, values and integrity questionnaires
There are absolute right and wrong answers	There is no one 'correct' answer to a question
Usually have a time limit	Are generally untimed

Ability tests

Ability tests are tests of numerical reasoning (see Chapter 21), verbal reasoning (Chapter 22), abstract reasoning (Chapter 23) and specific types of skills and knowledge (Chapter 24). When used for recruitment, ability tests can serve two purposes. The first is to help employers understand how capable you are at demonstrating a specific skill that is relevant to the job you are applying for. See the case study below.

Case study – Testing specific abilities

Oliver is applying for a graduate position at a major accountancy firm. The firm uses a test of numerical reasoning ability. As the name implies, the questions in this test measure Oliver's ability to use and reason with numbers, for example, by performing calculations, interpreting sets of numbers, and checking for differences. Because work as a trainee accountant involves these types of task, Oliver's results tell the employer something useful about his ability to do well in the job. If Oliver's score is on the 15th percentile, then the employer would know that many more graduates will be better than him at working with numerical data.

Employers can also use ability tests to measure your overall level of intelligence. This is useful because more intelligent people tend to be quicker learners and are generally better at solving complex problems. See the case study below for more details.

Case study – Testing general intelligence

Samantha is applying for a position at a management consulting firm, which uses ability tests for checking out applicants' general intelligence. The firm's consultants need to get to grips with new clients very quickly and understand how they operate. They have to solve problems and present solutions to their clients, who are often working in sectors and markets that the consultants may not be familiar with. As part of her application, Samantha is asked to complete verbal and numerical reasoning tests. While both of these abilities are relevant to the role of a management consultant, the firm is more interested in her overall intelligence, which it estimates by combining the scores on both tests. Her combined score is on the 80th percentile, so the firm can be very confident about employing her intellectual capacity.

How can psychometric tests measure specific abilities like numerical reasoning and verbal reasoning as well as something called general intelligence? It all comes down to the relationship – the correlation – between different abilities. Think back to school. Were the people who were good at one subject also good at others? Generally, the answer is 'yes'. This is because of general intelligence. Different mental abilities correlate well, and this is shown by the overlapping circles in the diagram opposite. Each circle covers some unique ground – this is information only that test provides. The accountancy firm that Oliver applied to was only concerned with numerical ability. For this reason they only needed a numerical reasoning test. In contrast the management consulting firm was interested in measuring general intelligence and so they used two tests. This meant that they had a more accurate assessment of candidates' overall intelligence.

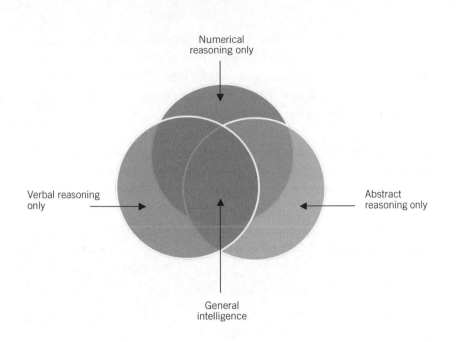

Whatever reason employers have for using psychometric ability tests, you can see from the case studies that your test scores will directly affect hiring decisions. Later on in this chapter, we will describe how employers use psychometric test scores to reach hiring decisions.

Preference tests

Now let's look at the psychometric tests that measure preferences. The most common type of preference test is a personality questionnaire. The idea behind these tests is that we are all reasonably consistent in our behaviour, and this is because our behaviours are shaped, in part, by our personality. Think about your own personality traits:

- Do you tend to arrive early or turn up late?
- Will you stay calm in a crisis or wear your heart on your sleeve?
- Are you naturally talkative or reserved in a crowd?

People who know you well will know what to expect from you – and could probably answer these questions on your behalf! Of course we all do different things on different occasions, but our behaviour is far from random. Our personality drives the preferences that shape our behaviour in one direction, and move us away from another direction. Employers are interested in measuring your personality because it provides them with information about your personal style – the sorts of tasks and activities that you naturally enjoy and those situations that you may wish to avoid.

So what do personality questionnaires actually measure? Usually the questions you answer will correspond to five broad domains. These are shown in the table below, along with example questions.

Personality domain	Example questions	Answer	
		Yes	No
Openness to experience	I prefer to have variety in my day		
	I enjoy hearing new ideas		
	I have a vivid imagination		
Conscientiousness	I like working towards a plan		
	I always keep my promises		
	I pay attention to the details		
Extraversion	I want to be the centre of attention		
	I like having lots to do		
	I enjoy being around other people		
Agreeableness	I believe that other people are trustworthy		
	I try to avoid getting into disagreements		
	I feel sorry for people less fortunate than me		
Emotional stability	I rarely worry about things		
	I find it easy to get over setbacks		
	It takes a lot to make me feel angry		

When you complete a personality questionnaire you might wonder – most people do – why the same sorts of questions come up so regularly. Contrary to popular belief, this is not a cunning method to catch people out if they give different answers. In fact, you might well respond differently to similar questions and that's how the questionnaire works.

In the case study overleaf, Charlotte completed a personality questionnaire as part of a promotions process by a book publisher in Paris.

Case study – Matching the right personality to the job

Charlotte has taken a personality test that her employer uses to assess employees' suitability for a particular job. The test consisted of 20 statements describing different aspects of socialising or working with others (e.g. 'I quickly get bored when I am alone') and Charlotte had to indicate whether she agreed or disagreed with them. Charlotte tended to agree with statements about wanting to spend time with others and she tended to disagree with statements about spending time alone.

So is she an introvert (someone who is comfortable in her own company) or an extravert (someone who prefers to be around others)? That depends how her responses match-up with the comparison group. Her employer used a comparison group of 2,000 managers and professionals based in France. Because Charlotte endorsed more extravert-related questions than 80% of the comparison group, we can say that she has a strong preference towards extraversion.

Charlotte's colleagues Tomas and Sebastian also completed the questionnaire. Tomas endorsed some statements relating to extraversion and some statements about introversion. This does not mean that Tomas is indecisive, or, indeed, schizophrenic. In fact, most people prefer a balance between the two extremes of highly sociable or hermit-like. Because Tomas' responses were similar to many people in the comparison group he was close to the average, which is 50%. This shows that Tomas has a balanced preference, suggesting that there are times when he enjoys being with other people and times when he is comfortable in his own company.

Finally, Sebastian endorsed fewer questions relating to extraversion than either Tomas or Charlotte. Based on the comparison group he is on the 20th percentile for extraversion. This shows that Sebastian has a strong preference towards introversion.

It's important to note that personality test results are interpreted differently from the ability tests, where higher scores are better. In the above case study example, we cannot say that Charlotte is somehow 'better' than Tomas or

Sebastian. What we can say is that she is more extraverted than most other managers and professionals working in France. Tomas has a similar level of extraversion to most managers and professionals, whilst Sebastian is more introverted than many of his peers.

Why employers use psychometric tests

There are two main reasons why employers use these tests early on in the selction process:

- **Cost-effectiveness** – ability-based psychometric tests can be completed online by candidates and automatically scored, without human intervention. Because the early stages of a recruitment process involve screening the largest number of candidates, employers prefer to use highly efficient selection methods, such as psychometric tests, which incur relatively small financial costs and no time costs. The figure below is an illustration of a typical recruitment process, showing where psychometric tests usually occur within a selection process.
- **Better assessment of candidates' suitability** – ability-based psychometric tests are, when used appropriately, among the best methods for predicting how well a candidate will perform on the job. It makes sense to use the most accurate selection tests early on because this is when the most candidates are screened out. By taking this approach employers reduce the number of unsuitable candidates who will attend the latter stages of a recruitment process, as well as avoiding mistakenly screening out suitable candidates.

A typical recruitment process

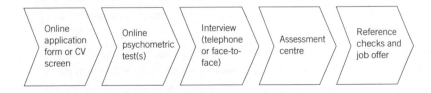

| Online application form or CV screen | Online psychometric test(s) | Interview (telephone or face-to-face) | Assessment centre | Reference checks and job offer |

How employers use psychometric tests

Preference tests

In the case study in the previous section, the book publisher in Paris can use Charlotte, Tomas and Sebastian's personality profiles in two ways. The first, and most common, is to use the results to help generate questions for the next stage – the interview. The key tasks of the job that they all have applied for are:

- Networking and forging new relationships with authors and retailers.
- Setting and planning the budgets for a major department within the publishing company.

From the preference test results, the hiring manager knows that Charlotte is likely to enjoy networking and relationship building. However, given the strength of her extraversion he decides to ask Charlotte about her approach in two areas:

- He asks her how she goes about building new relationships with others and, in particular, how she balances talking with listening. This is because some people with a strong preference for extraversion can also be very talkative – possibly to the point that they can dominate conversations. It will therefore be useful to understand how she does this in practice.

Preference tests are used mainly as a tool by recruiters to shape their interview questions

- He also asks her how she manages tasks that require individual work. The budget planning process will involve spending considerable time working at a desk, without the direct involvement of others. Will Charlotte be able to work like this without being distracted by opportunities for social contact?

In the same way, the hiring manager can identify useful interview questions for Tomas and Sebastian by comparing their personality profiles with the key activities on the job description. You will notice in this example that the employer does not make assumptions about the candidates' abilities based on their personality profiles. This is because the personality questionnaire is a test of preferences and not a test of ability!

Using the test results to create shortlists of candidates

The second way employers can use preference test scores is as a direct 'cut-off', which means the hiring manager can screen out those candidates whose profiles suggest that they are unlikely to fit in well with important aspects of a job. This usually happens where there are thousands of candidates applying for only a few vacancies, or when the vacancy is for a very specific and important task that favours a particular type of personality.

For example, maintenance engineers in the nuclear industry may, in a rare emergency, have to perform critical tasks under extreme pressure in order to avert a major incident. Don't drop that spanner! We saw in the table on page 322 that one dimension of personality is known as 'emotional stability'. People who are low on this scale tend to be anxious and prone to worry. As a result, an employer filling that vacancy may decide to sift out candidates who have a low score on emotional stability.

However, for most jobs, it's hard to justify a black and white approach to using preference tests – they are used mainly as a tool that helps recruiters shape their interviews.

Ability tests

When employers use ability tests they need to select the most appropriate test or tests and then decide on an appropriate 'cut-off' score. This is the minimum score that candidates must achieve in order to pass a test. In setting a cut-off score, recruiters want to ensure that suitable candidates are retained and as many unsuitable candidates as possible are selected out. The case study below shows how employers make these decisions.

Case study

Christian works for a large government department in the UK. He is responsible for the recruitment of experienced staff within the policy and advisory unit. Christian has five vacancies for senior policy officers which he needs to fill from the 300 candidates who have applied. Like many recruiters, Christian decides to use an ability-based psychometric test early on in the selection process.

Christian examines the job description for a senior policy officer. The main responsibilities of the role are:

■ Conducting research on important social, environmental and financial issues
■ Analysing complex research data to draw conclusions
■ Writing clear and comprehensive policy documents to inform decision makers

Christian decides to use a psychometric test of verbal reasoning. These tests measure people's ability to use and reason with written words, for example, by comprehending passages of text, making inferences, and comparing arguments.

Christian wishes to use a verbal reasoning test for two reasons.

■ Firstly, the specific skills that the test measures are relevant to writing policy documents.
■ Secondly, the test also provides a measure of intelligence, which will affect the ability to conduct research and to make sense of complex results.

Christian also needs to decide on a 'cut-off score'. Remember that psychometric tests work by comparing candidates' scores with those of a comparison group. In this case, Christian is using a comparison group of managers and professionals based in the UK.

The data for the comparison group will be provided by the publisher of the test he is using. Employers can choose to set their cut-off scores at any percentile, and most organisations set a cut-off somewhere between the 30th and the 60th percentiles. Because Christian believes that good verbal reasoning is an important skill for senior policy officers, he sets the cut-off score at the 50th percentile, which is relatively high. This means that only candidates who have at least average verbal reasoning skills, in comparison with managers and professionals in the UK, will pass the test.

If we assume that almost all of Christian's 300 candidates are currently managers or professionals in the UK, we can expect about 150 of them to pass the test by scoring on, or above, the 50th percentile cut-off. In theory, all 300 candidates could pass or fail the test, although this would indicate that the pool of applicants is of an unusually high, or low, calibre.

As we have seen, recruiters often use ability and preference based psychometric tests in very different ways. Ability tests provide an absolute 'pass' or 'fail' decision, whilst preference tests are generally used in an advisory capacity.

IN A NUTSHELL

Psychometric tests are a widely used tool in employment. This chapter gave an overview of what psychometric tests are and how they are used:

- There are two main types of psychometric tests – ability tests and preference tests.
- Psychometric tests work by comparing your responses with those of other, similar people.
- For ability tests, employers use cut-off scores (a minimum percentile score) to screen out low-scoring candidates.
- For preference tests, employers most commonly use the scores to generate interview questions.

21 NUMERICAL REASONING TESTS

How good do you think you are with numbers: confident, average, panicky?

In our experience, people tend to be more nervous about numerical ability tests than any other element of a selection process. So if you are anxious about this kind of question, be reassured that you are not alone! Whether this is because of dark memories of maths classes in school or because they just seem intrinsically more daunting, the reality is that our own anxiety is often the biggest barrier to doing well in this kind of test. This chapter will try to remove some of that anxiety. Specifically, we will cover:

- Types of numerical test and what they try to measure

- Familiarisation and preparation

- Practice test items

Types of numerical test and what they measure

Businesses use a range of numerical tests to assess how able you are in dealing with different kinds of numerical information. Whether the tests are delivered online or in pencil and paper format, they have a lot in common, and this chapter is designed to help you become familiar with the most frequently used kinds of numerical items.

It's worth remembering that businesses using these tests are not usually concerned about your mathematical ability as such – they are not interested in how well you can do algebra or solve equations (unless you are applying for a role where there is a clear mathematics specialism such as engineering). What they are concerned about is your ability to use and interpret the kinds of numbers that come up in the running of a business. In practice this means:

- Identifying relevant facts from tables provided
- Working out percentages
- Working out averages
- Using basic ratios, decimals and fractions

Only a few tests nowadays – typically much older tests – use items such as arithmetic or geometric progression (i.e. can you work out the next number in a sequence of numbers). The great majority present you with work/business-related number problems. (We give you a few examples of the older-style questions at the end of this chapter.)

The most regularly used tests will present you with one of two formats:

- Table-based formats – the test will present you with information – usually in a table – and then ask you a number of questions relating to that table (or sometimes tables).
- Specific-question-based formats – these tests will ask you specific questions of the kind you are probably familiar with from school, but presented in business terminology.

Here is an example of a question-based format test question.

In an average week the production line is down for 3.5 hours. Lost production, per hour, is 1,200 units. How many units are lost in an average week?

A – 3,800   B – 4,200   C – 4,000   D – 2,400   E – 2,4000

(The answer is B: 3.5 × 1,200 = 4,200)

The skills needed for these questions are broadly the same; the main difference being that in the table-based formats you have to first identify the relevant information before you can calculate your answer.

This chapter concentrates on these practical, business-focused tests, which are by far the most common. For the number 'puzzle' kinds of tests, we recommend reading the 'test your own IQ' books, which still contain these kinds of items.

Practising numerical tests

Anyone can improve their ability to perform well when working on numerical problems. In everyday life we are constantly provided with opportunities to flex our numerical muscles but technology has also encouraged us to become lazy when working with numbers. How many of us bother to work out the correct change when we are shopping? Fewer and fewer I suspect because we trust computerised tills to do the work for us. How many of us bother to work out time and distance when we are driving? Again, I suspect, fewer and fewer because our car milometers and our satellite navigation systems do it for us. Refreshing your memory of the 'times tables, taking the opportunity to do basic mental arithmetic and looking for chances to estimate a numerical answer (for example, estimating roughly how much you expect your shopping to cost) are all helpful ways to get more numerically 'fit' in addition to looking at numerical test items.

Your state of mind is a big factor in doing well in this kind of test. Probably the best thing you can do to get yourself in a good state of mind is to practise! The example questions in the following sections should help you to feel more at ease with business-focused numerical tests but remember you should also take as many other opportunities to practise as you can.

GETTING FAMILIAR WITH THE TASKS

- Practise identifying relevant information from tables: if you look at the financial press, there is no shortage of projections in table form, so get used to reading them and extrapolating some of the basic facts they contain.
- Brush up your mental arithmetic: practise working out rough percentages in your head or practise roughly totting up figures and working out an average.
- Do numerical puzzles: for example Sudoku or the numerical puzzles contained in games such as 'Brain Training' on Nintendo DS.
- The BBC's Skillswise website is also a good resource for freshening up your numerical skills (www.bbc.co.uk/skillswise/).

Practice will also help you to become familiar with the kind of language used in the tests. Some tests will deliberately use business terminology in the questions. This can be off-putting if you aren't used to using this kind of language every day: terms such as 'capital ratios', 'partner equity', 'sales revenue', 'profit margin'. Don't be fazed by this terminology, it is usually easy to work out what the question is getting at without having to have an accountant's understanding of specific business terms. Again, practice and familiarity are the key.

CALCULATORS

A lot of tests allow you to use calculators if you wish and these will often be provided. If you are told that calculators are permitted then it is better to use your own – one that you are familiar with – rather than having to get to know a new instrument in 'real time' during the test! Unless you are accustomed to using complex calculators, choose a simple machine with large buttons and practise using it in advance, particularly how to work out percentages.

A lot of the more complex numerical tests actually rely on increasing the complexity of the wording in the questions to achieve a higher difficulty level. Now, it is arguable whether this is a real test of numerical ability. However, it does mean that you need to read the questions very carefully to make sure you understand what is being asked. If you are puzzled, looking at the multiple choice answers will give you a clue. For example, are the possible answers all percentages; are they all numbers in the thousands; are they all decimals? Knowing this can often help you to interpret even quite verbally complex questions.

Tips for top scores

In the following sections we give you a number of examples of different formats to try out, together with correct answers (at the end of the chapter) and the steps needed to get to the right answer. We have also rated the questions as easy, moderate or hard. This will help you to get a sense of the questions or question formats you find easiest or most difficult and plan your practice accordingly.

Assess the information provided

For table-based questions, look at the tables before you start on each question. Getting a sense of the information they are giving you (or not giving you) will make it easier to understand the questions. For example, if you have looked through the tables and can see that the information relates to sales figures (in millions) and profitability (in £ per item sold), this will enable you to interpret each question more easily and to head more quickly for the table that contains the information you need to work out the answer.

Get a sense of the questions or question formats you find easiest or most difficult and plan your practice accordingly

It is all too easy to get flustered when faced by a page of tables; don't rush, give yourself some time to navigate your way around the information and to understand the format the tables are using. For example, in business tables it is very common to keep the information in the columns and rows as simple as possible by putting a heading on the column explaining that the numbers in the tables are in thousands ('000') in millions ('000,000') or that they refer to percentages. Give yourself time to read these headings so that you can make sure you are using the right information in your calculations.

Visualise the question

People sometimes find it difficult to deal with the 'abstract' nature of numbers – particularly large numbers – saying things like 'the numbers all just get jumbled up in my head' or 'halfway through the calculation I just lost track of what I was doing'. Turning numbers into something more concrete is one way of reducing this problem. You may remember this technique from school, where turning 'a' 'b' or 'x' and 'y' into apples or bananas seemed to make the problem less daunting!

For some people, it also helps to 'visualise' the question rather than just think about the numbers in front of you. So, for example, in the table in Section A (page 341) – Crowbridge Hotel room figures – imagine the hotel, picture it in your mind. The double rooms are probably bigger than the single rooms; perhaps the suites – there are only eight of them – are all on the top floor. Doing this helps to make the questions more practical and less abstract, and a lot of people find this helpful.

Now try the same technique for the information in the Adams Heaters example on page 343.

Remember there is no 'one right way' of doing this, you need to try it out and see if it helps. Here is our 'visualised' response to the information in the Adams Heaters tables.

- Perhaps the 20 watt heaters are about the size of a matchbox.
- Perhaps the 1 kilowatt heaters are about the size of a suitcase.
- They sell a lot of the 120 watt heaters so perhaps they have better packaging?
- They don't sell many of the 40 watt heaters so perhaps it is an old model?

The idea, remember, is to make the information less abstract – not just numbers on a page – and more real. For people who are not particularly confident in working with numbers this helps to 'de-mystify' this kind of question.

Using these tips will help you in two ways. Firstly, of course, we know that they work and will help you to find the right answers more quickly and with greater confidence. Secondly, simply having a method – a set of tools that you can easily use – is often the crucial difference between focused problem solving and increasingly anxious floundering. When you do get stuck on a question, as everyone does from time to time, it really helps to have a systematic approach to get you back on track. Both of these tips give you that clear 'back to first principles' approach.

As you work through the practice examples on the following pages make use of these tips as often as you can. As you gain in experience, notice how you start to apply the techniques without having to consciously 'use' them. The easier this becomes, the more fluent you will be in working through each type of question. Ultimately this means that you will have time to answer more questions and increase your score.

PRACTICE QUESTIONS

(answers can be found at the end of the chapter on page 353)

A. Table-based formats (easy)

Crowbridge Hotel room figures 2010

Type of room	Number of rooms available	Average number of days per year each room occupied
Single rooms	25	245
Double rooms	20	260
Family rooms (four beds)	20	310
Suites (four beds)	8	190

1. On average, how many days in the year were the family rooms occupied?

    A – 300   B – 260   C – 390   D – 310   E – 245

2. Excluding suites, how many rooms are available in the hotel?

    A – 48   B – 65   C – 60   D – 75   E – 55

3. If every family room held its maximum number of occupants, how many people could the hotel accommodate in family rooms on any given night?

    A – 80   B – 32   C – 88   D – 100   E – Can't say

4. Assuming that the average occupancy applies to every room, which type of room had the greatest total number of occupied days?

    A – Double   B – Single   C – Family   D – Suite   E – Can't say

5. To the nearest whole number, what percentage of the hotel's rooms is made up of family rooms?

    A – 20%   B – 25%   C – 30%   D – 27%   E – 33%

Crowbridge River Ferry Statistics

Season	Number of crossings per day	Average number of passengers per crossing
Spring	20	12
Summer	24	18
Autumn	18	12
Winter	16	10

6. In spring, how many passengers – on average – use the ferry each day?

    A – 12   B – 120   C – 240   D – 220   E – 180

7. Across all seasons, what is the average number of passengers per crossing?

    A – 12   B – 13   C – 18   D – 16   E – Can't say

8. If each passenger is charged £3.00 to use the ferry, what is the average revenue per day in the winter season?

    A – £480   B – £560   C – £460   D – £510   E – £490

9. On average, how many more passengers per day use the ferry in the spring + summer seasons as compared with the autumn + winter seasons?

    A – 309   B – 298   C – 296   D – 291   E – Can't say

10. Assuming there are 90 days in each season, what is the total number of crossings each year?

    A – 6800   B – 6950   C – 7200   D – 7250   E – 7020

B. Table-based formats (easy/moderate)

Adams Heaters: sales figures for 2010

Heater type	Profit per heater
20 W	£5.00
40 W	£5.00
80 W	£4.00
120 W	£3.50
1 kW	£7.50

Sales in 000s of units – 2010

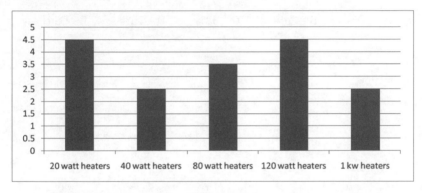

Note, in the following questions you might have to use information from either the table or the figure or both kinds of information.

1. **How much total profit was generated by 1 kilowatt heaters?**

   A – £18,750   B – £25,000   C – £2,500   D – £17,500   E – £19,750

2. **Which type of heater generated the greatest total profit?**

   A – 20 watt   B – 40 watt   C – 80 watt   D – 120 watt   E – 1 kilowatt

3. **If the sales of 1 kilowatt heaters were doubled, how much more profit would they make than the current sales of 80 watt heaters?**

   A – £6,500   B – £32,000   C – £25,500   D – £22,250   E – £23,500

4. What is the average profitability across all the heater types?

    A – £4.50   B – £5.00   C – £4.25   D – £6.00   E – £6.25

5. If 1 kilowatt heaters sold 20% less than they currently do, what would
    the total sales of 40 watt heaters have to be to achieve the same overall
    profit?

    A – 750   B – 3,000   C – 3,250   D – 3,750   E – 4,750

6. If improved production methods enabled the profitability of 20 watt
    heaters to be raised to £6.00 per unit, and this was sustained for 6
    months of next year (2011), what percentage of total profitability for
    2011 would be accounted for by 20 watt heaters?

    A – 20%   B – 24%   C – 32%   D – 15%   E – Can't say

C. Table-based formats (moderate/hard)

Vale Foods Ltd – Year on year sales (millions of units)

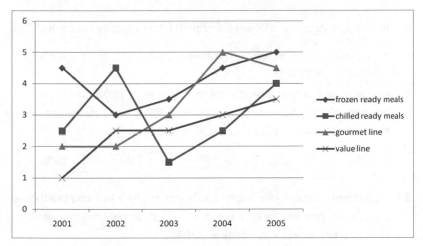

Production capacity in 2005

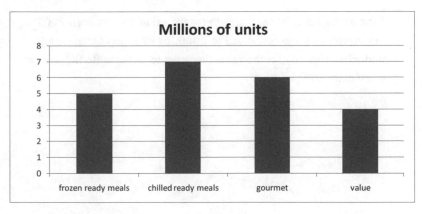

1. **Which was the most profitable product line in 2003?**

    A – Frozen   B – Chilled   C – Can't say   D – Gourmet   E – Value

2. **Across all product lines, what was the difference between total sales in 2001 and 2002?**

    A – 5 million   B – 3 million   C – 1.5 million   D – 2 million   E – 1 million

3. Across the 5 years for which information is available, which product has the highest sales?

    A – Value   B – Can't say   C – Chilled   D – Frozen   E – Gourmet

4. In 2005, what is the total excess of production capacity over sales?

    A – 6 million   B – 8 million   C – 5 million   D – Can't say   E – 4 million

5. Assuming production capacity was the same as in 2005, what percentage of production capacity for the chilled ready meals line – to the nearest whole number – was sold in 2002?

    A – 64%   B – 70%   C – 62%   D – 68%   E – 69%

6. If production capacity for frozen meals was cut by a half and production capacity for gourmet meals was cut by a third, by what amount would total capacity exceed total sales in 2005?

    A – 1 million   B – 500,000   C – 750,000   D – 1.5 million   E – 250,000

7. If the average annual sales growth for the value line between 2001 and 2005 was projected ahead to 2006, by what percentage would production capacity for the value line have to increase (to the nearest whole number)?

    A – 12%   B – 5%   C – 3%   D – 7%   E – 2%

D. Specific-question-based formats

(easy)

1. How many employees, at a recruitment cost of £3,000 each, can be hired if the recruitment budget is £261,000?

   A – 76   B – 87   C – 78   D – 74   E – 82

2. If sales of toys grew by 26% this year, from last year's figure of 820,000, what is the figure for this year's sales?

   A – 1,033,200   B – 1,133,200   C – 1,230,000
   D – 1,123,000   E – 1,280,300

3. Productivity for the last 5 years has been 78%, 74%, 81%, 80% and 84%. What has been the average productivity over this period?

   A – 81%   B – 78.9%   C – 80.5 %   D – 79.9%   E – 79.4%

4. There are 7 people working in your team; in total they worked for 270.9 hours last week. What was the average number of hours worked per person?

   A – 37.8 hours   B – 38.7 hours   C – 38 hours
   D – 36.8 hours   E – 38.6 hours

5. Your Band 1 staff earn on average 34% more than your Band 2 staff. If the average salary for Band 2 staff is £31,000, what is the average salary of a Band 1 employee?

   A – £40,450   B – £41,750   C – £40,750   D – £41,540   E – £41,175

E. Specific-question-based formats
(moderate)

1. Your factory has three production lines – A, B and C – producing 104, 127 and 94 units per hour, respectively. In an 8-hour shift how many more units will lines A and B combined produce compared with line C?

    A – 1,750   B – 1,096   C – 1,607   D – 1,960   E – 1,069

2. The average age of employees in your business is 38.5 years. The average age for men is 40.5 years; what is the average age for women?

    A – 38 years   B – 36.5 years   C – 35.5 years
    D – 37 years   E – Can't say

3. Anderson, Hilton and Weston are the three partners in a firm of solicitors, owning 40%, 35% and 25% of the equity in the business, respectively. Profits are divided up in proportion to each partner's equity in the business. If the business makes a profit of £475,600 then how much more will Hilton receive compared with Weston?

    A – £43,750 B – £47,560   C – £35,500 D – £39,470 E – Can't say

4. Your business currently borrows £350,000 at an annual interest rate of 6% on the first £200,000 and 7.5% on the remainder. You have the opportunity to pay off this debt by selling one of your retail units although you will be selling the unit at a loss of £58,000. How many years will it take for the saving in interest to cover the loss (to the nearest decimal place)?

    A – 2 years   B – 2.2 years   C – 2.7 years D – 3.1 years E – 2.5 years

5. The annual profits made by two London stores are £2,340,000 for the Oxford Street branch and £1,920,000 for the Strand branch. These profits are spread equally across all 12 months of the year. Both stores need to be refurbished; this will involve closing them for a period. If Oxford Street is closed for 2.5 months and the Strand is closed for 1.5 months, how much profit will be lost?

    A – £727,500 B – £750,000   C – £687,500 D – £770,500 E – £690,500

F. Specific-question-based formats

(hard)

1. On a turnover of £8.5 million, the gross profit made by your business is £2.7 million. From this figure must be taken overhead costs of £1,425,000 to arrive at net profit. What is the net profit to turnover ratio?

    A – 17.5%   B – 15.5%   C – 15%   D – 16.5%   E – 16%

2. In your sales team Andy sells 43 units per month, Ajaz sells 52 units per month and Sue sells 62 units per month: they offer discounts of £18, £23 and £21, respectively, per unit they sell. The total value (undiscounted) of units sold by the three in a month is £25,905. In a full year, by how much will the amount of Ajaz's and Sue's discount together exceed Andy's?

    A – £25,600   B – £20,688   C – £21,645   D – £22,555   E – £20,750

3. The total spend of the marketing department of your firm last year was 1.6 million on advertising, 0.8 million on public relations, 0.3 million on brochures and 0.7 million on corporate events. The marketing budget represents 13% of the firm's turnover. If the marketing budget for last year was underspent by 20%, what was the firm's turnover to the nearest million?

    A – 30 million B – 34 million   C – 38 million D – 33 million   E – 31 million

4. Every year your business sets aside £750,000 to cover legal costs. The money is spent with three separate law firms: Williams Partners (Litigation), Singh Partners (Employment Law) and Brace Brothers (Contract Law) in the proportion 5:3:2, respectively. Brace Brothers is proposing to increase its charges by 15%, while Singh Partners is proposing to reduce its by 5%. In total, how much money would you save by giving your contract law business to Singh Partners?

    A – £30,000   B – £18,750   C – £25,000   D – £35,500   E – £27,550

G. Other numerical formats

We mentioned at the start of this chapter that some, usually older, tests make use of items that are based on 'pure' numerical reasoning. You are much less likely to run across this kind of item but just so that you recognise them if they do come up, this section gives them some brief coverage.

You will occasionally see tests that are essentially about basic arithmetic; the format is usually as follows:

$56 - 9 = 7 + ?$	Answer = 40
$18 \times 5 = 9 \times ?$	Answer = 10
$5 \times 13 + 27 = 11 \times 8 + ?$	Answer = 4
$6.3 \times 2.9 \times 4.8 = ?$	Answer = 87.69
$4 \times ? = 47 + 9 \times 8$	Answer = 112

There is no real trick to items like this: it is simply a matter of working through the calculation, making sure you are accurate about whether you are adding, subtracting, multiplying or dividing to work out the unknown number. Such tests often don't allow you to use a calculator, so make sure your long division and long multiplication are up to scratch!

Another category of test – again asking you to identify a missing number – is based on you having to identify the rule that lets you predict the missing number. Here are some examples:

6	9	12	15	18	?

This is a simple arithmetic progression: you get the next number by adding 3 each time so the missing value is 21. So the rule here is 'add 3'. Here are some more examples of arithmetic progressions:

1.	225	200	175	150	?
2.	9	19	28	36	?
3.	13	20	27	34	?

Slightly more complex are geometric progressions where you have to multiply or divide to get the next number: again, the trick is to work out the rule that lets you predict the missing value. Here are some examples:

4. 3   9   27   81   ?

5. 4   16   256   ?

6. 480   120   30   7.5   ?

Another category of test is the number 'puzzle' kind of test. These are usually just a combination of arithmetic and/or geometric progressions – so again the issue is to find the rule that is being applied. Some of the formats in which these tests are presented can be quite novel, however. It is not possible to cover every variation you might encounter but here are some representative examples:

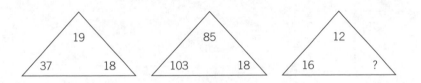

Here the rule is to take the smaller from the larger number on the left in each triangle, to get the number on the bottom right in each triangle. The answer is 4. Remember that the rule will probably change from item to item so you will need to work it out each time. Here are some more examples:

7.

8.

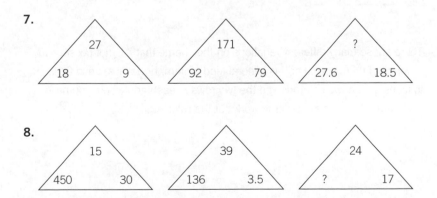

A final format you might see is a 'puzzle' presented in table format as follows:

2	4	6
5	7	9
8	10	?

Here, the rule is that numbers increase by 2 from left to right and by three from top to bottom. In this case it doesn't matter which rule you apply, you still get the answer 12. As before, however, the rule will usually change from item to item so you need to work it out each time. Here are some more examples:

9.

2	4	6
5	7	9
7	11	?

10.

7	10	70
8	8	64
4	13	?

There are so many different variations on this theme that it is not possible to cover all of them here. For this general kind of item, however, a good tip is to focus on the two columns and the two rows in each grid where you have complete information in order to work out the rule.

Numerical Tests – Answers

A.1 **D – 310 days** (This is simply a matter of reading the right line in the table; namely that the family rooms were occupied for an average of 310 days.)

A.2 **B – 65** (Adding the numbers in column one but excluding the 8 for suites to get the total.)

A.3 **A – 80** (20 family rooms × 4 possible occupants.)

A.4 **C – Family room** (note that they are asking about the *type* of room). To get total occupancy you multiply column one by column two for each type of room thus:

Single   25 × 245 = 6,125
Double   20 × 260 = 5,200
Family   20 × 310 = 6,200
Suite   8 × 190 = 1,520

A.5 **D – 27%** (Calculated by dividing the number of family rooms (20) by the total number of rooms (73) and multiplying by 100. The accurate answer is 27.3972%, but they only want it to the nearest whole number!)

A.6 **C – 240** (The calculation is simply the number of crossings per day in spring(20) multiplied by the average number of passengers per crossing in spring(12): the only thing to watch out for is to notice that they are asking for passengers per day not per crossing.)

A.7 **B – 13** (The calculation is to add the average number of passengers per crossing across all seasons (12+18+12+10) and then divide by 4 to get the answer)

A.8 **A – £480** (Simply 16 x 10 to give the average number of passengers per day in winter, multiplied by £3.00 to give the revenue.)

A.9 **C – 296** (20 × 12 plus 24 × 18, minus 18 × 12 plus 16 × 10.)

A.10 **E – 7020** (You need to multiply each of the seasonal crossings per day by 90 and then add these together)

B.1 **A – £18,750** (The answer is simply the profit per 1 kilowatt heater (£7.50 from the first table) multiplied by the number of units sold (2,500 from the first figure) to get the answer.)

B.2 **A – 20 watt heater** (The answer again is simply the profit per heater multiplied by the number sold and then looking for the highest figure. However, you can save some time here by estimating. Looking at the numbers, you should be able to estimate that the 20 watt and 1 kilowatt heaters are the only real contenders; the 40 watt heater doesn't sell enough, the 80 watt heater sells less and is less profitable and the 120 watt has the same volume as the 20 watt but is much less profitable. The complete total profit table is as follows:

20 watt	£22,500
40 watt	£12,500
80 watt	£14,000
120 watt	£15,750
1 kW	£18,750

So the answer is the 20 watt heater with a total profit of £22,500.)

B.3 **E – £23,500** (You have probably done a lot of this calculation already in answering question B2. Current total profit for 80 watt heaters is £14,000 (3,500 × £4); doubling the current total profit of 1 kilowatt heaters is £37,500 (2,500 × £7.5 × 2) and then subtracting one from the other to get the answer.)

B.4 **B – £5.00** (This is an easy question so don't make it more complicated; they are asking about profit per *type* of heater so it is simply the average of the figures in the first table.)

B.5 **C – 3,250** (Now this looks nasty but it's not that bad. 1 kilowatt heaters currently sell 2,500 units; 20% less than this is 2,000. So, if you are selling 500 less of them at £7.50 each you have a profit shortfall of

£3,750 (500 × £7.5). So, how many more of the 40 watt heaters – at a profit of £5.00 each – do you have to sell to make up the difference? Simply 3,750 divided by 5 which equals 750, but this is not the answer! They ask for the *total* sales of 40 watt heaters, not additional sales, so you have to add 750 to the current sales (2,500) to get the answer. See what we mean about reading the question carefully?)

B.6 **E – Can't say** (You are not given sales figures for next year so you can't calculate total profitability, so you can't say what percentage the profit for 20 watt heaters would account for. To make this calculation possible they would either have had to give you projected sales figures for 2011, or told you to assume the same sales figures as the current year. They didn't, so you can't say!)

C.1   **C – Can't say** (They do not give you any information about profitability, only about sales.)

C.2   **D – 2 million** (Simply calculated by adding up the sales figures for 2001 (1 + 2 + 2.5 + 4.5 = 10), adding up the sales figures for 2002 (2 + 2.5 + 3 + 4.5 = 12) and taking one from the other to get the answer.)

C.3   **D – Frozen** (Calculated by adding the sales figures for each product for each year as follows:

Frozen   =   20.5 million
Chilled   =   15 million
Gourmet   =   16.5 million
Value   =   12.5 million)

C.4   **C – 5 million** (Calculated by comparing the two graphs and noting that:

Frozen   production capacity and sales are the same
Chilled   production capacity exceeds sales by 3 million
Gourmet   production capacity exceeds sales by 1.5 million
Value   production capacity exceeds sales by 0.5 million

Giving an excess of 5 million in total.)

C.5   **A – 64%** (64.28 to be accurate; calculated by assuming that production capacity in 2002 was 7 million (they tell you to assume this), of which 4.5 million was sold, so 4.5 divided by 7 × 100 = 64)

C.6   **B – 500,000** (Calculated as follows: cutting frozen meals capacity by half means production capacity is now 2.5 million (down from 5 million), cutting gourmet meals capacity by a third means production capacity is now 4 million (down from 6 million). So, 4.5 million has been cut from production capacity; 2005 capacity is currently 22 million; take away 4.5 million and you are left with a total production capacity of 17.5 million. Total sales in 2005 are 17 million, so capacity exceeds sales by 500,000!)

C.7 **C – 3%** (Worked out as follows: first you need to know the average sales growth for the value line, like this:

2001–2002 growth = 1.5 million
2002–2003 growth = 0
2003–2004 growth = 0.5 million
2004–2005 growth = 0.5 million

Add up (to get 2.5 million) and divide by 4 to get an average sales growth of 0.625 million per year. If you now add this to the 2005 figure (3.5 million) you get a projected figure for 2006 of 4.125 million. So how much more is this than the current production capacity of 4 million? Time for percentages again: 4 million divided by 4.125 million × 100 = 96.96% (rounded up to 97%). This means you can currently only produce 97% of what you predict will be needed in 2006, so production capacity has to increase by 3%.)

D.1 **B – 87** (The calculation is 261,000 divided by 3,000.)

D.2 **A – 1,033,200** (The calculation is 820,000 divided by 100 × 26 added to the original 820,000.)

D.3 **E – 79.4%** (The calculation is 78 + 74 + 81 + 80 + 84 divided by 5.)

D.4 **B – 38.7 hours** (The calculation is 270.9 divided by 7.)

D.5 **D – £41,540** (The calculation is 31,000 divided by 100, multiplied by 34, added to the original 31,000.)

E.1 **B – 1096** (The calculation is (104 × 8) + (127 × 8) minus (94 × 8).)

E.2 **E – Can't say** (Without knowing the numbers of male and female employees there is no way of calculating a precise answer. You can estimate that the average age of women must be less than 38.5 years – given that men have a higher average age – but you can't put a figure on it.)

E.3   **B – £47,560** (The calculation is 35% of £475,600 (= 166,460) minus 25% of £475,600 (= 118,900) to give a difference of £47,560. This is actually a straightforward percentages question but it is made to appear more complicated by the use of terms like 'equity' and by the option of a 'Can't say' answer. The moral of the tale is look for the simple route to the answer.)

E.4   **E – 2.5 years** (The calculation is first, the annual cost of borrowing, which is 6% of 200,000 plus 7.5% of 150,000 (12,000 + 11,250) to get a total cost of borrowing of £23,250. Divide this into 58,000 to see how long it will take to get your money back. The accurate answer is 2.4946 years but the question only asks for accuracy to one decimal place.)

E.5   **A – £727,500** (The calculation is to work out the monthly profitability of each store (simply dividing the annual profit by 12) then multiply the monthly profit by the number of months the store will be closed as follows. Monthly profitability of Oxford Street is £195,000 × 2.5 months closed, added to the monthly profitability of the Strand, which is £160,000 × 1.5 months closed to get the answer.)

F.1   **C – 15%** (The calculation is first to work out net profit (simply 2,700,000 minus 1,425,000 = 1,275,000) and then to present this number as a percentage of 8.5 million. (1,275,000 divided by 8,500,000 × 100) The only complication here is the slightly intimidating language.)

F.2   **B – £20,688** (The calculation is the number of units sold × the discount value for each person, multiplied by 12 to get the total for each person for a year. It is then simply a matter of adding Ajaz's and Sue's totals together and subtracting the total for Andy to get the answer. The challenge with this question is too much information: it tempts you to work out the sale price of each unit through the information given in the second sentence but this information is redundant! You can calculate the answer through the very complicated route of working out the undiscounted value of each person's sales, then removing the discount, but you don't need to do this. A good example of where a couple of minutes given to understanding the gist of the question can save you a lot of calculator time!)

F.3   **D – 33 million** (The calculation is first to get the total marketing spend (1.6 + 0.8 + 0.3 + 0.7 = 3.4 million), this represents 80% of the marketing budget so the total marketing budget would have been 3.4 million divided by 80 × 100 = 4,250,000. This number in turn is 13% of turnover so total turnover will be 4,250,000 divided by 13 × 100. The accurate answer is 32,692,307 but the question only asks for the nearest million.)

F.4   **A – £30,000** (The calculation is first to work out the amount spent with each law firm. To do this, translate proportions into percentages thus: 5 + 3 + 2 = 10, so Williams has 5 tenths of the budget (50%), Singh has 3 tenths (30%) and Brace has 2 tenths (20%). As percentages of the total budget this equates to:

Williams	=	£375,000
Singh	=	£225,000
Brace	=	£150,000

From this basis you can work out what the proposed increases and decreases mean if you apportion work as you do currently, so your costs will be £11,250 less with Singh but £22,500 more with Brace. The secret here is to recognise that one option leads to an increase in cost while the other leads to a reduction and you must put the two together to get the difference or total saving. If things stay the same, Singh will be charging you £11,250 less but Brace will be charging you £22,500 more, in total an increase of £11,250. By moving the contract business to Singh and away from Brace you will be getting a 5% discount on a new total of £375,000 which equals £18,750 less. Thus the total difference (saving) is £18,750 + £11,250 = £30,000 less compared with what you would have had to spend otherwise.)

G.1   **125** (The rule is subtract 25.)

G.2   **43** (The rule is add 1 less each time: 10, 9, 8, 7, 6.)

G.3   **41** (The rule is add 7.)

G.4   **243** (The rule is multiply by 3.)

G.5   **65,536** (The rule is multiply each number by itself.)

G.6   **1.875** (The rule is divide by 4.)

G.7   **46.1** (Here the rule is to add the two lower numbers in each triangle to get the number at the apex.)

G.8   **408** (Here the rule is to multiply the two numbers on the right in each triangle to get the number on the bottom left.)

G.9   **15** (Here the rule is simply to add up the top two numbers in each column to get the bottom number.)

G.10   **52** (Here the rule is to multiply the first two numbers in each row to get the third number.)

IN A NUTSHELL

Numerical reasoning tests are used to measure your ability to interpret the kinds of number work that you would encounter in the running of a business.

- Practise using numerical information; for example, increase your familiarity with extracting information from tables. For table based questions, give yourself a minute to familiarise yourself with the information they contain.
- Make sure you can work out percentages and brush up on your long division and long multiplication; get to know and trust your calculator.
- Read the questions carefully, don't do calculations that you don't have to!
- Make full use of the practice items you will be given at the start of any test; make sure you understand the format.
- Don't be fazed by business language and terminology; if you have found any of the language in the example questions intimidating, then make time during your preparation to look up specific words or practise reading business-related material.

22 VERBAL REASONING TESTS

Employers will often want to make an assessment of prospective employees' reasoning skills, and verbal reasoning tests are the most common way that they try to do this. In this chapter we will:

■ Explain what the commonly used tests are trying to measure

■ Familiarise you with different response formats

■ Give you the opportunity to practise verbal reasoning tests

What verbal reasoning tests measure

Verbal tests are designed to assess how well you use vocabulary, solve problems, reason and apply logic using words. Sometimes they are described as 'logical reasoning' or 'critical thinking' tests but they all depend on use and understanding of words to assess your thinking. As you can probably tell from this mixture of abilities, verbally based tests are often trying to measure more than one thing at the same time. Essentially, they usually try to measure the following aspects of your verbal ability, sometimes in combination and sometimes separately:

- **Comprehension** – can you read a short passage and accurately find required information or facts within it?
- **Logic and logical relationships** – can you deduce a conclusion based on the information you are given?
- **Word meaning/vocabulary** – do you understand the precise meaning of words, can you select substitute words that mean the same thing?

By far the most common form of these tests is to present you with a passage of information and then to ask you a number of questions about it; either comprehension questions or logic questions and sometimes a combination of the two. As before, a potential employer is much less interested in your literary skills – unless you are applying for a specific role which involves writing, such as journalism – and much more interested in whether you can understand and extract the relevant information from written material.

Employers are interested in whether you can understand and extract relevant information from written material

We will concentrate on giving you examples of these most commonly used test formats.

Once again, preparation, practice and familiarity are important factors in doing well in verbal tests. Take advantage of the sample items on test publishers' websites. People vary a great deal in terms of how much time they spend reading – at work or as a leisure activity. There is no doubt that your confidence and comfort in reading is a big factor in doing well in such tests, so, if you do not read a great deal, additional practice here is likely to pay off.

Response formats

All the verbal tests you encounter will ask you to respond in multiple choice format, selecting the option that you think is correct. The most common format is to ask you to read a short passage of information and then answer questions based on the information.

Comprehension tests

In comprehension tests, i.e. finding the right information in the passage, you will be given the usual choice of answers, usually between three and five, and asked to select the one you think is most accurate.

Logic tests

In logic tests you will be asked to look at a statement they give you and to respond:

- **True** – if you think the statement is correct and/or follows logically from the information given.
- **False** – if you think the statement is incorrect or does not follow on logically from the information given.
- **Can't say** – if you can't tell whether the statement is correct or otherwise based on the information given.

STICK TO THE GIVEN FACTS

Most verbal tests will warn you to base your answers on the information given and not on your own knowledge or opinions about the subject matter of the passage. So, for example, you might be asked to read a passage about a subject on which you are well informed, having your own views and knowledge; you must base your answers on the information given and not on your own opinions even if, factually, your view is more accurate.

Word meaning tests

In word meaning tests you will usually be asked to:

- **Replace words** – by selecting an alternative word from a list.
- **Identify synonyms and antonyms** – words that mean the same or opposite of a given word, again selected from a list of alternatives.

You might also – increasingly rarely these days – come across old-fashioned IQ type verbal items such as:

Dog is to puppy as cat is to:

- ☐ Small
- ☐ Furry
- ☐ Kitten
- ☐ Pet
- ☐ Parent

These are now so uncommon that we won't cover them here but plenty of items of this kind are available online if you want to explore them.

Tips for top scores

- Practise – use the example items to improve your speed at pulling out key information.
- Read questions very carefully; make sure you understand what is being asked for.
- If you do not read a great deal, then set aside time for reading to increase the speed at which you can spot relevant information.
- Improving your 'lexicon' of word meanings can take time; again, reading more will help but challenge yourself by reading material where you will encounter words that are unfamiliar and that you will need to look up.

PRACTICE QUESTIONS

(answers can be found at the end of the chapter on page 384)

The following sections have a number of examples of different formats to try out, together with correct answers and the logic used to get to the right answer. We have rated the questions as easy, moderate or hard. This will help you to get a sense of which questions or question formats you find easiest or most difficult so that you can plan your practice accordingly.

In turn, the practice examples will include:

- Comprehension questions – finding information in a passage of writing
- Logic questions – drawing conclusions about what is correct or incorrect based on information given
- Word meaning/vocabulary

Comprehension (easy)

Example A

Read the passage below and then answer the following questions:

'These days, most areas of science have become so specialised that it is no longer possible to be an "all rounder". Our Victorian predecessors had the luxury of being able to span physics, chemistry and the natural sciences and develop a respectable knowledge across a number of disciplines. For example, Lord Kelvin made vital contributions to physics, engineering and geology; Sir Francis Galton made important contributions to meteorology, psychology and biology. Such polymaths were relatively common in the 19th century but are hard to find now.'

1. **Which of these disciplines is not mentioned in the passage?**

    a. Biology
    b. Astronomy
    c. Physics
    d. Chemistry
    e. Natural sciences

2. **Which one of these statements most accurately reflects the key points of the passage?**

    a. Victorians were great scientists
    b. It is important to know more than one science
    c. Victorian scientists were greatly respected
    d. It is harder now to be a scientific generalist than it was in the past
    e. Science is too specialised

3. **For which one of the following reasons is it harder to find polymaths now?**

    a. There was more time to study in the 19th century
    b. People such as Lord Kelvin had wider interests
    c. Individual sciences have become much more specialised
    d. People are less interested in science now
    e. Science used to be taught better

Example B

Read the passage below and then answer the following questions:

'Few people can afford to be complacent about their pensions in the current situation, particularly those of us depending on private pensions. The poor performance of the stock market over the last 10 years means that pension funds have not delivered their promised rates of return and for a lot of us this means substantially less income to see us through retirement. Most independent pensions advisers are saying that private pensions are underinvested by about 40%, meaning that the average saver needs to be investing £5,000 more each year than they currently do if they want to protect their retirement income. Whether you are planning to buy an annuity or whether you have other plans for investing your pension pot on retirement, chances are that it will not deliver what you expect.'

1. **Which one of the following reasons best explains why pension funds have underperformed?**

   a. Pension investors have been too cautious
   b. People are not listening to their independent financial advisers
   c. Private pensions are not as good as state pensions
   d. People cannot afford to invest enough
   e. The stock market has performed poorly

2. **Which one of these sentences most accurately paraphrases the first sentence in the passage?**

   a. Currently, people with private pensions are especially at risk if they are too complacent
   b. All pensioners need to be more vigilant about future earnings
   c. Poor stock market performance puts us all at risk
   d. People with private pensions will have problems buying annuities
   e. It is dangerous to depend on private pensions

3. **Which one of these headlines most accurately summarises the content of the passage?**

   a. 'Pensions funds are in trouble'
   b. 'Pensions advisers warn of need for more investment'
   c. 'Annuities are 40% down on predictions'
   d. 'Stock market still down after 10 years'
   e. 'Bad time to invest in pensions'

Comprehension (moderate/hard)

Example C

Read the passage below and then answer the following questions:

'Everyone is capable of creativity and innovation. Although it comes more easily to some than others – dependent on personality, aptitude and motivation – we all have brains that are evolved for creative problem solving. So why don't we all get the chance? Some of the answer lies in the stereotypes we have of ourselves or our roles, but what is R&D if not a creative activity; what is enterprise if not a creative activity; what is writing just a memo if not a creative activity? All these are about making something, whether it is a compound, a business or an idea. The environment and the climate that we work in are key determinants of how much of our creativity we bring to work. Do we work in a highly controlling environment where analysis overrides original thinking? Are we managed in a way that focuses on control, metrics and short term deliverables rather than on broader, more open ended thinking? Does our business climate reward systematisation more than speculation? An unsupportive creativity climate makes it all the more likely that we will save our moments of inspiration for the weekend!'

1. **Which pair of statements best describe reasons for a lack of creativity?**

    a. Everyone can be creative + an unsupportive creativity climate
    b. Our stereotypes of ourselves + our brains are evolved to be creative
    c. A highly controlling environment + management focused on the short term
    d. Too much analysis + everyone is capable of innovation

2. **According to the information provided, why does creativity come more easily to some people than to others?**

    a. We have brains evolved for problem solving
    b. It depends on personality, aptitude and motivation
    c. Businesses focus on short-term deliverables
    d. Not everyone gets the chance

3. **Which of the following phrases best captures the meaning of the phrase** '*we will save our moments of inspiration for the weekend*' **at the end of the passage?**

    a. People tend to be more creative in their own time
    b. Businesses miss an opportunity if they don't support creativity
    c. People resent being controlled
    d. Creativity depends on a lot of different factors

4. **Which of the following statements is closest in meaning to the phrase** '*The environment and the climate that we work in are key determinants of how much of our creativity we bring to work.*'

    a. How we are feeling makes a difference to how creative we are
    b. Company culture and the way we are managed are important influences on our creativity at work
    c. Most of us are more creative at home than we are at work
    d. If we are determined we can all overcome barriers to creativity

Example D

Read the following passage then answer the questions:

'Arguments in health economics are always challenging ones; the fundamental difficulty of aligning scarce resources with apparently infinite demand means that prioritising – in itself problematic and subject to multiple sources of influence – becomes as much a political as a scientific or strictly rational process. Health economists find relatively little difficulty in calculating return on investment for a particular therapeutic intervention (for example in terms of speed of recovery), or in estimating average individual benefit in terms of quality of life or extended life expectancy, but find it much more difficult to provide an "economic" answer as to the value of newer therapeutic options such as fertility treatment where the payoff is hard to define in individual or societal terms but is, rather, a matter of personal well-being or even human rights. As a result, the economic arguments for supporting or proscribing a therapy will never be the only consideration when it comes to making difficult decisions about how to ration health care.'

1. **Which of these statements best explains why health economics decisions are difficult?**

    a. Political factors are as important as economic ones
    b. Demand for treatment exceeds supply
    c. New therapies are always being developed
    d. There are a wide range of factors that have to be considered

2. **Which of these sentences would best replace the final sentence in the passage?**

    a. As a result difficult decisions about health care will always involve a lot of factors
    b. As a result economics will be only one of the factors influencing health care decisions
    c. As a result decisions about how to ration health care will always be difficult
    d. As a result there are always economic arguments for supporting or proscribing a particular therapy

3. **Which of these phrases best summarises the content of the passage?**

   a. Some therapies, such as fertility treatment, are harder to justify than others
   b. Health economists find it difficult to take account of factors such as personal well-being
   c. The economic case is only part of the argument when it comes to decisions about health care
   d. Tangible benefits such as increased life expectancy should get a higher priority when it comes to decisions about health care

4. **Which of these statements is factually accurate based on the information in the passage?**

   a. Decisions about how to prioritise are subject to political influence
   b. It is difficult to calculate return on investment for most therapies
   c. Average extended life expectancy is the most frequently used measure of patient benefit
   d. Newer therapies will inevitably take time to prove their value

Logic and logical relationships (easy)

In these questions, read the passage provided and then decide whether each of the statements following the passage is:

- **True** – if you think the statement is correct and/or follows logically from the information given.
- **False** – if you think the statement is incorrect or does not follow on logically from the information given.
- **Can't say** – if you can't tell whether the statement is correct or otherwise based on the information given.

Example E

'Situated close to the river Thames, the Tower of London is home to the Crown Jewels and one of the most famous castles in England. Founded by William the Conqueror in about 1070, the Tower has been at the centre of English history for almost 1,000 years; over this period it has served as a fortress, a royal palace, a prison and an armoury. William's first construction on the site would have been a relatively hastily erected building of timber and stone; the White Tower – the main central keep – was started in 1078, taking about 10 years to build, and has been significantly added to and improved since.'

For each statement answer A – True; B – False or C – Can't say.

1. William's first construction on the site was built relatively quickly
2. The Crown Jewels are kept close to the river Thames
3. There was already a building on the site before 1070
4. The White Tower has not changed much since 1078
5. The White Tower is the largest structure on the site

Example F

'The genetic health of many breeds of dog has come under the spotlight recently; critics point to inbred defects that have a serious impact on the health and well-being of a significant number of pedigree animals. Defects such as hip dysplasia, breathing problems and syringomyelia (a particular problem in King Charles Spaniels) are held to be the result of breeding programmes that are aimed at producing aesthetically "perfect" dogs in terms of the breed standard rather than healthy animals. The BBC and the RSPCA have recently decided to withdraw support for Crufts, the premier dog show, in response to widespread disquiet that the Kennel Club and the dog breeding fraternity have done too little to tackle the issue.'

For each statement answer A – True; B – False or C – Can't say.

1. Non-pedigree dogs do not suffer from genetic defects
2. The RSPCA still support Crufts despite criticisms about dog health
3. Defects caused by breeding programmes include hip dysplasia and breathing problems
4. Some dog breeders have focused on the breed standard at the expense of animal health
5. The Kennel Club and Crufts are working to remedy the problem of inbreeding

Logic and logical relationships
(moderate/hard)

Example G

'The process of developing new drugs and new therapies is long and expensive. Pharmaceutical companies must overcome many obstacles before they can market a new drug. First they have to discover a new molecule which is not already the intellectual property of another company; they then have to prove that it is effective and safe. Many years are needed to complete all the trials required before a drug can be taken to market and most compounds – even promising ones – don't make it to the prescription list. The hit rate is low and people can spend their whole careers in pharmaceutical research and development without ever taking a drug all the way through this process. So expensive is drug development that big pharmaceutical companies need to be confident that the drug will have a large market when it has completed all the testing stages. For this reason, important areas of therapy can be neglected because too few people suffer from the illness to make it worth the investment. Large companies have to answer to their shareholders and, cynically, it can be argued that from a drug company point of view, the ideal drug is one that moderates symptoms – and thus has to be taken over a long period of time – rather than one which cures the disease and never needs to be taken again.'

For each statement answer A – True; B – False or C – Can't say.

1. Market factors will influence which drugs companies are willing to invest in
2. It cannot be said that drug companies need to be confident of a large market for their products
3. Most drugs have side effects so they have to be rigorously tested
4. The prescription list is made up of only a small proportion of the drugs that go through trials and testing
5. Discovering a new molecule is not the first stage in developing a new drug

Example H

'The Fender Stratocaster is probably the most widely used electric guitar in the world. It has been in continuous production since it was first designed by Leo Fender and his colleagues in 1954. It differs from earlier designs – such as the Telecaster – in a number of important ways, including the more comfortable contoured shape of the body and in terms of its electrical components. The Stratocaster has three single coil pick-ups in contrast to the Telecaster's two, and while the Telecaster can claim to be the solid-bodied guitar that has been in continuous production for longer, the 'Strat' – as the Stratocaster is usually known – has eclipsed it in terms of sales and fame. Strats are only built in the USA, Mexico, Japan and Korea, while a cheaper version – known as the Squier Strat – is also built under licence in China, Indonesia and India. The Stratocaster is known for its very clean, bright sound and the flexibility of tone provided by its three-way selector switch, which allows the player to decide which of the three pick-ups is being used to amplify the signal. Guitarists also discovered that by putting the switch in an intermediate position between pick-ups, a unique growling sound could be produced.'

For each statement answer A – True; B – False or C – Can't say.

1. It is not true to say that the Telecaster and the Stratocaster are broadly similar in design
2. The guitar that has been in production for longer also has three pick-ups
3. The contoured body and the number of pick-ups are only two of the ways in which the Strat and the Telecaster differ
4. Comfort is one of the factors that has led to increased sales of Stratocasters as compared to Telecasters
5. The Stratocaster gives guitarists more scope for experimentation and modification of the guitar

Example I

'The invention of the steam engine is most commonly associated with the names of Thomas Newcomen and James Watt, though in fact it was James Savery who first patented a crude steam engine in 1698. The industrial revolution and its demand for mineral resources meant that coal mining was a crucial enterprise and one of its most significant challenges was that of pumping water out of deep mines: it was this problem that Savery's steam engine solved. While Newcomen later improved this pump design and while the more charismatic applications of steam were to be credited to people such as James Watt and George Stephenson, the initial groundbreaking work was Savery's. Watt's key contribution – in his patent of 1769 – was the addition of a separate condenser that made steam engines much more efficient: this became the predominant design which served as the powerhouse for the industrial revolution. The expiry of this patent in 1800 opened the doors to inventors such as Trevithic and Stephenson who, with their patents for high-pressure engines, were then able to lay the foundations for the age of steam locomotion.'

For each statement answer A – True; B – False or C – Can't say.

1. People who built on the work of James Savery became more famous than Savery himself
2. Watt's patent was intermediate between those of Savery and Stephenson
3. Trevithic and Stephenson had been working on their steam engine designs prior to 1800
4. Savery's steam engine design was too weak to be used in deep mines
5. It would not be true to say that Watt's contribution made steam engines slightly more effective
6. Watt and Stephenson were more charismatic than Savery and Newcomen
7. A number of people deserve credit for developing the steam engine, no one person made a pioneering contribution

Word meaning/vocabulary

The format of word meaning or vocabulary tests you will most commonly encounter is, again, based on reading a short passage but this time being asked questions about specific words in the passage. As usual you will be given a multiple response choice from which to select your answer. An easy and a hard example are given below.

Example J (easy)

*'Few people can afford to be **complacent** about their pensions in the current situation, particularly those of us depending on private pensions. The poor performance of the stock market over the last 10 years means that pension funds have not delivered their promised rates of return and for a lot of us this means substantially less income to see us through retirement. Most **independent** pensions advisers are saying that private pensions are underinvested by about 40%, meaning that the **average** saver needs to be investing £5,000 more each year than they currently do if they want to protect their retirement income. Whether you are planning to buy an annuity or whether you have other plans for investing your pension pot on retirement, chances are that it will not deliver what you expect.'*

1. **Which of these words would best replace the word *complacent* in the first sentence?**

    a. Easy
    b. Satisfied
    c. Compliant
    d. Anxious
    e. Conducive

2. **Which of these words would best replace the word *average* in the third sentence?**

    a. Mean
    b. Typical
    c. Normal
    d. Irregular
    e. Concerned

3. **Which of these words means the opposite of *independent*?**

   a. Reliant
   b. Qualified
   c. Self-sufficient
   d. Objective
   e. Isolated

Example K (hard)

*'Arguments in health economics are always challenging ones; the fundamental difficulty of **aligning** scarce resources with apparently infinite demand means that prioritising – in itself problematic and subject to multiple sources of influence – becomes as much a political as a scientific or strictly **rational** process. Health economists find relatively little difficulty in calculating return on investment for a particular **therapeutic** intervention (for example in terms of speed of recovery), or in estimating average individual benefit in terms of quality of life or extended life expectancy, but find it much more difficult to provide an "economic" answer as to the value of newer therapeutic options such as fertility treatment where the payoff is hard to define in individual or societal terms but is, rather, a matter of personal well-being or even human rights. As a result, the economic arguments for supporting or **proscribing** a therapy will never be the only consideration when it comes to making difficult decisions about how to ration health care.'*

1. **Which of these words is closest in meaning to the word 'aligning' in the first sentence?**

   a. Comparing
   b. Agreeing
   c. Convincing
   d. Matching
   e. Accepting

2. Which of these words would best replace the word 'rational' in the first sentence?

   a. Cognitive
   b. Objective
   c. Decisive
   d. Numerical
   e. Reasonable

3. Which of these words means the opposite of 'therapeutic' in the second sentence?

   a. Injurious
   b. Restorative
   c. Remedial
   d. Alternative
   e. Harmless

4. Which of these words means the same as 'proscribing' in the final sentence?

   a. Permitting
   b. Legalising
   c. Undermining
   d. Prohibiting
   e. Preventing

Remember that some tests combine all these formats; in other words, a passage is followed by questions about comprehension, logic and word meanings. The principles are exactly the same as above, however, and familiarity with these items should help to remove a lot of the anxiety about this kind of test.

Verbal Tests – Answers

Example A

The answers are   1 – b   2 – d   3 – c

The answers are simply based on an accurate reading of the passage; the only point to watch out for here is to make sure you base your answer to Q3 purely on the passage and not on your own views – for example regarding whether science used to be taught better!

Example B

The answers are   1 – e   2 – a   3 – b

Again, accurate reading of the passage and careful reading of the question is what is needed here. For Q1, only choice (e) is factually correct based on the information in the passage; some of the other statements might be possible explanations but not from the facts given. For Q2, choice (a) has the same meaning as the first sentence in the passage because it is the only statement that points out that complacency is a particular problem for people with private pensions. For Q3, answer (b) is the fullest summary; the other options make reference to only a small part of the passage, or are offering an opinion rather than a summary.

Example C

The answers are   1 – c   2 – b   3 – b   4 – b

Careful reading of the question becomes still more important as the items become more complex. Often, the difficulty level comes from having to choose a 'best fit' answer rather than one that is absolutely correct. One of the alternatives they give you will be better than the others, however, and this is what you must look out for. For example, in Q1 above, none of the pairs provides a complete answer to the question 'what are the reasons for a lack of creativity', but this is not what they are asking! They are asking for which pair *best* describes reasons for a lack of creativity – in other words which pair comes closest to explaining – and (c) is the only answer that contains two inhibitors of creativity.

Example D

The answers are: 1 – b   2 – b   3 – c   4 – a

The principles here are the same as for the other passages – namely, the need for careful reading and the need to base your answers only on the information provided. The challenge here is that the passage is more complex, with more sub-clauses and trickier language. If we unpick the specific questions:

- Q1 – all of the potential answers are plausible conclusions that you could draw from the information given, but only (b) is an *explanation* of why health care decisions are difficult and this is what the question asks for.
- Q2 – answer (a) is a close replacement for the final sentence but answer (b) is better because it makes specific reference to one of the factors – namely economics – which is a closer paraphrasing of the final sentence. Answer (c) is a broad conclusion not a paraphrasing of the last sentence and answer (d) does not make any of the same points as are covered in the last sentence.
- Q3 – the first three option answers are all conclusions you could reasonably draw from the passage but only answer (c) summarises the gist of what has been said. Answer (d) is a statement of opinion and not a summary.
- Q4 – only answer (a) is factually accurate; the others are plausible – even common sense – opinions but you can't defend them purely based on the information given.

Example E

The answers are: 1 – A   2 – A   3 – C   4 – B   5 – C

Hopefully you won't have had too much trouble with these questions, but just to help you check the logic:

Q1 True: the passage clearly states this.

Q2 True: the passage tells you that the Crown Jewels are in the Tower and that the Tower is close to the Thames, it follows logically that the jewels are kept close to the Thames.

Q3 Can't say: there is no information in the passage about any earlier building; now, you might happen to know that there was a Roman fort on the site 1,000 years earlier, but *you can't deduce this from the information in the passage*!

Q4 False: the passage clearly states that the White Tower has been added to and improved; therefore it is incorrect to say that it has not changed much.

Q5 Can't say: again, the passage gives you no information about this.

Example F

The answers are: 1 – C   2 – B   3 – A   4 – A   5 – C
Here is a quick walk through the logic of these answers:

Q1 Can't say: the passage makes no mention of problems with non-pedigree dogs; it might be implied that pedigree animals have more problems, but from the passage alone, you can't say. Watch out too for double negatives in this kind of question – non-pedigree ... do not suffer – they are sometimes used to make interpretation more difficult.

Q2 False: the passage is clear that the RSPCA has withdrawn support.

Q3 True: factually true based on the information given.

Q4 True: this is a clear logical conclusion you can draw from the information given.

Q5 Can't say: while it might be likely that these organisations are working on the problem, you do not have any evidence of it from the passage.

Example G

The answers are: 1 – A   2 – B   3 – C   4 – A   5 – B
Once again, the logic is as follows:

Q1 True: the passage states that companies need to be confident of a large market so it follows that this will influence which drugs they invest in.

Q2 False: it *can* be said that drug companies need a large market, so this statement is false.

Q3 Can't say: you might think this from your own knowledge but you are not explicitly told it in the passage.

Q4 True: you are told that most drugs don't make it to the prescription list so it follows logically that only a small proportion of the drugs tested do make it through to the list.

Q5 False: you are told that discovering a new molecule *is* the first stage; this statement contradicts that so it must be false.

Example H

The answers are: 1 – A   2 – B   3 – A   4 – A   5 – C
Here is a quick run through the logic:

Q1 True: here is another of those double negatives – it is true to say that it is not true to say – the passage tells you that there are important differences in design, so a statement saying that 'it is not true to say that they are broadly similar' has to be true.

Q2 False: the guitar that has been in production for longer is the Telecaster and the passage tells you that the Telecaster has only two pick-ups.

Q3 True: the passage tells you that 'there are a number of ways' in which they differ of which contour and number of pick-ups are only two, therefore the statement is true.

Q4 True: the passage tells you that the Stratocaster has 'eclipsed' sales of the Telecaster (meaning it sells a lot more) and that the comfortable contoured shape is one of the improvements over the Telecaster; it therefore follows logically that comfort *is* one of the factors leading to increased sales.

Q5 Can't say: the passage does not give you enough information to draw this conclusion; while the passage does state that guitarists have discovered novel ways of using the controls on the Stratocaster, it says nothing about how much it is possible to experiment with the Telecaster.

Example I

The answers are: 1 – A   2 – A   3 – C   4 – B   5 – A   6 – C
7 – B

Once again, here is the logic:

Q1 True: it is a reasonable inference from the information in the passage, namely that developments in early steam engine design are more often associated with names other than Savery's. You may need to be careful with this question because it is an example of one where – for once – your common sense and the requirements of the question might line up. In other words, your common knowledge might tell you that Watt is more famous than Savery (and could lead you to second-guess the question as in earlier examples) but in fact this conclusion is *also* a logical conclusion from the information you are given!

Q2 True: careful reading is all that is required here; Watt's patent came after Savery's and before Stephenson's.

Q3 Can't say: the information in the passage does not tell you what Trevithic and Stephenson were up to before 1800.

Q4 False: the passage clearly states that the problem of pumping water out of deep mines was what Savery's engine solved.

Q5 True: this is another of those double negatives; Watt's design made steam engines considerably more effective (not slightly more), so it is true to say that a statement claiming this to be false is indeed correct (or true!).

Q6 Can't say: the passage does not give you any information about this, it mentions *more charismatic applications* but does not comment on the charisma of the individuals.

Q7 False: the passage clearly states that 'the groundbreaking work was Savery's', telling us that he did indeed make a pioneering contribution, so the statement is false.

Example J

The answers are: 1 – b   2 – b   3 – a

Hopefully, not too much of a problem with these: as usual you need to read the question carefully. In the first two questions you are asked for the best replacement word – meaning that you have to take the context into account. In other words, which of the alternatives would work best *in this sentence*? You can sometimes be asked to identify a word of similar or opposite meaning without reference to the context, so watch out for these.

Example K

The answers are: 1 – d   2 – b   3 – a   4 – d

The harder questions of this type usually depend on more obscure words or on more subtle differences in meaning, for example, the difference between 'prohibiting' and 'preventing' in question 4. (To be pedantic – prevent is a more causative verb implying direct intervention to stop something from happening; prohibit implies a rule or law to more indirectly stop something from happening – this is the meaning that is closest to the context of the example.) Once again, careful reading of the question is important.

IN A NUTSHELL

There are a number of reasons why you might get a score lower than you deserve when completing verbal reasoning tests, for example: lack of familiarity with the test format, nervousness and poor preparation. Avoid these pitfalls by:

■ Practising – make sure you understand the logic of the examples contained in this chapter.

■ Developing your test taking skills as you work through the examples. Recognise when you tend to get stuck and you are better served by moving on to the next item.

■ Reading questions very carefully to make sure you understand what is being asked of you, you can waste a lot of time otherwise.

■ Developing your own sense of which kinds of item you find easy or hard – use this to focus your practice.

Above all – don't panic!

23 ABSTRACT REASONING TESTS

This chapter aims to familiarise you with the different types of abstract reasoning tests. You will also get a chance to practise them extensively. You will understand:

■ The different types of 'rules' that are used in abstract reasoning questions

■ How to do your best by focusing on one aspect of the question at a time

■ How to use the multiple-choice options to help identify the correct answer

■ Which types of questions you are best at and where you need to gain more practice

What abstract reasoning tests measure

Of all the psychometric tests you might complete, abstract reasoning tests will 'look' the most unusual and unconventional, that is the questions do not look like typical business problems. Instead, you will be given diagrams consisting of shapes, signs or symbols, as you will see from the practice questions in this chapter. So why are these tests used? Despite their strange appearance, the questions in abstract reasoning tests measure important qualities. Employers use these tests when they want to understand how well you can:

- Identify patterns or 'rules' in complex data
- Separate what is important from what is irrelevant
- Deal with and interpret complexity
- Apply insights to solve problems

In abstract reasoning tests, each question works by following a particular rule or set of rules

How abstract reasoning tests work

Although there are many different formats, abstract reasoning tests involve one of two general methods:

- **Series** – identifying the next pattern in a series of patterns.
- **Categories** – identifying which pattern 'belongs' to a group of patterns.

Whichever method tests use, each question works by following a particular rule or set of rules. To answer the questions successfully you will need to identify which rule or rules are being used.

Let's look at an example of a series-based question:

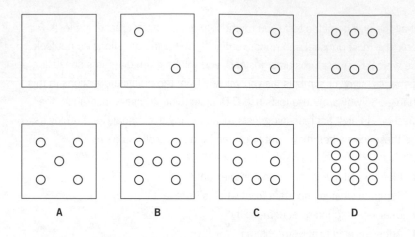

Here there is only one rule operating and that rule quickly becomes apparent. We can see that two circles are added each time, so the correct answer is option C – the next pattern in the sequence is 8 circles.

Let's look at an example of a category-based question.

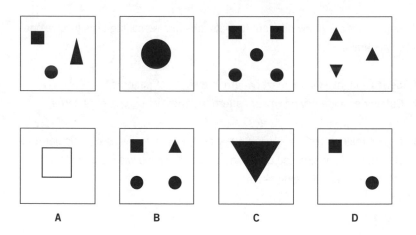

Here there are two rules in operation. The first, and most obvious, is that all of the shapes are black. The second is that there are an odd number of shapes in each pattern. So the correct answer is option C. The questions become harder if the rule is more difficult to spot or if more than one rule is applied at the same time. What might make a rule more difficult to spot? Rules can be based on any aspect of the shapes within a pattern. The table below shows just some of the ways in which rules can be applied.

Rule	Examples
Shape	The shape remains consistent, e.g. all triangles
	The shapes change in a cyclical pattern, e.g. square, then circle, then triangle, then back to square
	The shapes share common features, e.g. all are curved, straight-lined, or enclosed
Colour	Colour remains constant
	Colours change in a cyclical pattern
	Colours combine to form a new colour
Size	Size remains constant
	Size changes in a progressive pattern (e.g. small, medium, large)
Number	Each pattern has a constant number of shapes
	The number of shapes changes in a progressive or cyclical pattern
Rotation	Patterns revolve clockwise or anti-clockwise
	Patterns are inverted
Lines of symmetry	Patterns are symmetrical or non-symmetrical
	Patterns share the same lines of symmetry
	Lines of symmetry rotate
Merging	Two shapes overlap to form a new pattern
	Two shapes overlap and cancel each other out (e.g. two squares overlap exactly and disappear)

Remember, the above table shows just some of the rules that are used in abstract reasoning questions. In practice, you are likely to come across these and other rules. So what is the best way to tackle these types of questions?

Tips for top scores

Focus on one rule at a time

As you will see from the practice questions in this chapter, harder questions tend to have more complicated patterns where there is lots of information to take in. When faced with questions like these, it is all too easy to panic and stare at the shapes without taking anything in.

The most important tactic is to work systematically – like a detective – through one possibility at a time. Focus on one hypothesis and investigate until you have proved or discounted it. This disciplined, systematic approach will allow you to work through the questions as quickly and clearly as possible. It saves the confusion and wasted effort of half-exploring a possibility, moving on to others, and then having to revisit it again.

Work systematically through one possibility at a time

Use the 'answer patterns' to help

Whichever format an abstract reasoning test uses, each question will have two components:

- Question patterns – which present the problem that needs to be solved
- Answer patterns – which are the multiple choice answers that can be given

Some answer patterns will be related to the question patterns and others won't. The most obvious approach is to examine the question patterns and try to determine the link between them, which will then show which of the answer patterns are correct. A better approach, however, is to make full use of all the data you have available – the question patterns and the answer patterns. Knowing that some of the answer patterns will be right and some of them will be wrong means that you can look for differences between them.

A good starting point is to check if any of the answer patterns are obviously different from the other answer and question patterns. If you can spot the difference, it's often easy to identify the rule or rules at play. For example, one of the answer patterns may miss an element that is included in most of the other patterns, such as a black triangle, or a line of symmetry. Remember when using this technique that the 'odd' answer patterns may be different because they exclude or include elements.

PRACTICE QUESTIONS

(answers can be found at the end of the chapter on page 416)

In the rest of this chapter we give you a number of examples of abstract reasoning questions to try out, together with correct answers and the logic used to solve the question. We have rated the questions as easy, moderate and hard. This will help you to get a sense of which questions or question formats you find easiest or most difficult and to plan your practice accordingly.

In turn, the practice examples will cover:

- Series-based formats
- Category-based formats

Series

In each of these practice questions there are eight patterns. The four patterns that run along the top are the 'question patterns'. The four patterns in the row beneath are the multiple choice 'answer patterns' which are labelled A, B, C and D. To answer the question correctly you need to identify which one of the answer patterns in the bottom row continues the series in the top row.

(...sy)

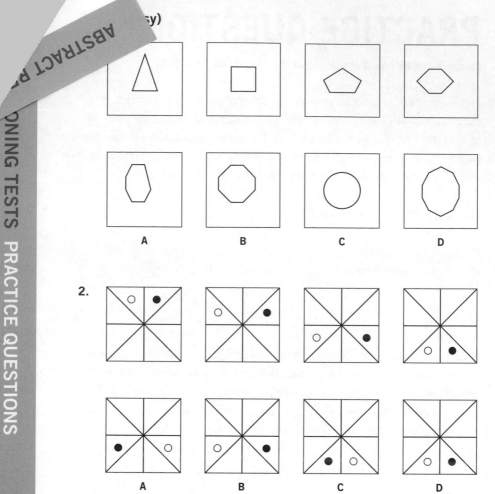

2.

3.

4.

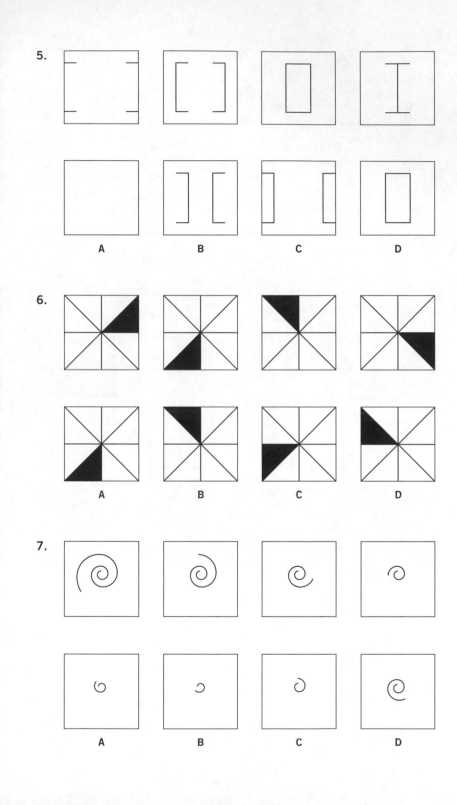

Series (moderate)

8.

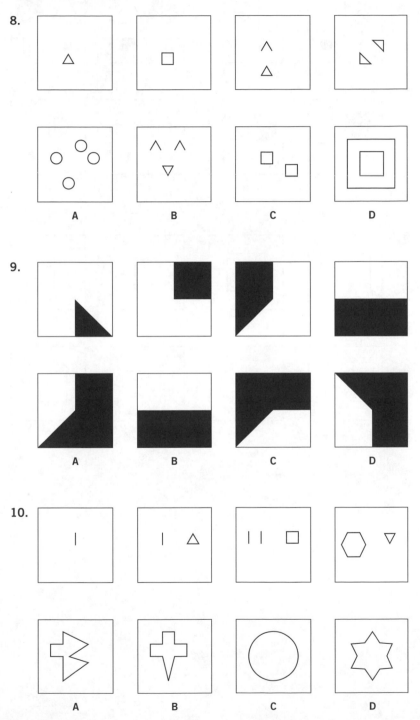

11.

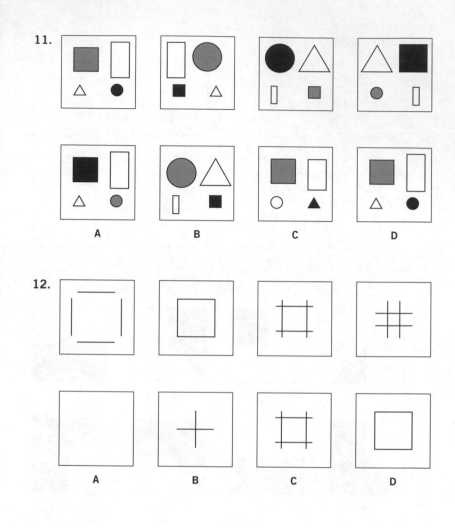

12.

13.

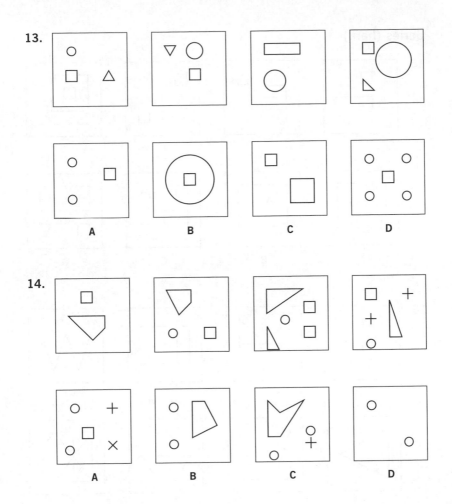

14.

Series (hard)

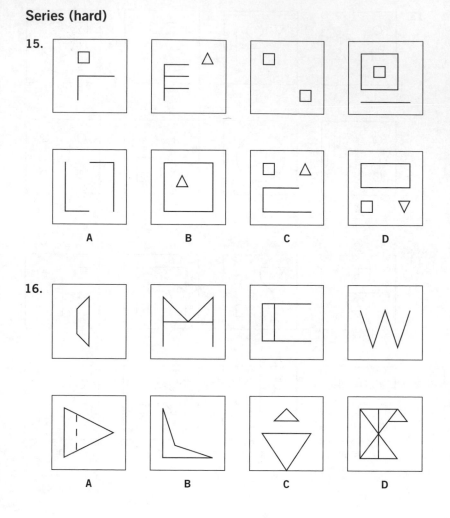

17.

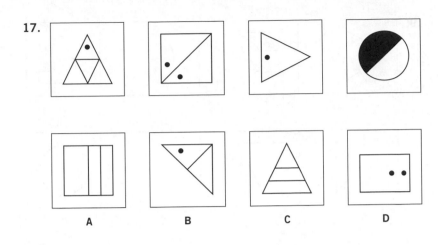

A   B   C   D

18.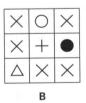

A   B   C   D

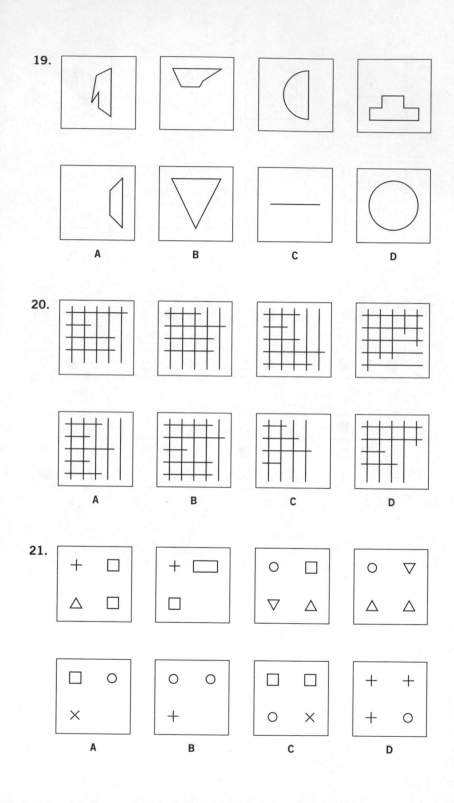

19.

A   B   C   D

20.

A   B   C   D

21.

A   B   C   D

Categories

The four patterns that run along the top are the 'question patterns'. The four patterns in the row beneath are the multiple choice 'answer patterns', which are labelled A, B, C and D. The question patterns always have at least one characteristic in common. To answer each question correctly, you need to identify which two of the answer patterns shares that same characteristic.

Categories (easy)

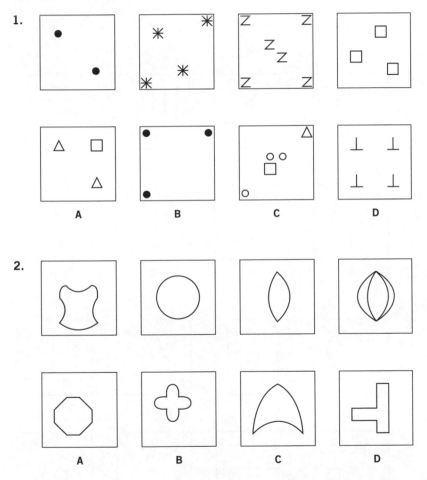

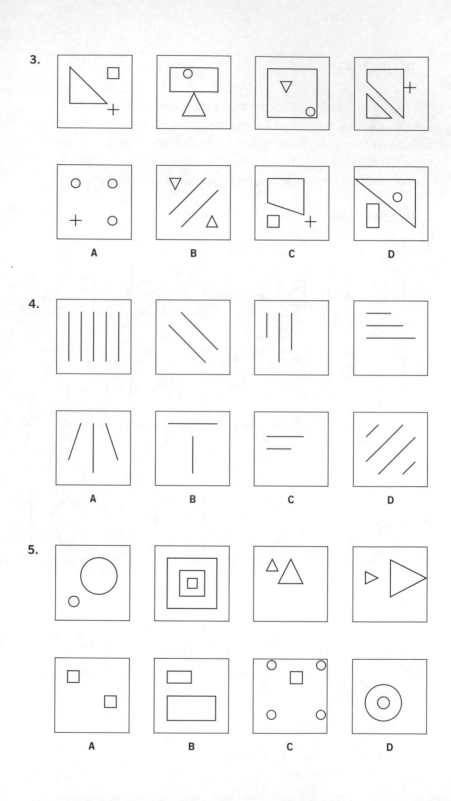

6.

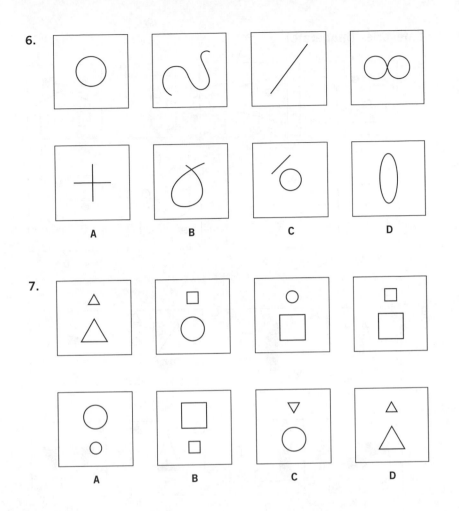

7.

Categories (moderate)

8.

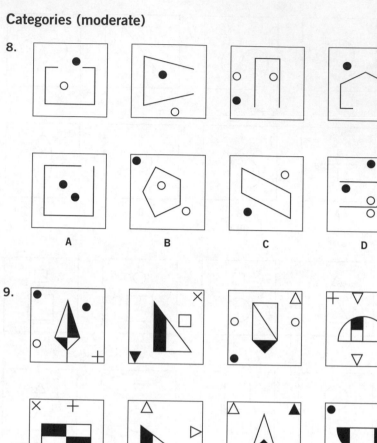

9.

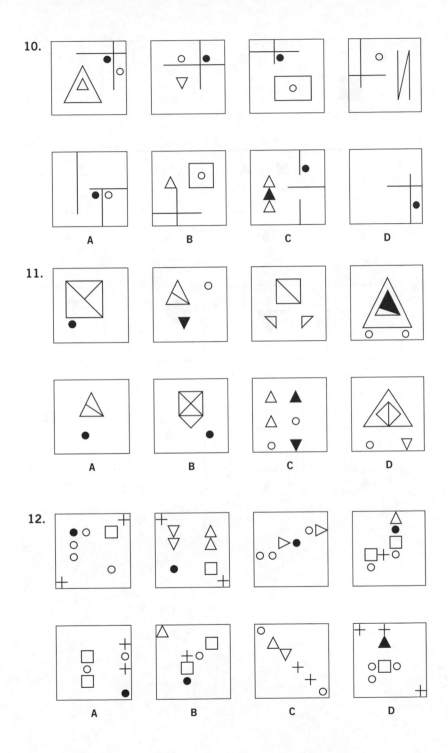

10.

11.

12.

A   B   C   D

13.

14.

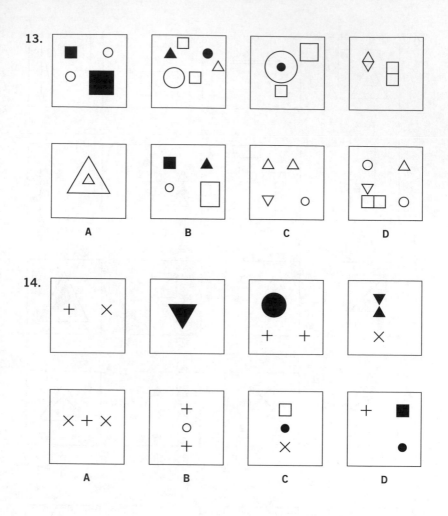

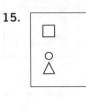

Categories (hard)

15.

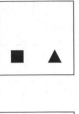
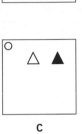
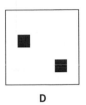

A   B   C   D

16.

A   B   C   D

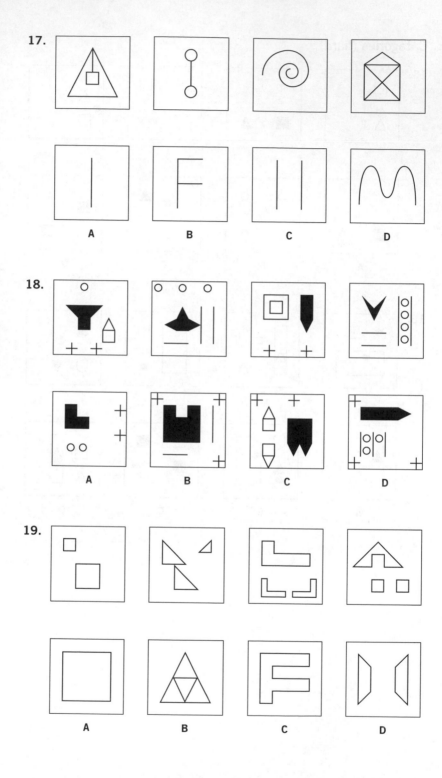

17.

18.

19.

20.

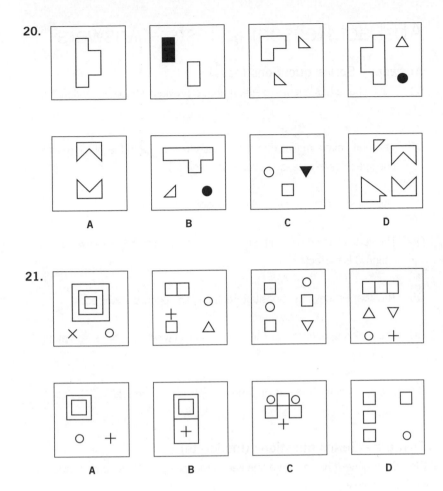

A   B   C   D

21.

A   B   C   D

Abstract Reasoning Tests – Answers

Answers – Series questions (easy)

Q1   Each shape has one more side than the previous shape, so option A is correct.

Q2   The white circle moves one space anti-clockwise and the black moves one space clockwise, so option C is correct.

Q3   The objects follow the triangle, so option B is correct.

Q4   The vertical line moves right and the horizontal line moves down, so option C is correct.

Q5   The shapes move in opposite directions, so option B is correct.

Q6   The dark segment moves three spaces clockwise each time, so option C is correct.

Q7   The spiral gets shorter each time, so option C is correct.

Answers – Series questions (moderate)

Q8   Each pattern has an extra line each time, so option B is correct as it has seven lines.

Q9   The black area grows by one-eighth and the pattern rotates 90 degrees anti-clockwise, so option D is correct.

Q10   The shape on the left of each pattern has the same number of lines as all of the shapes in the previous pattern combined. So option A is correct as it has nine lines.

Q11   The shapes rotate anti-clockwise, the patterns rotate clockwise, and the shapes on the top are always larger, so option D is correct.

Q12   The four lines gradually converge, so option B is correct.

Q13 The circle gets bigger each time, so option B is correct.

Q14 The number of symmetrical shapes increases by one each time, so option A is correct.

Answers – Series questions (hard)

Q15 Each pattern has one more line than the previous pattern, so option C is correct as it comprises 10 lines.

Q16 The line of symmetry in each pattern alternates between horizontal and vertical, so option A is correct as it has a horizontal line of symmetry.

Q17 The line of symmetry rotates 45 degrees clockwise, starting with a vertical line of symmetry for the first pattern, so option C is correct as it has a vertical (180 degrees) line of symmetry.

Q18 An extra 'X' is added each time, so option B is correct.

Q19 The longest line of each shape rotates 90 degrees anti-clockwise, so option A is correct.

Q20 The number of times that two lines cross increases by one each time, so option B is correct.

Q21 The number of horizontal lines decreases by one each time, so option A is correct.

Answers – Categories questions (easy)

Q1 Each pattern is made up of identical shapes, so options B and D are correct.

Q2 Each pattern is made up of curved lines, so options B and C are correct.

Q3 Each pattern contains a triangle, so options B and D are correct.

Q4 The lines in each pattern are always parallel, so options C and D are correct.

Q5 The shapes in each pattern get bigger, so options B and D are correct.

Q6 Each shape contains only one line, so options B and D are correct.

Q7 In each pattern the largest shape is at the bottom, so options C and D are correct.

Answers – Categories questions (moderate)

Q8 Each pattern has a shape which is 'open', so options A and D are correct.

Q9 Each pattern has a shape or symbol in one corner with another shape or symbol diagonally opposite, so options A and D are correct. Notice how many other shapes there are to distract your attention.

Q10 Each pattern contains lines that cross, so options B and D are correct.

Q11 Each pattern contains four triangles, so options C and D are correct.

Q12 Each pattern contains a black circle, so options A and B are correct.

Q13 In each pattern there is two of every shape, so options A and D are correct.

Q14 None of the shapes are 'hollow', so options A and D are correct.

Answers – Categories questions (hard)

Q15 The shapes in each pattern only occupy one half of the box, so options A and C are correct.

Q16 Each pattern contains a vowel, so options B and D are correct. Note that most abstract reasoning questions are designed so that they can be solved without any prior knowledge (e.g. about vowels and consonants), although this is not always the case.

Q17 Each pattern can be drawn without going over the same line twice, or taking the pencil off the paper, so options A and D are correct.

Q18 All of the black shapes in each pattern have a vertical line of symmetry, so options B and C are correct.

Q19 All of the patterns contain at least one right angle, so options A and C are correct.

Q20 Each pattern contains eight right-angles, so options C and D are correct.

Q21 Each pattern contains three squares, so options B and C are correct.

IN A NUTSHELL

In abstract reasoning tests, each question works by following a particular rule or set of rules.

- The key to answering abstract reasoning questions correctly is identifying the 'rules' that are being used.
- Remember that the rules can go from the tangible (e.g. the number of shapes) through to the very abstract (e.g. patterns that can only be drawn by taking your pencil off the paper, or going over the same line twice!).
- Use the 'answer patterns' as well as the 'question patterns' to identify the rules by spotting the odd one out.
- Don't become overwhelmed by complex patterns – focus on just one hypothesis at a time.

24 KNOWLEDGE AND SKILLS TESTS

In this chapter you will be introduced to knowledge and skills tests that are sometimes used by employers. You will understand:

■ The differences between knowledge and skills tests

■ The most common types of knowledge and skills tests

■ How to perform at your best in these tests

What are tests of knowledge and skills?

The three most common types of ability tests are numerical, verbal and abstract reasoning, which are covered in Chapters 21, 22 and 23. Although they are much less common, you might come across other types of psychometric tests designed to measure specific knowledge and skills. Remember to always ask the recruiter what kind of test you will be taking!

Tests of knowledge

Tests of knowledge measure how much information, or expertise, a candidate has about a specific business area.

Tests of knowledge include:

- Mechanical comprehension
- Book-keeping and payroll
- Linguistics (e.g. ability to speak and understand a foreign language such as German or Mandarin)
- Computer programming and website design

A knowledge test will include multiple-choice or 'yes/no' questions about specific aspects of a business area. An example is given below.

International Financial Reporting Standards (IFRS) financial statements consist of which of the following?

Item	Yes	No
A Statement of Financial Position		
A comprehensive income statement		
Either a statement of changes in equity (SOCE) or a statement of recognised income or expense (SORIE)		
Receipts for expenses		
The home address of the chief finance officer		
A cashflow statement or statement of cashflows		
Notes, including a summary of the significant accounting policies		

Unlike other psychometric tests, knowledge tests are very specific in that they focus on a specialist area of knowledge or expertise. As a result, the answers cannot easily be guessed. However, unlike other tests we have described, the information that these tests deal with is learnable, given sufficient time.

Tests of skill

Tests of skill measure how well a candidate can execute a certain task. Skills that employers may wish to test include:

- **Emotional intelligence** – the ability to identify and understand emotions.
- **Spatial awareness** – the ability to understand the relative position and rotation of objects.
- **Touch-typing** – the ability to type quickly and accurately use the touch-typing technique.

For example, given three pages of handwritten notes, or a 20-minute recording of a meeting, how quickly and accurately can a candidate type this information? An emotional intelligence test presents pictures and written scenarios and requires candidates to identify the emotions (or the most appropriate emotions) given the picture shown or the situation described. See the example below.

Simon is about to meet his new line manager for the first time. As he knocks to enter the office, Simon can hear him shouting angrily down the telephone. To what extent will Simon feel the following?

	Not at all		Moderately		Very strongly
	1	2	3	4	5
Anxious					
Angry					
Self-conscious					
Relieved					

This question is about understanding emotions – recognising which emotions are most likely to occur in different situations. In this question we would expect Simon to feel anxious and, as a result, somewhat self-conscious, although he is unlikely to feel relieved or angry. Let's look at another example.

Alice is about to give a presentation at a conference where many of the delegates are potential customers. How helpful will the following emotions be?

	Not helpful at all		Somewhat helpful		Very helpful
	1	2	3	4	5
Apprehension					
Acceptance					
Joy					
Vigilance					
Surprise					
Boredom					
Serenity					

In this question, we can expect positive emotions such as joy to be helpful, along with some degree of nervousness which will provide the necessary urgency and adrenaline! Less helpful will be emotions that can serve to inhibit or distract, such as surprise and boredom. To see other examples of emotional intelligence questions, visit the Emotional Intelligence & MSCEIT 2, 3, 4 website (www.emotionaliq.org/MSCEITExamples.htm).

Remember to always ask the recruiter what kind of test you will be taking.

Unlike the tests described in chapters 21, 22 and 23, which are used by recruiters for a wide variety of roles and industries, knowledge and skill tests tend to be used in more specific circumstances and within specific industries. For example, we worked with a telecoms business to develop a skills test for recruiting call centre staff. The test simulated the computer systems that the staff used when taking customer calls. The company wanted to select candidates who were able to use Information Technology effectively to provide excellent customer service. Candidates who took the test were shown how to use the simulated computer system. They then received calls from assessors, who were acting as customers. Using the test the company was able to assess how well candidates navigated the computer system to find the relevant information, and how accurately and quickly they relayed it.

Tips for top scores

Practice

Like all skills, we can improve our abilities – and therefore our scores in the knowledge and skills types of test – through practice. If you are considering a career which has specific skill requirements, think about activities that you can practise, which will develop your skills. This could involve at-work tasks or social activities such as volunteering or sports.

Make full use of free resources

Aside from paid-for professional training courses, there are several excellent – and free – sources of information if you need to improve your knowledge in a specific area. The following list gives just some examples:

- iTunes U (www.apple.com/support/itunes_u/) – this service is provided as part of Apple's iTunes software and is free to download from the Apple website. From iTunes you can access sound recordings and accompanying course notes from a wide range of educational lectures and topics. These resources are provided by many leading universities including Harvard, Yale, Stanford, Oxford and Cambridge.
- Open Yale Courses (http://oyc.yale.edu) – this website is hosted by Yale University and includes course materials and videos of lectures on a range of introductory courses.
- Google Scholar beta (http://scholar.google.co.uk) – the Google scholar website searches many journals and peer-reviewed articles based on the key words you enter. Although some of the content is restricted access, for example because it is sold by publishers, look for PDF format articles that are downloadable for free. Let's say you want to learn about the Prince2 project management methodology. Typing 'Prince2' into Google Scholar returns a few books and citations, but the fifth link (at the time of writing) is a free-access PDF document titled 'Understanding Prince2'. At 247 pages, it should be enough to give you a thorough introduction!

IN A NUTSHELL

For certain jobs that require specific knowledge and skills, potential employers can ask you to take a test that examines your existing knowledge and skills in that area. Remember that:

- Tests of knowledge ask very specific questions about an area of expertise, such as financial reporting, web design or project management methodology.
- Tests of skill measure how well something can be done, such as recognising emotions or touch-typing.
- Knowledge and skills can be improved through practice – take advantage of freely available online resources, work-based projects and social activities.

25 PERSONALITY AND PREFERENCE TESTS

As well as measures of specific ability such as numerical and verbal reasoning, it is now common for organisations to include measures of personality as part of their selection processes. So what are they trying to discover about you by using such tests? In this chapter we will:

■ Explain what these tests are trying to measure and how these tests are used by organisations

■ Give you the chance to rate yourself on some of the main personality dimensions

■ Help you to build your self-awareness

■ Explain different response formats and the main tests you can expect to encounter

What personality and preference tests measure

As mentioned in Chapter 20, personality and preference tests are based on the idea that there are elements of our character, personality, habits or work style that are relatively stable across our life, and that these have some bearing on how effectively we will perform in a job. So, for example, personality tests try to explore qualities such as:

- How well are you likely to work as part of a team?
- Do you have a strong preference for independence and autonomy or do you prefer to work collaboratively?
- Are you extraverted and talkative or do you prefer quiet time in which to reflect?
- Are you the big-picture thinker who gets frustrated by detail or are you structured and a perfectionist?
- Are you an analytical problem-solver who likes data or are you a creative and imaginative problem-solver?
- Do you prefer to work in a focused way, concentrating on one thing at a time, or do you value flexibility and the chance to multi-task?

These are the kinds of 'preferences' that personality tests are trying to get at.

There are important differences between personality tests and ability tests. Perhaps the most important difference is that preference tests do not have an objectively 'right' answer; however, employers would not be using them if they did not think that they provided information that helps them to differentiate between people who are more or less suited to a particular role. This said, in general you should not worry about answering questions in the way that you think they want – there are dangers in doing this. It also means that for personality tests there is only one top tip, namely – BE YOURSELF!

ASSESSING PERSONALITY

When employers are recruiting, they are often just as worried about making a mistake and getting the wrong person – someone who just won't fit in – as they are about selecting the best person for the job. When we talk to employers, they usually have a broad idea about the kinds of personal characteristics that they think a given job requires, but they also have a view about the kind of person who is unlikely to do well. For example, in a recent project we worked with a large retailer to identify the key attributes needed by its managers. Just as important as any specific experience or knowledge was their approach to customer service and their approach to working with their colleagues. While they wanted people who were commercially competitive, they certainly did not want people who would be selfish at the expense of their team mates or at the expense of customer service. They felt that getting this wrong would be a bigger risk than any particular knowledge that a new manager might be missing. For this employer, assessing a potential recruit's personality, style or preferences is a way of helping to manage this risk.

Personality tests are based on your self-report; in other words, the interpretation of your 'style' that they give can only be as accurate as your responses to the questions. (There is no evidence for so-called 'objective' measures of personality, such as interpretation of handwriting or ink blots. You should be suspicious of any organisation that uses them.)

Being yourself

For some of us this is easier said than done. The reason is that some of us are just more self-aware than others and find it easier to answer questions about how we would respond 'on average' or about our 'typical' preferences or ways of responding to certain situations.

Take a question like the following one – it is quite typical of the kind of question you find in personality tests:

'In social situations I usually prefer to wait for others to approach me rather than actively joining the conversation'

Here comes the usual multiple-choice response format:

1. Strongly agree
2. Agree
3. Neither agree nor disagree
4. Disagree
5. Strongly disagree

Now, suppose you answer 'strongly disagree': in other words you feel you **are** the kind of person who quickly goes up to other people and starts chatting to them. But are you right? How much insight do you have to your behaviour in situations like this? Is it something you have thought about? What if sometimes you do, and sometimes you don't? What if it depends on the kind of social situation or the kind of people involved?

Good test designers go to a lot of trouble to create questions that people will be able to relate to and that they will find relatively easy to answer. However, they depend on your ability to answer such questions 'on average' or in terms of what you would typically do. This in turn depends on your ability to look at your own behaviour fairly objectively. So, how can you tell how self-aware you are?

One way is to ask yourself or your friends the questions overleaf; rate yourself – or get them to rate you – on a 10-point scale.

How open to new experiences am I – am I typically quite adventurous or more cautious in the kinds of situations I seek out?

Cautious   Adventurous

1   2   3   4   5   6   7   8   9   10

How conscientious am I – am I usually pretty organised, punctual and disciplined in the way I go about things or am I typically more free-wheeling in my approach?

Free-wheeling   Conscientious

1   2   3   4   5   6   7   8   9   10

How extraverted am I – am I usually a very sociable person, seeking out people and being chatty, or am I usually more reserved, quiet and needing time on my own?

Reserved   Extraverted

1   2   3   4   5   6   7   8   9   10

How agreeable am I – would people describe me as kind, thoughtful and considerate or am I seen as more objective, critical and 'tell it like it is'?

Critical   Agreeable

1   2   3   4   5   6   7   8   9   10

How anxious am I – am I the kind of person who is seldom stressed or nervous, or am I more emotional, showing my feelings and often working under a lot of pressure?

Calm   Anxious

1   2   3   4   5   6   7   8   9   10

If you and your friends' ratings are within a couple of points of each other, you probably have pretty good self-awareness. This means that when you fill out a personality test, the results will be in line with what you would expect. If there are significant differences between your ratings and your friends' ratings, this suggests that you might have some 'blind spots' in terms of your self-assessment. This exercise in itself will help you to re-evaluate and re-calibrate your perception of yourself.

How the test results are used

Unlike ability tests, personality tests are harder to use to predict work performance, for the simple reason that there is often more than one 'right way' to do a job well. Thus it isn't easy to say what kinds of personality characteristics will predict effective job performance. For example, suppose a recruiter is looking for sales representatives; you might think it would make sense for them to look for extraverted, sociable, talkative people who will have the 'gift of the gab' and will relate well to customers. This is fine in theory, but in reality, if that person is going to have to spend much of the working day alone in a car, driving from customer to customer, what is that going to do for their motivation and effectiveness?

Remember that an extravert is someone who needs people, who likes sociable working environments. A well-advised recruiter might recognise this and avoid people who are too extraverted. You, on the other hand, as an applicant, might be assuming that they will value extraverted tendencies and, as a result might try to enhance this aspect of your style as you fill out a personality test. This is why we say – BE YOURSELF. It seldom pays to second-guess the test or what an employer is looking for.

Personality tests are quite expensive for employers to use because the test publishers and the British Psychological Society insist that people should be trained to use and interpret them. So how – and – why do businesses use them?

Most business psychologists would not recommend that people be selected for jobs on the basis of personality tests alone. More typical uses for personality tests as part of selection are given below.

Screening

Some employers will use questionnaires about motivation and preferences as a way of sifting out people who they think will be unsuited to a particular task. They might, for example, disregard the applicants who are highly strategic and conceptual for a role which is operational, repetitive and administrative.

If you fill out such tests honestly you will be doing yourself a favour as you would be unlikely to enjoy or perform well in any kind of work which requires you to behave in ways that are completely contrary to your preferences.

Employers who use tests in this way are running the risk of recruiting 'clones' rather than people who can grow and develop in their business. However, be aware that they will usually be basing this practice on past experience of the kind of people who thrive or who flourish or wither in a particular role.

Fitting in

Sometimes employers will be looking for an individual to fit in to a particular team or work group. At senior level this might be a specific search for someone strategic to balance the skills of a team that is very operational, or for someone very creative to enhance a team that is very practical. The personality test will never be the only source of information they are using but it will often be used to back up other data. (See the section 'Additional information to support other selection techniques' below.)

Worrying signs

For some roles, again usually at middle to senior level, the employer might be looking for signs of any extreme characteristics – sometimes called de-railing characteristics – such as extreme competitiveness or extreme non-compliance with rules and procedures. People with such 'dark side' characteristics often do quite well in organisations – up to a point. This is because it can make them very entrepreneurial and willing to take risks. However, at some point these extremes usually get them – and the organisation – into trouble. An employer seeing signs of these characteristics will usually want to explore the tendencies at an in-depth interview. (See 'Integrity testing' below.)

Additional information to support other selection techniques

This is the most common – and recommended – way of using personality measures. Typically, the results from a personality questionnaire will be used to support an interview, or will be added to all the other information the employer might have based on your CV, or from your performance at a presentation or from your attendance at an assessment centre.

So, for example, here you are, a well-qualified and plausible candidate for a job, you have been selected for an interview and asked to complete a personality test before you attend; how are they going to use it? The most common way is for the person who has interpreted the test to identify particular areas they want to explore with you at the interview – sometimes in person or sometimes by passing questions to the interviewer. It might be, for example, that your test profile gives a picture of you as someone who is particularly task focused and a bit of a perfectionist in your work style. While this won't rule you out (after all you have been selected for interview!) the interviewer might want to ask you about how this characteristic actually shows itself at work. Do you manage it or do you get too hung up on detail? Can you delegate or does your perfectionism mean that you try to do everything yourself? Your self-awareness comes into play again here; it will reassure the interviewer if you recognise the tendency in yourself and can show that you have developed options for mitigating any down sides.

Case study – knowing me, knowing you

Most employers who use psychometrics for middle or senior level recruitment will be particularly interested in the 'fitting in' and 'worrying signs' aspects of a potential recruit's personality. In a recent assignment we worked with an engineering employer where it was essential that a new technical specialist – Director of Research and Development – would be able to quickly fit in to an established senior team. By using a personality measure they were able to identify that the applicant with the best technical qualifications had strong preferences for independent working and for a great deal of autonomy in terms of setting the business direction. Armed with this information, the final interview panel was able to probe these areas in order to assess the difficulty this person might have in fitting in to a very cohesive team. In the end both parties agreed that the 'fit' with this particular role was not good but were able to discuss alternative jobs where this person's strengths would be better used.

Types of personality test

There is much literature on personality and personality measurement which we won't trouble you with here. (Wikipedia is a good starting place if you want to know more.) It is useful, however, to know about the main characteristics of the tests you are likely to come across.

HONESTY *IS* THE BEST POLICY

Can you 'fake' a personality test so that you appear to have characteristics that are not like you? The answer is; yes you can; but it is difficult, you will usually be caught out and ultimately it is pointless! The personality questionnaires most frequently used as part of selection procedures all have sophisticated measures of 'response bias' built in to them – psychologists' speak for 'lying through your teeth'!

In a selection situation it is understandable that people want to present themselves in the best possible light, and tests will take account of this, but they are also clever at assessing whether this is being taken to an extreme, whether there are inconsistencies in the way you respond to questions when they are put in several different ways, and whether you are trying to please the tester rather than tell the truth. In the old days, these used to be called 'lie scales' and were based on your responses to statements such as:

- I am always on time for meetings
- I have never stolen anything
- I sometimes tell lies

(We've always thought that this last item was a little paradoxical!)

These days, measures of response bias are a lot more subtle and you will tie yourself in knots trying to unravel them if you are aiming to respond in anything other than an honest way. So – BE YOURSELF.

Trait tests and type tests

Most of the tests you encounter in selection situations are, in the psychometric jargon, trait tests. This means that they are aiming to assess where you sit on a number of scales that are deemed relevant to your work performance; in other words where you sit in relation to relevant personality characteristics, habits or preferences.

Another category of measures are called 'type' tests; while similar in format, these tests try to assign you to a particular 'type'; in other words to group you with other people who have similar characteristics, values or preferences.

TRAIT vs TYPE

You *have* a trait (among many others) but you *fit* a type.

The most commonly used *type* test is the MBTI (Myers Briggs Type Indicator). It assigns you to one of 16 'boxes' based on your scores relating to four basic preferences. We do not recommend *type* tests for selection purposes; they are best reserved for training, development and for building self-awareness.

For the rest of this chapter we will focus on trait tests. Trait tests contain items (questions) that are relevant to work situations. Broadly, these usually cluster into questions about your:

- Thinking style
- Preferences for interacting with people
- Style in terms of delivering tasks
- Emotions

Examples of traits (characteristics) or dimensions that are included in tests are:

- Operational versus strategic
- Collaborative versus independent
- Structured versus flexible
- Obedient versus challenging
- Conceptual versus practical

- Ambitious versus contented
- Controlling versus democratic

By asking you to answer a number of questions – usually several questions per trait – the testers are trying to see what your personality profile looks like. That is, the pattern that you show in terms of all the traits. So, using the example traits listed above, a profile might look something like this:

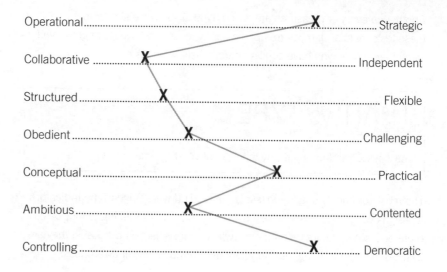

Operational	Strategic
Collaborative	Independent
Structured	Flexible
Obedient	Challenging
Conceptual	Practical
Ambitious	Contented
Controlling	Democratic

Test designers try to make sure that the scales are relatively independent of each other. By this we mean that you can be high, low, or average on any of the scales *regardless* of the other scales. So, the fact that you might score high on *strategic* should not influence whether you score high or low on *obedient*. (In practice, however, personality test scales often do have some small correlation with each other.)

Most of the best tests are built on the foundation of something called 'Big five' personality theory. You have already met the big five – they are the basis for the short self-completion test on page 322. Briefly, these are the five most consistent and well-researched fundamental personality characteristics that underpin a lot of our behaviour:

Openness – this refers to how open you are to new experiences, new ideas and change as well as to your intellectual curiosity.

Conscientiousness – this refers to your tendency to be organised, structured, detail conscious and reliable in meeting commitments.

Extraversion – this refers to your sociability, gregariousness, need for attention, tendency to be talkative and enthusiastic.

Agreeableness – this refers to how empathetic, understanding and keen to please you are, as opposed to tough minded and dominant.

Emotional stability – this refers to how confident, stable and emotionally cool you are as opposed to anxious and more prone to mood swings.

As ever, there are dangers in making value judgements about which ends of these scales are 'good' or 'bad'. Neuroticism in particular comes with a lot of value 'baggage', so much so that the scale is often called something else, such as confidence. When you ask people to 'fake good' in completing these tests they usually try to raise their extraversion and lower their neuroticism score but, for the reasons we have already seen, there are dangers in this. If, for example, you are somewhat stress prone, why would you seek to 'fool' an employer into giving you a job where you might continually be under pressure! So, if you try to 'fake' a low score on such anxiety or confidence scales you might not be doing yourself a favour.

Another reason for not trying to 'massage' your personality profile is that skilled interpreters of any psychometric test will not be looking at any one scale in isolation; they will be looking at combinations of factors. For example, someone who is low on conscientiousness and high on agreeableness might still be relied on to deliver because they will not want to let people down.

INTERPRETING PROFILES

The various preferences or habits we have do not operate in isolation to influence our behaviour; our traits interact with each other. For example, in terms of the Big 5 characteristics described on page 441, someone who has a strong preference to be highly conscientious and rule following, who is highly agreeable and eager to please and who is also quite anxious, may make life difficult for themselves by taking on too much, by trying to deliver it somewhat perfectionistically and by becoming stressed when they can't meet all their obligations. At the same time the introverted but highly conscientious person need not necessarily become isolated if they recognise communication as an important part of their job description. As with all interpretations, the profile can show you the building blocks of someone's personality but only by speaking with them can you flesh this out to understand the real impact on their behaviour.

The kinds of personality measures you are most likely to encounter in selection situations will drill down from these scales into more specifically work-related characteristics. For example, agreeableness might be broken down into scales relating to autocratic versus democratic management styles, or how willing you are to take unpopular decisions.

For more details, or indeed to try out a short Big five test, visit the 'Big five personality test' website (www.outofservice.com/bigfive/) or the Signal Patterns website (www.signalpatterns.com), where you can find out how you score in terms of these characteristics. No harm in continuing to develop that self-awareness!

Reputable trait tests include:

- Occupational Personality Questionnaire (OPQ)
- Saville Consulting Wave
- Hogan Personality Inventory (HPI)
- Hogan Development Survey (HDS)
- NEO PI-R
- California Psychological Inventory (CPI)

Enter these names into your favourite search engine for more information. While there are lots of other tests, of varying quality and validity, these are the ones you are most likely to encounter.

Integrity testing

One category of personality tests focuses specifically on aspects of our personality that relate to honesty and integrity. These typically follow the standard test format but concentrate on questions about our attitudes to honesty, following rules and procedures, and about our emotions and proneness to stress.

The response bias scales in these tests are usually particularly sensitive, so again the best advice is to complete them as openly and as straightforwardly as you can.

Other measures on the market aim to explore some more extreme personality traits that research has shown to be related to career derailment or other performance problems at work. Sometimes referred to as 'dark side' characteristics, they are aspects of our 'style' or habits that we find hard to control when we are under pressure. Examples would include extreme stubbornness, perfectionism, risk taking or dominance. The HDS (mentioned above) is one example of such a measure.

Case study – managing the boss

We have already mentioned that employers are on the look out for 'worrying signs' in their recruitment processes and 'dark side' characteristics certainly provide these. Interestingly, however, many senior business leaders possess one or more dark side characteristics; for example extreme ambition or self confidence taken to the point that they find it hard to accept advice. In our experience the extent to which these characteristics represent assets or risks is often based on the resilience and indeed courage of the people working around them: again emphasising the importance of 'fit' when selecting people for senior teams. Another factor which can mitigate the risk of these characteristics is the degree of self awareness that the person shows: can they recognise those situations where their dark side characteristics might come into play and do something about it? We recently worked with a client where both of these safeguards were available and where the person in question was able to perform well.

Norming

Most of the best tests will have been tried out on a range of different people, in different jobs; this process is called 'norming'. In practice it means that an employer will not be comparing your scores with the scores of the general population, but with the scores of people in relevant comparison groups such as sales professionals, senior managers or graduates. This means that your profile or your position on a particular scale is based on how it compares with the relevant reference group and not with the general population. So, if you score 'low' on a scale relating to how ambitious you are, and the reference (or norm) group is senior managers, then this would probably mean that you are still averagely ambitious in relation to the general population but not in terms of comparison with a group of people who collectively score high in terms of ambition.

When you fill out the test or questionnaire you probably won't know which norm group is being used to provide the base line for your scores. Once again, the best advice is to be yourself rather than to answer questions in the way you think may be desirable.

Response formats

Personality tests are not usually timed (typically they take about 40 minutes). So familiarity with different response formats is much less of an issue than it is for tests of ability. However, there is no harm in being aware of the most common methods of responding.

The agree/disagree format

By far the most common response format is one where you are given a statement and then asked to indicate, using the scale provided, how much you agree or disagree with the statement. For example:

I enjoy making new friends

☐ Strongly agree
☐ Agree
☐ Don't know
☐ Disagree
☐ Strongly disagree

Most tests will encourage you to follow your gut reaction when answering the questions but it's worth pausing to think how true the statement is of you 'on average'.

Like you/not like you format

Another response format is one that 'forces' you to make choices about which ones of a series of statements are most or least like you. For example:

*For each of the statements below please indicate which **one** is most like you and which **one** is least like you. Only tick one statement in each column.*

I am the kind of person who prefers to:

	Most like me	Least like me
Work at a steady pace	☐	☐
Have a wide circle of friends	☐	☐
Have a lot of interests	☐	☐
Help people with their problems	☐	☐

This 'forced choice' format is designed to assess the relative strength of your preferences in relation to each other.

True/false format

One last format you might come across provides you – as usual – with a long list of statements, but this time you are asked to answer 'true' or 'false' to each item depending on which is most like you or which best represents your belief. For example:

	True	False
Most people are honest	☐	☐
I often feel sad	☐	☐
It is better to live life day by day	☐	☐
You should always tell people the truth	☐	☐

IN A NUTSHELL

This chapter has shown you some of the most commonly used personality and preference measures, how they are typically used and the response formats you can expect to encounter. To summarise our top tips for this chapter:

■ Be yourself.
■ Don't second-guess the test or the person who is interpreting the test; trying to give them what they want by massaging your answers will rarely pay off.
■ Think about your behaviour or your attitude 'on average' but otherwise don't worry about consistency. If you answer straightforwardly this will take care of itself.

26 PEFORMING AT YOUR BEST

This chapter is about what you can do to perform at the very best of your ability when taking a psychometric test. You will understand:

- How to develop a positive mindset

- How to get the environment right before taking a test – including having the right equipment

- Important test taking strategies such as the 'one-minute rule' and guessing wisely

- Your personal test taking style and how it could impact on your performance

Successful test taking

A key theme in this chapter is that it takes a long time to get significantly better at using numbers, understanding words or reasoning with abstract concepts. However, there are lots of reasons why people get lower test scores than they deserve.

In this chapter we explain, step by step, what you can do to avoid these pitfalls when taking psychometric tests so that your test score is your best score. Let's start with preparation and then move on to test taking.

Preparation

Becoming familiar with the various test formats

Becoming familiar with the 'look and feel' of psychometric tests, especially ability tests, is crucial. The vast majority of tests that you encounter will be in multiple-choice response format, having between four and eight possible answers to choose from. For online tests, you will be asked to check the appropriate box; for paper and pencil tests you will usually be asked to tick or shade a box on a separate answer sheet. It's always worth checking that you are putting your response in the right box. In the heat of the moment it is surprisingly easy to make a mistake, especially if you decide to skip a question, so keep checking.

It's always worth checking that you are putting your response in the right box.

Note that as well as possible answers, the options sometimes contain a 'Can't say' response (see Practice Questions). You should choose this option when the question cannot be answered from the information given; remember – it is a test of your logic and it is not meant to be an 'I don't know' option!

Make use of the websites given in Chapters 23–25, to familiarise yourself with the different question and response formats.

Practising core skills

Completing psychometric ability tests involves using skills that can be practised and improved. For example:

- Numerical tests – calculating percentages
- Verbal tests – understanding word meanings
- Abstract tests – identifying different types of rules (e.g. similarities and progressions)

Case study – Martin and percentages

Martin is due to sit a numerical reasoning test in two weeks. He knows that he will have to calculate percentages to answer some of the questions. Although he knows how percentages work, it is not a skill that he often uses. Martin wants to ensure that he is as quick and error-free as possible. He identifies and regularly practises different types of percentage calculations in the run-up to taking the test (the answers are at the end of this chapter):

1. Ordinary percentages – for example, finding 35% of 5,000.
2. Increase percentages – for example, finding the previous cost of a car when it is now £15,640, which is a 15% increase on the previous cost.
3. Missing percentages – for example, if 12 of the items on sale cost less than £100 and there are 40 items in total, working out what percentage of items cost less than £100.
4. Missing whole – for example, if 20% of sales are in France and there were 50,000 sales in France, working out the total number of sales.

For a few days or weeks – while the practice is still fresh in his mind – Martin can solve these percentage problems more quickly, accurately and confidently than he normally would. Also, because he has been practising using his calculator, he knows exactly which buttons to use.

The kinds of computation required in ability tests are relatively straightforward, and most people can answer these test questions if given enough time. However, the speed at which you complete them is important because this will affect the number of items you finish (hopefully all correctly) and so finally your score. As Martin in the case study above found, practice increases speed and accuracy.

Positive mindset

Psychological research shows that emotion has an important influence on our performance. When we are very anxious or filled with self-doubt, distracting thoughts are triggered, which take our attention away from what we are doing. These are known as performance-inhibiting thoughts, or PITs.

Compare the impact of PITs to running an unwanted application on a computer. An unwanted application takes up valuable resources such as memory and processing time which then can't be used by the computer for other, more important, tasks. PITs have the same effect on test takers.

AVOID PERFORMANCE-INHIBITING THOUGHTS, OR PITS

- Notice how much quicker and more accurate you are as you become more practised.
- Remember that some questions are designed to be very difficult – you should not expect to answer every one.
- Remember that tests are designed to have very tight timings – you may not have time to fully consider all of the questions.
- Remind yourself why you are well suited to the job you are applying for – ideally hold two or three specific reasons in your mind.
- When we are in an optimistic mindset we are more likely to perform at our best.

Communicating disabilities

If you have a disability it is important to let employers know about this before you take a psychometric test – or any type of recruitment activity. This allows employers to consider making what are known as 'reasonable adjustments', which they are legally obliged to do for certain types of disability.

Test taking strategies

The environment

Once it is time to take the test there is some information you will be given upfront: you will be told how long the test lasts and you will be given some practice questions to complete. You might also be told how many questions there are in the test itself.

Before the test begins, it is important to check your environment. If you are completing a paper and pencil test make sure you:

- Can hear what the test administrator is saying.
- Have plenty of room – remember that you will have a question book, an answer book, rough paper, two pencils and possibly a calculator.
- Have the equipment listed above – this is usually provided by the administrator but we strongly advise you to bring your own calculator that you are fully familiar with.
- Know how to properly mark your answers in the answer sheet.
- Are comfortable and do not need a toilet break or a drink, etc.

If you are working online, make sure to check:

- That you will not be disturbed.
- That your laptop (if you are using one) is plugged into the mains.
- That your mouse or cursor control is working well.
- That you have paper and a pen or pencil available for making notes.
- That you have a calculator you are familiar with if you are completing a numerical reasoning test.
- That you are comfortable and do not need a toilet break or a drink, etc.

Timings

When you are told how long the test takes to complete note down what time you will finish. This allows you to easily check how long you have left at any point in time. Set a few simple 'check-in' points during the test. For example, if the test has 40 questions, check how you are progressing when you get to questions 10, 20 and 30. If you are halfway through the allotted time at question 15, then you know you'll need to speed-up.

The one-minute rule

If you are stuck on one question and you are losing time, remember not to panic. Instead, move on to the next question – it might suit you better. Most test scores are based on how many correct answers you have given. Read the case study below and compare John and Lisa's approach.

Case study – Effective time management while test taking

John is methodical and accurate whereas Lisa moves on when she gets stuck and guesses when she is about to run out of time. They both take a 10-question test with an eight-minute time limit.

Here is John's approach:

Question number	1	2	3	4	5	6	7	8	9	10
Time spent (in minutes and seconds)	0.31	0.25	2.26	0.49	2.55	0.52	0.02	0.00	0.00	0.00
Correct?	Yes	Yes	Yes	No	No	Yes	No	No	No	No

Total score: 4 out of 10

As expected, John worked methodically through each question. But he spent more than half of the available time answering just two questions – questions 3 and 5. He did not finish question 7 and ran out of time before he could look at the last three questions.

Here is Lisa's approach:

Question number	1	2	3	4	5	6	7	8	9	10
Time spent	0.29	0.33	0.44	0.55	0.51	0.47	0.51	1.15	0.42	0.53
Correct?	Yes	No	No	Yes	No	Yes	Yes	Yes	No	Yes

Total score: 6 out of 10

As she worked through the test Lisa realised that question 3 was very difficult and moved on to the next question. She did the same for question 5. Although she didn't answer these difficult questions correctly, she did leave herself much more time than John did to answer questions 7, 8 and 10, which were all relatively easy. She also realised that question 9 was very difficult and tried to correctly guess the answer. Overall, she was much more flexible than John in completing the test and scored two points more than him.

Lisa followed one of our test taking tips – the one-minute rule. If you are nowhere near answering a question after one minute then move on to the next. Remember, this doesn't mean that you should abandon a question that you are about to finish! The one-minute rule is about recognising when you are stuck and moving on in good time.

Guessing wisely

There are two reasons why you might need to guess the answer to a question on a psychometric ability test:

- You can't work out the correct answer
- You do not have enough time left to work out the answer fully.

When you do need to guess, remember that it is best not to guess randomly. Let's look at another case study.

Case study – Smart guessing in psychometric tests (1)

Kieran is taking a numerical reasoning test. One of the questions has five possible answers and only one is correct.

Credit-Flex is a loans company specialising in debt consolidation. It allows customers to pool all of their debts so that only one monthly interest payment is needed. Credit-Flex customers have loans with an average value of £5,150. Every month, customers are charged 9.25% interest on the value of their loan. Based on the average loan value, how much money in interest payments will Credit-Flex receive this month for every 1,000 customers?

A	B	C	D	E
£51,125	£476,375	£610,070	£489,875	£501,700

If Kieran makes a random guess, he has just a one in five chance of being right. By taking just a few seconds longer, Kieran can estimate the answer without performing the whole calculation. By quickly reading the question he realises that he can estimate the answer by finding 10% of £5,000, which is £500, and multiplying this by 1,000. In a few seconds he has worked out that the answer is close to £500,000. This immediately excludes options A and C which are too far away from this estimate to be correct. Without taking the time to find the precise answer he has narrowed it down to three options. In doing so, he has increased his chances of guessing correctly from one question in every five, to one question in every three.

You can use the same rules for abstract reasoning tests. Look at the next case study about a 'category'-based question (see Chapter 23 for more details about these).

Case study – Smart guessing in psychometric tests (2)

Raj is taking an abstract reasoning test as shown below.

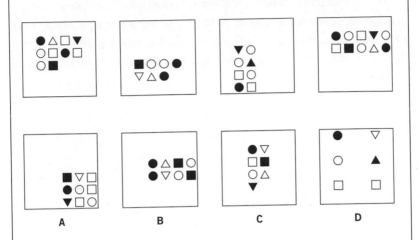

A   B   C   D

In this question there are two 'rules' in operation. The first, and most obvious, is that all of the shapes are closely grouped together. The second, less obvious rule is that there are two white shapes between every black shape, as you move from left to right and then down. From the four possible answers two are correct and two are incorrect. Raj has reached this question in the test, but he has less than 20 seconds before the time runs out, so he has to guess. One random guess gives Raj a 50% chance of choosing one of the correct options. But by spotting and using the first rule in this question – that the shapes are grouped closely together – Raj can guess smartly. He can see that option D is different from all of the other patterns because the shapes are spaced out. If he discounts this option, it gives him a 66% chance of getting one right answer.

Remember – when you need to guess don't act randomly! There are often one or two options that are obviously incorrect with just a cursory reading of the question.

Know your test taking style

What is your test taking style? And will it help you to pass a psychometric test, or might it reduce your chances? Whether you have taken psychometric tests before or if your only experience is taking school or university exams, use the questionnaire opposite to better understand your test taking style. Simply read each statement and tick the box that best describes your approach. Complete the four sections and read our analysis and recommendations to help improve your test taking.

Test taking style questionnaire 1

		Strongly disagree	Disagree	Neither agree nor disagree	Agree	Strongly agree
A1	I feel that if I start answering a question I have to get it right					
A2	I am the sort of person who double checks my answers					
A3	I hate answering a question if I'm not sure what the correct answer is					
A4	Most people take less care over their work than I do					

If you **mostly agreed or strongly agreed** with the statements then you are likely to have a perfectionist test taking style that prioritises accuracy over speed. You should bear the following points in mind:

- Your natural tendency will be to preserve and get each question correct – so if you get stuck, remember to move on!
- Remember that some questions are designed to be very difficult – it is not unusual or a 'failure' if you don't know every answer.

If you **mostly disagreed or strongly disagreed** with the statements then you are likely to have an expedient test taking style that prioritises speed over accuracy. Consider the following points:

- Take care while considering which of the multiple-choice answers you select. The option that looks correct at the first glance can be incorrect.
- Make sure you know how to answer the test properly. For example, some tests require that you clearly mark a box next to your chosen multiple-choice option by completely blacking-out the appropriate box. If you are too hasty you may not indicate your choice clearly enough.

If your answers to the statements were mixed then you probably have a test taking style which balances a concern for accuracy with a willingness to work quickly.

Test taking style questionnaire 2

		Strongly disagree	Disagree	Neither agree nor disagree	Agree	Strongly agree
B1	The thought of completing a timed test makes me feel sick with nerves					
B2	I often feel anxious before important events					
B3	Sometimes I lose sleep because I feel worried					
B4	I often expect things to go wrong					

If you **mostly agreed or strongly agreed** with the statements above you are likely to have an anxious test taking style. Consider the following points:

- Excessive nervousness is distracting and can prevent you from doing your best.
- Regular practice will help you feel better prepared and calmer.
- You are not supposed to get all of the questions right – don't panic if you can't answer one, just move on!

If you **mostly disagreed or strongly disagreed** with the statements then you are likely to have a calm test taking style. Remember that:

- You will get benefit from practising extensively before taking a psychometric test. Without sufficient impetus, you may underplay the need to practise.
- If you can combine your ability to stay calm and focused with an appropriate sense of urgency in completing psychometric tests, you will be well placed to perform to the best of your ability.

If your answers to the statements were mixed then you probably have a 'keyed-up' test taking style, where you will experience a degree of nervousness and adrenaline without being overly distracted by these feelings.

Test taking style questionnaire 3

	Strongly disagree	Disagree	Neither agree nor disagree	Agree	Strongly agree
C1	When I start a test, I rarely work out how long I have to answer each question				
C2	I find it hard to keep an eye on the time as I work through a test				
C3	I often get so engrossed in the test questions that I lose all track of time				
C4	I have been surprised that I ran out of time when completing a test				

If you **mostly agreed or strongly agreed** with the statements then you are likely to have an unsystematic test taking style. Consider the following points:

- When you are told how long the psychometric test takes to complete, note down what time you will finish. For example, if the test starts at 10.15 in the morning and takes 30 minutes to complete, write down 10.45. This allows you to easily check how long you have left at any point in time.
- Try setting a few simple 'check-in' points during the test. For example, if the test has 30 questions, check how you are progressing when you get to questions 10 and 20. If you are halfway through the allotted time at question 10, then you know you'll need to speed up.

If you **mostly disagreed or strongly disagreed** with the statements then you are likely to have a structured test taking style. Remember the following points:

- In your planning allow one minute at the end to guess any uncompleted questions.
- Use your systematic approach to your advantage – if you can't answer a question, but have narrowed down the right answer to two or three of the multiple-choice options, make a quick note of these. If you finish the other questions this will allow you to focus on fewer options, or, if you run out of time and need to guess, you will have a better chance of guessing correctly.

If your answers to the statements varied, you probably have a test taking style that balances a degree of structure with some impulsivity. If this is the case, take care to check timings and progress as you complete the test, but don't allow yourself to become distracted from the test questions.

Test taking style questionnaire 4

	Strongly disagree	Disagree	Neither agree nor disagree	Agree	Strongly agree
D1	I like to answer test questions in the order that they are given				
D2	I expect sufficient time to complete all of the questions in a test				
D3	When completing a test I will try to complete the question I have started before moving on				
D4	I expect that I should be able to answer any question in a test correctly				

If you **mostly agreed or strongly agreed** with the statements then you have a 'traditional' test taking style. You should bear the following points in mind:

- Psychometric tests are rarely designed to be completed in the allotted time. This is done to prevent a 'ceiling effect', where too many people answer all of the questions correctly. As well as working quickly, you should be prepared to guess if you start running out of time.
- Answer the easiest questions first – this stops you getting stuck on one difficult question and running out of time. You should be fully prepared to skip difficult questions.
- Don't be concerned if you can't solve a particular question. Some questions are designed to be very difficult as another method of preventing a 'ceiling effect'. If you take it as a sign of failure, you are likely to become flustered and distract yourself. Instead, realise that it is normal to find some questions that are too difficult.

If you **mostly disagreed or strongly disagreed** with the statements then you are likely to have a flexible test taking style. Remember the following point:

- To get the best from your approach you should ensure that you move between questions in a disciplined way, rather than leaving too many questions unfinished.

If your answers to the statements were mixed then you are likely to respond flexibly to some aspects of psychometric tests, while slipping into a more formal, linear style of responding at other times. Think about when the formal approach is most likely to happen – perhaps when you are nervous, or feeling under pressure? Whatever the stimulus, remember to take a flexible approach when you can, as you will get the most benefit from answering as many questions as possible – in whatever order that entails.

Preference test tips

Completing preference tests, like personality questionnaires, is a much easier proposition than ability tests. The main point we like to emphasise is that personality questionnaires should be completed as openly and candidly as possible. We realise that there is always the temptation to second-guess what an employer is looking for – an outgoing person perhaps? Someone who has a strong attention to detail? Perhaps someone who is open to new ideas and situations?

THE PROBLEM WITH SECOND-GUESSING

- Poor fit – what if a job involves meeting new people day-in and day-out? If this would genuinely be uncomfortable for you, why pretend otherwise? A great deal of research shows that people are happier, more productive and stay longer in jobs that are well suited to their personality preferences.
- Inaccurate guessing – what you think an employer is looking for and what they are actually looking for could be entirely different! It would be most unfortunate to paint yourself in a different light if, in fact, your natural preferences are more suitable.

Other points that will help you in completing preference tests are:

- Work quickly – your 'gut instinct' is often the most accurate reflection of your true preferences. When we over-analyse our own preferences we often end up losing rather than gaining accuracy.
- Think with your 'shoes off' – we often find that the more experienced our clients are, the harder they find it to separate their 'true' preferences from the habits they have built up over many years in the workplace. To help, think about what you want to do when you get home and take your shoes off. In other words, how do you like to behave when there are no external pressures driving you – the 'shoulds' and the 'musts'. Do you seek others' company or prefer to spend some time alone? Do you make plans for the

future or tend to keep your options open? Answering in this way ensures that you reflect your natural rather than your learned style of behaving.

Answers

1. Ordinary percentages – finding 35% of 5,000. To answer this question, first find 1% of 5,000 (5,000 divided by 100, which equals 50). Then multiply 50 by 35, which equals 1,750.

2. Increase percentages – finding the previous cost of a car when it is now £15,640 which is a 15% increase on the previous cost. To answer this question we start by knowing that £15,640 is a 15% increase on an unknown figure. Another way of saying this is that £15,640 is 115% of an unknown figure. We divide £15,640 by 115, which equals £136. We then multiply £136 by 100, which gives us £13,600.

3. Missing percentages – if 12 of the items on sale cost less than £100 and there are 40 items in total, work out what percentage of items cost less than £100. There are 40 items in total so start by finding how many percentage points are represented by our smallest unit, which is one item (100 divided by 40, which equals 2.5). So if one item is 2.5% and there are 12 items costing less than £100, we then multiply 2.5 by 12 which equals 30%. So 30% of items cost less than £100.

4. Missing whole – if 20% of sales are in France and there were 50,000 sales in France, work out the total number of sales. We start by finding 1% of our missing total (50,000 divided by 20). This gives us 2,500. We then find the total by multiplying by 100, which gives 250,000 sales.

IN A NUTSHELL

There are lots of reasons why candidates get a lower score than they should on psychometric ability tests. All of these pitfalls can be avoided.

- Practise core skills such as calculating percentages and word meanings.
- Avoid performance-inhibiting thoughts through realistic test expectations and reminding yourself why you are well suited to the job.
- Set 'check points' so you can keep an eye on your progress during a test.
- Use the 'one-minute rule' – do not get stuck on difficult questions.
- Never guess randomly.
- Answer preference tests as honestly as you can – with your 'shoes off'.

27 AND FINALLY...

"Preparation makes no difference, you've either got it or you haven't." Wrong!

A key theme of Part III is that there are lots of reasons for getting a score lower than you deserve. These include:

- Lack of familiarity with psychometric tests
- Anxiety
- Poor test taking strategy
- Lack of practice

It is important to recognise that all of these reasons can be influenced. By taking action to prepare effectively you will be able to perform to the best of your abilities.

Psychometric tests are being used more often than ever by employers to recruit and promote staff. As a result, people who can pass these tests are in stronger positions to secure the jobs they want.

By reading this part and completing the practice questions you have already taken a significant step to performing at your very best when completing psychometric tests. You now know:

- How psychometric tests work – there is no 'black magic' and nothing to be afraid of!
- How to prepare yourself and your environment
- What the test questions look like and how to complete them
- About your own test taking style
- Where to access online practice tests

When we started writing Part III we knew that many candidates under performed on psychometric tests, for a variety of reasons. With that in mind our aim was to give clear, easy to use advice, which will help candidates to show employers what they are really capable of.

An interesting side-effect is this: when candidates complete psychometric tests to the very best of their ability, it means that employers make better decisions because the scores they have are entirely accurate. Now that's a win–win.

The knowledge and confidence you will have gained from using Part III means that when you complete psychometric tests in the future your concentration will be focused on answering the questions and you will not be distracted by uncertainty or over anxiety.

These skills of test taking will be useful to you throughout your career whether you are joining a new employer, competing for internal positions, or engaging in a talent management process.

We leave you with the reminder that it is often the most well prepared who succeed in passing psychometric tests. With this in mind we wish you all the best!

Ceri Roderick and James Meachin
www.pearnkandola.com

28 Further Resources

Websites

Recruitment sites

- www.monster.co.uk
- www.jobsite.co.uk
- www.totaljobs.com
- www.manpowergroup.com
- www.topjobs.co.uk
- www.exec-appointments.com
- www.fish4.co.uk
- www.reed.co.uk
- www.education-jobs.co.uk
- www.charityjob.co.uk
- www.redgoldfish.co.uk
- www.hays.com

Professional associations

- Association of Chartered Certified Accountants: www.acca.co.uk
- British Computer Society: www.bcs.org
- Call Centre Association: www.cca-global.com
- Chartered Institute of Building: www.ciob.org.uk
- Chartered Institute of Management Accountants: www.cima.org.uk
- Chartered Institute of Marketing: www.cim.co.uk
- Chartered Institute of Personnel and Development: www.cipd.co.uk

- Chartered Institute of Public Finance and Accounting: www.cipfa.org.uk
- Chartered Institute of Purchasing and Supply: www.cips.org
- Chartered Institute of Taxation: www.tax.org.uk
- Chartered Management Institute: www.inst-mgt.org.uk
- Communications Management Association: www.thecma.com
- Institute of Directors: www.iod.com
- Institute of Electrical Engineers: www.iie.com
- Institute of Legal Executives: www.ilex.org.uk
- Institute of Leisure and Amenity Management: www.ilam.ie
- Institute of Physics: www.iop.org
- Periodicals Training Council: www.ppa.co.uk
- Public Relations Consultants' Association: www.prca.org.uk
- Royal Institution of Chartered Surveyors: www.rics.org
- The College of Law of England and Wales: www.college-of-law.co.uk
- The Engineering Council: www.engc.org.uk
- The Royal Society of Chemistry: www.rsc.org
- Women's National Commission: www.thewnc.org.uk
- Young Professionals Network: www.una.org.uk

Test provider websites

- Kenexa online practice tests (www.psl.com/practice) – this website provides practice numerical, verbal and abstract reasoning test questions.
- SHL Practice tests (www.shldirect.com/practice_tests.html) – this website includes information about tests, tips on coping with the tests, and practice verbal, numerical and abstract reasoning questions. It also includes practice personality and motivation questionnaires with free feedback.
- PreVisor Talent Measurement (www.previsor.co.uk/products/certifications) – includes a wide range of sample tests on abstract, verbal and numerical reasoning.
- Morrisby (www.morrisby.com – click on 'Try taking a test') – this website provides practice tests, plus guidance on test taking.

University career services

- Brunel University, Placement and Careers Centre, Psychometric tests (www.brunel.ac.uk/pcc/students/psychometrictest.shtml – click on 'Try some practice tests') – this website links to a wide range of practice tests from test publishers and employers.
- University of Kent, 'How to pass graduate aptitude tests' (www.kent.ac.uk/careers) – you can practise on a range of tests that were developed specifically by the university.

- Imperial College Business School, Psychometric tests (www3.imperial. ac.uk/business-school/currentstudents/careers) – this website has links to practice tests from major test publishers, as well as employers such as the Civil Service, Barclays Capital and McKinsey.
- University of Liverpool, Centre for Lifelong Learning, Practice Psychometric Tests Online (www.liv.ac.uk/careers/students/cvs_applications_interviews/ psychometric/links.htm) – this website has links to a variety of ability and personality-based psychometric tests.

Other resources

- IQtext.dk (http://iqtest.dk/main.swf) – this website has a good-quality, free abstract reasoning test that produces an IQ score.
- AssessmentDay (www.assessmentday.co.uk) – this website has free practice questions for numerical, verbal and abstract reasoning.

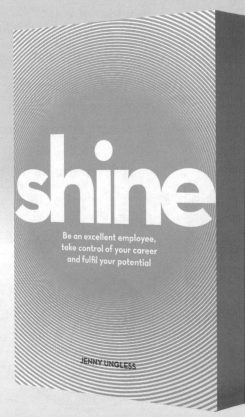

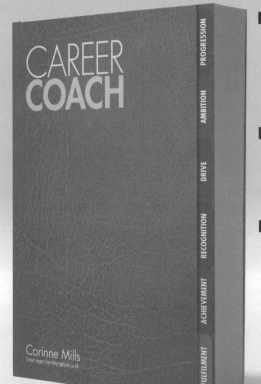

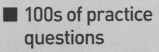